Cooperative Learning & Social Studies
Towards Excellence & Equity

Tom Morton

With contributions by John Myers
In consultation with Dr. Spencer Kagan

©1998 by *Kagan Publishing*

This book is published by *Kagan Publishing*. All rights are reserved by *Kagan Publishing*. No part of this publication may be reproduced or transmitted in any form by any means, electronic or mechanical, including photocopy, recording, or any information storage and retrieval system, without prior written permission from *Kagan Publishing*. The blackline masters included in this book are intended for duplication only by classroom teachers who purchase the book, for use limited to their own classrooms. To obtain additional copies of this book, or information regarding workshops in cooperative learning, contact:

Kagan Publishing
1160 Calle Cordillera
San Clemente, CA 92673
1(800) 933-2667
www.KaganOnline.com

ISBN: 1-879097-32-X

Table of Contents

PART ONE: INTRODUCTION
CHART OF THEMES IV
FOREWORD—DR. SPENCER KAGAN V
INTRODUCTION 1
CHAPTER 1: OVERVIEW 3
CHAPTER 2: COOPERATIVE STRUCTURES AND THE GOALS OF SOCIAL STUDIES 7
CHAPTER 3: CROSSING THE IMPLEMENTATION DIP—HOW DO I GET STARTED? 13
CHAPTER 4: EVALUATION 21
    Handouts: Geography Project: A Metaphor for the World 24
    Performance Rubric for a Visual Metaphor 25
    Participation Pie/Individual Reflection 29
    Group Evaluation Form 30

PART TWO: STRUCTURES AND STORIES
1. COLOR-CODED CO-OP CARDS 31
    Narrative: Geoflash on Europe 35
    Handout: Mini-maps of Europe 37
2. CO-OP CO-OP 39
    Handout: Museum Project on Immigration 45
    Narrative: Immigration from Latin America 46
3. CORNERS 49
    Narrative: Multiple Intelligences and Metaphors 52
4. CREATIVE CONTROVERSY 55
    Narrative: Christopher Columbus: Was He a Great Man? 62
    Handouts: Guidelines for a Good Argument 60
        Processing Questionnaire for after a Creative Controversy 61
        Christopher Columbus: Was He a Great Man? 64
        Children of Columbus 65
        Tainos 66
5. FIND MY RULE 67
    Narrative: Assimilation 73
    Handouts: Topics for Find My Rule 72
    Find My Rule 75

Table of Contents

6. FIND-SOMEONE-WHO **77**
    Narrative: Globingo and Lobingo... 81
    Handouts: People Hunt.. 79
        Human Intelligence Hunt/Energy Hunt 80
        Globingo 82
        Lobingo 83

7. FORMATIONS **85**
    Narrative: Demonstrating Orographic Rainfall 89

8. INSIDE-OUTSIDE CIRCLE **91**
    Variations: Team Inside-Outside Circle, Role Play Inside-Outside Circle 92
    Narrative: Teaching about Revolutions... 94

9. JIGSAW **97**
    Variation: Scavenger Hunt 99
    Narrative: The Underground Railroad 102
    Handouts: Scavenger Hunt-Citizenship: Government and Law 101
        Expert Sheets: Harriet Tubman 104
        Alexander Milton Ross 105
        Follow the Drinking Gourd... 106
        Escape Routes of Underground Railroad 107
        Henry "Box" Brown 108

10. MIX-N-MATCH **109**
    Narrative: Rhythms of Resistance in South Africa... 111
    Handouts: Mix-N-Match Materials 112

11. MYSTERY GAME **115**
    Narrative: Images of the World 120
    Handout: Guess the Country 122

12. NUMBERED HEADS TOGETHER **123**
    Variations: Stand and Deliver, Simultaneous Numbered Heads Together, Stir-The-Class 124
    Narrative: Neighborhood Field Study 126

13. PAIRS CHECK **129**
    Narrative: Reading Strategies 131
    Handout: Finding the Main Idea 133

14. PAIRS COMPARE **137**
    Narrative: Land and Logging 140
    Handout: Decision-Making Model 142

15. PAIRS READ AND PAIRS VIEW **143**
    Narrative: The Return of Martin Guerre 147
    Handouts: Anticipation Guide for "The Return of Martin Guerre" 149
        The Return of Martin Guerre 150

16. ROUNDROBIN AND ROUNDTABLE **153**
    Variations: Simultaneous Roundtable, Reaction Wheel, RallyRobin, RallyTable, Team Boggle .. 154
    Narrative: Current Events Study 158

17. Sequencing 161
- Narrative: Forest Ecology 164
- Handout: The Forest System 165

18. Simultaneous Sharing: Ten Variations 167
- Blackboard Sharing, Carousel Sharing, Choral Speaking, Gallery Tour, Neighbor Show and Tell, Showing, Stand-N-Share, Team Inside-Outside Circle, Teams Tour, Voting 168

19. Sort 171
- Variations: Structured Sort, People Sort, Sort and Predict 172
- Narrative: Economic Field Study of the Parking Lot 174

20. Team Discussion 177
- Variations: Teammates Consult, Team Project, Team Statement, Team Thesis 178
- Narrative: Analyzing Arguments on Women's Role 181
- Handouts: MARKER 183
  - The Woman's Sphere/The Suffragist Position 184

21. Team Web 185
- Variations: Team Graphic, Future Wheel, Woolly Thinking 187
- Narrative: On China 192

22. Think-Pair-Share 193
- Variations: Think-Pair-Square, Sketch-Pair-Write-Pair-Share 194
- Narrative: Cartoon Analysis 196

23. Three-Step Interview 199
- Narrative: Personal and Political Change 202

24. Value Lines 205
- Variations: Human Graph, Pro-Con Dialogue 207
- Narrative: Case Studies on Violence and Rebellion 210
- Handout: Case Studies on Violent Rebellion 212

Part Three: Conclusion

Conclusion 213
References 215
Recommended Sources 219

Chart of Themes
National Council for Social Studies Curriculum Standards

NARRATIVE	Civic ideals and practices	Time, continuity and change	People, places and environment	Individual development and identity	Individuals, groups and institutions	Production, distribution and consumption	Power, authority and governance	Science, technology and society	Global connections	Culture
1. Geoflash on Europe			✓							
2. Immigration from Latin America			✓						✓	
3. Multiple Intelligences and Metaphors		✓								
4. Christopher Columbus: Was He a Great Man?		✓								
5. Assimilation				✓	✓					✓
6. Globingo and Lobingo			✓	✓					✓	
7. Demonstrating Orographic Rainfall			✓							
8. Teaching about Revolutions		✓					✓			
9. The Underground Railroad		✓		✓			✓			
10. Rhythms of Resistance in Southern Africa			✓				✓		✓	✓
11. Images of the World			✓							
12. Neighborhood Field Study	✓		✓							
13. Reading Strategies										
14. Land and Logging			✓		✓					
15. The Return of Martin Guerre		✓		✓	✓					
16. Current Events Study	✓									
17. Forest Ecology			✓						✓	
19. Economic Field Study of the Parking Lot	✓				✓	✓			✓	✓
20. Analyzing Arguments on Women's Role		✓								
21. On China		✓	✓					✓	✓	✓
22. Cartoon Analysis										
23. Personal and Political Change	✓	✓		✓	✓		✓			
24. Case Studies on Violence and Rebellion							✓			

Cooperative Learning and Social Studies: Towards Excellence and Equity by Tom Morton
Kagan Publishing • 1(800) 933-2667 • www.KaganOnline.com

Foreword

by Dr. Spencer Kagan

The single most important function of an educational system in any democracy is to prepare students to fulfill the office of citizen. The wisdom and democratic habits we provide for our students today will determine whether we as a democracy flourish or fail when those students begin to chart our future tomorrow.

There is no more important function we as educators can fulfill than creating an informed, wise, democratic electorate. It rests with us to create the next generation electorate—an electorate committed to preserving a respect for the delicate balance between the will of the majority and the rights of the minority; respectful of the needs and opinions of an increasingly diverse population; willing and able to assume the stewardship of the nation and, together with those of other nations, the planet.

It is one of the greatest ironies and tragedies of our educational system that we come to settle generally and almost exclusively on autocratic classroom structures as methods to prepare students for participation in a democracy! It is a practice destined for failure: What we do, screams louder than what we say.

How can we prepare students to listen to, respect, and weigh a range of opinions, if we rely on classroom instructional strategies in which the teacher does most of the talking? If student-student interaction remains the occasional, exceptional event, we cannot hope to create a generation of students prepared for democracy. How can we prepare students to reach reasoned decisions based on the needs of all if we use classroom structures in which only the teacher decides what and how to study, how to evaluate the product, and the content of the classroom rules of conduct?

What a missed opportunity! With traditional methods we miss the opportunity to make our classrooms active labs in which to practice the process of democracy.

The traditional approach is absurd not only philosophically, but practically. Let's take one example: Current events. If we want our students to become an informed electorate, we need to have them report often on the events of the day. To that end, the presentation of "current events" is a time honored tradition in schools of every democracy. We attempt to have students read and report and think about the important events of the day so often that it becomes habitual. Unless we create in our students firm habits of reading and thinking about the events of the day, we cannot hope to create the wise, informed electorate of tomorrow.

If we choose the traditional structure for current events, each student in turn stands before the class to present for at least three minutes. Students each receive at least a minute of feedback from teacher and classmates. And then there is another minute of transition while the presenter retires to allow another to take his/her place. Five minutes a student multiplied by the thirty students in our classroom equal 150 minutes—three class periods. If it takes 150 minutes to do a round of current events, we can only have students reporting on current events occasionally, and reading about and thinking about the events of the day will not become habitual among our students. We will have failed in our mission of creating the informed electorate. And how have students spent their time during those three class periods? Three minutes each presenting, one minute each getting feedback, and the remaining 146 minutes waiting their turn! I challenge a talented behavioral engineer to come up with a structure more exquisitely designed to generate apathy and disinterest—qualities that spell doom in a democracy.

If we choose instead one of the many cooperative structures Tom Morton so well describes, the class comes alive. Discussion results. Students actively practice the skills of participants in a democracy. They hone their abilities to weigh competing ideas—abilities that spell a brighter future.

Consider what happens if we replace the traditional structure with a Three-Step Interview. Each student in the class is interviewed about his/her current event, interviews another, and then shares with the team what he/she has learned. The whole process takes less than 10 minutes. Within 10 minutes we accomplish more than with 150 minutes using the traditional approach.

When we adopt the cooperative alternative, how have students spent their time? They divide their time between presenting, listening carefully to others, and representing the point of view of others. They are held accountable for careful, accurate listening. They gain democratic values and skills.

If we are to fulfill our mission as educators in a democracy, we must walk the walk, not just talk the talk. We must restructure our classrooms so democracy is a living, breathing experience—not just words in a text. The alternative to making our classrooms active labs for acquiring democratic skills is to continue with our present autocratic classroom practices—practices which leave our students ill-prepared to shape a democratic future.

And Tom makes it easy. All we need to do is try any of his activities to discover how easily we can unleash the power of the cooperative, democratic alternative. This Canadian scholar and educator is a strong voice welcoming us to come to a more reasonable, responsible alternative. Morton's book provides us with a welcome invitation to make democracy come alive in our classrooms—to align our practices with our values.

The decision is as important as any we face as educators. In the balance hangs our future.

Part 1
INTRODUCTION:
ACKNOWLEDGEMENTS

That was the pattern of school life—a continuous triumph of the strong over the weak. Virtue consisted in winning: it consisted in being bigger, stronger, handsomer, richer, more popular, more elegant, more unscrupulous than other people—in dominating them, bullying them, making them suffer pain, making them look foolish, getting the better of them in every way.

—George Orwell, *Such Were the Days*, 1947

Orwell paints a horrid image of ruthless student competition, a school yard version of Picasso's Guernica. Most teachers would imagine a much more attractive picture of their own school, but many years later in his landmark study, *A Place Called School* (1984), John Goodlad presented a different, but equally unappealing portrait of school life in North America. Two images dominated, a teacher talking at students and students working alone. There was little cohesion or common purpose among class members in many of the hundreds of classrooms Goodlad's team visited. Though students saw social studies topics as potentially exciting, the classes were not. The emotional tone was flat. If this were the painting of classroom life, it would be an amorphous abstract done in beige and grey pastels.

Fortunately, many of the social studies teachers with whom I work are creating more vibrant classroom settings, far removed from either the brutal or the bland. They want classes characterized by lively, purposeful discussion about important content and issues, classes in which all students are contributing and using their minds well. They want caring classes where all students, regardless of ability or achievement level, are eager and able to learn—classes which value both excellence and equity. These teachers see cooperative learning approaches as their primary colors for painting such classes.

I wish to acknowledge especially the excellent teachers in the **British Columbia Cooperative Learning Association**, the students and teachers at **John Oliver Secondary School**, and **John Myers** of the Toronto Board of Education. **Jeanne Stone** gave useful ideas for revision, **Wendy Staroba Loreen** developed the layout, and **Catherine Hurlbert** formatted this book.

While *Cooperative Learning and Social Studies: A Guide for Secondary and Middle School Teachers* is based on **Spencer Kagan's** Structural Approach, I also should credit many other cooperative learning researchers, in particular **David** and **Roger Johnson** whose names and spirit appear throughout this guide. The book also reflects the work of **Elizabeth Cohen** and her colleagues at Stanford University who have given both John Myers and I an appreciation of how diversity can work in the classroom through using students' multiple abilities.

Above all, I wish to acknowledge the profound cooperation of my wife, **Rose-Hélène Gagné**, ma compagne de vie, and dedicate the book to her and our daughter **Chloé**.

Tom Morton
Vancouver, 1996

Chapter 1
OVERVIEW

> **Chapter at a Glance**
>
> Chapter 1, the Overview, contrasts a structure for "whole class teaching" with a cooperative learning structure and explains the key principles that define the Kagan Structural Approach. It also gives the purpose and organization of *Cooperative Learning and Social Studies*.

There are many models of cooperative learning and many good resource books for teachers. Yet there are few written specifically for high school teachers and students and few for social studies at the middle or high school levels.

Cooperative Learning and Social Studies: A Guide for Secondary and Middle School Teachers is intended for that audience. It is built on Spencer Kagan's Structural Approach that is explained in his book, *Cooperative Learning* (1992).

Cooperative Learning and Social Studies: A Guide for Secondary and Middle School Teachers is designed to do the following:

- Help teachers learn more about Kagan's Structural Approach to Cooperative Learning. Various different structures can help students learn important social studies content, master higher-level thinking skills and develop important habits of mind and character needed for effective learning and participation in democratic life.

- Show in story form how to make social studies exciting and active while still covering course content.

- Provide ideas for activities in history, geography and the social sciences, grades six to twelve, in a variety of classroom contexts.

Topics
- Purpose of this book

- Explanation of the structural approach

- Organization of this book

- Provide ideas for resolving such important classroom issues as management, assessment and evaluation.

Explanation of the Structural Approach

The following is an introduction to the components and vocabulary of the structural approach. A complete treatment can be found in Kagan's *Cooperative Learning* (1992).

Structures are content-free ways of organizing social interaction for the classrooms. They consist of a series of steps or elements. Structures are the "how" of instruction. The lesson content is the "what." The "how" and the "what" together, structure plus content, are an activity, but it is the structure which defines the student interaction. Consider the following comparison of a common, traditional structure and a cooperative structure for watching a videotape.

The traditional structure might be called Whole-Class View Question-Answer and it has four elements:

1. The teacher shows a film or video.
2. Students complete worksheets individually during and maybe after the showing.
3. When the video is over, the teacher calls on one student for an answer to a question on the worksheet.
4. The student attempts to state the correct answer.

During the show, there is usually no interaction among students or even with the teacher. If a section of the video or film is confusing or complex, the student gets no help or support to answer questions or clarify important issues. Habituated to television and couch potato viewing, some students do not even try to complete their worksheets.

The question and answer session can also frustrate many would-be learners. When students vie for the teacher's attention, student-student interaction becomes negative and the structure is competitive. Except for the strong few who continuously triumph, this competition works against learning as peer norms are established which discourage achievement for those not quick with the answer or not able to get the teacher's attention.

However, the viewing of a video and a question and answer session can also be structured cooperatively. Pairs View does this as follows:

1. The teacher pairs students A and B and tells the pairs that they have a common goal, a clear set of notes for each partner on the main ideas of the video.
2. The teacher shows the video and stops it every ten minutes or so (five minutes for younger students).
3. When the film is stopped for the first time, A:
   - Summarizes for B the information and ideas presented so far.
   - Tells B what s/he finds most interesting about what was presented.
   - Identifies anything that was confusing and tries to clarify, with B's help.
4. After three minutes of step 3, the film is turned on again.
5. After a suitable period the pause is repeated but with B taking the leading role.
6. The cycle repeats and the roles reverse with every pause until the film is finished;
7. With the whole class, the teacher randomly calls on different As or Bs to give their answers.

Pairs View illustrates the four key principles of the structural approach to cooperative learning, as defined by Kagan & Kagan:

Positive Interdependence: This is the heart of teamwork—when the success of one depends on the success of others. Sports teams, business organizations, unions, symphony orchestras, jazz ensembles, and dramatic productions work when interaction among all members is positive.

Notes

When team members work against each other, the whole team suffers. Pairs View has positive interdependence because there are complementary and alternating roles and a common goal, that both students have a complete set of notes.

Individual Accountability: When students know that they are accountable for their learning, they are more likely to achieve more. A group may also become resentful if all members are not pulling their own weight. In Pairs View both students learn from the film since their roles require them to take turns to explain to each other what they have learned. They are accountable too because the teacher can call on either to respond to any question about the film.

Equal Participation: In the traditional approach, only a few students actively participate during the class oral question-answer time. And it is often the same few, creating very unequal participation. In contrast, in Pairs View all students participate about equally.

Simultaneous Interaction: "The person who talks learns" is common wisdom since the stoic philosopher Seneca. Yet, in the final stage of Whole-Class View Question-Answer only the teacher or a single student talks about the film. The rest wait uninvolved and idle; and because we all know what happens to idle hands, management troubles can occur. In Pairs View, instead of one student talking about the video, half the class are talking simultaneously.

Organization of Cooperative Learning and Social Studies

Part One: Introduction presents brief chapters on a number of important topics such as how structures fit with Social Studies education, how to prepare your class for cooperation, how to manage the bustle of small group learning, how to implement new structures slowly and steadily, and how to assess and evaluate.

Part Two: Structures describes a variety of structures, the elements of each, and examples of Social Studies lesson activities. The activities for each structure include a "classroom narrative" that is a fictionalized account based on my own experiences and those of the teachers with whom I have worked.

The idea for using narratives rather than lesson plans to describe how the structures work in a classroom setting comes from *Expectations of Excellence: Curriculum Standards for Social Studies*, published in 1994 by the National Council for the Social Studies, and there are references to their intended outcomes in the margins.

Chapter 2

Cooperative Structures and the Goals of Social Studies

> **Chapter at a Glance**
>
> Chapter 2 explains how different structures can help students to acquire and apply social studies content and to develop the values and habits of responsible citizens. It also summarizes various ways that cooperative themes are featured in history, geography and the social sciences.

Social Studies is the integrated study of the social sciences and humanities to promote civic competence. Within the school program, Social Studies provides coordinated, systematic study drawing upon such disciplines as anthropology, archaeology, economics, geography, history, law, philosophy, political science, psychology, religion, and sociology, as well as appropriate content from the humanities, mathematics and natural sciences. The primary purpose of Social Studies is to help young people develop the ability to make informed and reasoned decisions for the public good as citizens of a culturally diverse, democratic society in an interdependent world.

—*National Council for the Social Studies (1994)*

We are doomed to live, so goes the ancient Chinese curse, in interesting times. And with a subject that the NCSS says draws systematically from more than eleven

Topics

- Acquiring social studies knowledge and skills

- Constructing meaning

- Developing responsible citizens

- The disciplines of social studies are also about cooperation

academic disciplines to help students be good citizens in such times, social studies teachers must sometimes feel that they are doomed to teach an interesting subject.

If "the primary purpose of social studies is to help young people... to make informed and reasoned decisions for the public good," there are three ways that social studies can do this. First, it can help students acquire knowledge from the academic disciplines and skills in research and communication so that they are informed about our civic culture and have the ability to continue informing themselves. Second, it can help them seek meaning in what they study so that they are willing and able to apply that knowledge to make reasoned decisions in and beyond the classroom. Finally, social studies can promote the public good by developing the values and dispositions of a responsible citizen. In the teaching of all three of these social studies goals cooperative learning structures can have important roles.

Acquiring Social Studies Knowledge and Skills

The first important and highly successful role for cooperative learning is to help students learn academic content. For example, Jigsaw is a well-known approach for acquiring information. Pairs Read, Pairs View, Inside-Outside Circle, and Team Discussion are also useful in the transmission of information.

As a class moves towards a summative evaluation, the teacher will want to ensure that students have mastered the knowledge or skills. The Geoflash narrative in Color Coded Co-op Cards is one example of how students can master basic geography facts. Numbered Head Together, RoundTable, and Pairs Compare are other ways for students in small groups to review factual

Notes

The Disciplines of Social Studies Are Also About Cooperation

Cooperative learning is more than just an effective teaching method. Cooperation is an important concept to explain the world both inside and outside the classroom. To better understand the world, students should know the content as well as the process of cooperation. Each of the disciplines which make up social studies contains cooperative themes of caring, belonging, interdependence, conflict resolution, equality, democracy, identity, diversity, and participation.
For example:

• **History:** Society's collective memory is an important source of knowledge for gaining insight into present circumstances, as well as future possibilities. On the one hand, history has traditionally provided us with knowledge of competition and conflict through the study of war and oppression. On the other hand, conflicts need to be resolved and history provides us with many examples, both good and bad, of how to do so. Moreover, conflicts often reflect themes of caring and struggles for equality and the right to participate in making decisions. For example, blacks and whites, slaves and citizens, Americans and Canadians worked together to build the Underground Railroad. In the years before the Civil War, they risked their lives in an intricate cooperative network in order to bring slaves to freedom. History has also become more democratic. "Who built the seven towers of Thebes? The books are filled with the names of kings. Was it kings who hauled the craggy blocks of stone?" wrote Bertolt Brecht a half century ago, but historians have started to fill modern books with more than the names of kings. Today's students are starting to learn that women, minorities, working people, children and even non-human species belong in history too.

• **Geography:** We live in a global village. Events around the world can have far-reaching impacts in our local communities. Geography can help us see the relationships between us and our wider world. Geographically and environmentally speaking, we live in an interdependent world. In fact, this global aspect of life has become so important that Global Studies and Ecology have

knowledge, while Pairs Check is useful for the mastery of skills. Mix-N-Match and Find-Someone-Who are energizing structures for whole class review.

Factual knowledge is organized into concepts. These need to be more deeply understood than the simple memorization required for important dates, places or statistics. Find-My-Rule helps students identify and explain major social studies concepts such as primary and secondary sources, tertiary industry, assimilation, scapegoating and renewable and non-renewable resources. Stir-The-Class, People Sort, Team Web, Team Discussion and Think-Pair-Share are useful too for helping a student's understanding of important ideas.

Constructing Meaning

No knowledge is an island unto itself. Students need to explore questions of importance to themselves and the disciplines, to seek connections to their own lives and to real world problems, and to apply, demonstrate and exhibit their learning in significant situations.

Ideally, students would seek much of their meaning outside the school educational programs organized around apprenticeship, mentoring, community service, and political action, but as exciting as these programs can be, they have limitations and, as yet, they are few in number. Inside the classroom, efforts to encourage teaching for meaning have blossomed into a hundred projects, programs and acronyms like HOTS (higher-order thinking); the Child Development Project; Project Zero; Program for Complex Instruction and its social studies hybrid, SPICE (Stanford Program on International and Cross-Cultural Education), which brings together multiple intelligences and cooperative learning; and the authentic instruction in social studies of emerged as new and important ways to organize Social Studies knowledge. Our current environmental challenges may be the result of an overemphasis on competing against, rather than cooperating with the forces of nature.

- **Civics/Political Science:** It seems that few voters these days are happy with those whom they elect to govern. On one hand, this may be a healthy impetus to change; on the other hand, this dissatisfaction may bode ill for democracy. The health of a democracy depends on what political scientists call the legitimacy of the government, what might be referred to in cooperative learning terms as trust. Participation is another issue common to cooperative learning and democracy. Alexis de Tocqueville wrote in 1840 that widespread participation in cooperative associations was the underpinning of American democracy. "Whenever at the head of some new undertaking you see the government in France, or a man of rank in England, in the United States you will be sure to find an association." While conflict is inherent in any civic society, democratic societies try to resolve it constructively.

- **Economics:** Our students will become employers, employees and consumers as well as citizens. Economic systems on one level are highly competitive as they are concerned with issues of distribution and scarcity. Yet, such systems also contain elements of interdependence and conflict resolution as governments, labor, and business cooperate to ensure that the system works and that competition is "fair." The hand of cooperation may seem invisible in classical economic explanations of the market, but there are countless examples of caring and interdependence from child rearing to helping a neighbor, all of which contribute to our economy. Moreover, most modern work places stress teamwork even when they embrace free enterprise.

- **Sociology, Psychology, Anthropology, Legal Education and World Religions:** Each of these areas also reflects cooperative themes. Sociology, psychology, and anthropology can develop our understanding of belonging, identity, interdependence and the influence of groups on behavior. Law considers questions of justice and the common good; the rule of law is part of the definition of democracy. Religion is about belonging to God's world and provides answers to important questions of ethics and meaning that are not found elsewhere. The study of other religions can also mean exploring themes of unity and diversity.

Fred Newmann and his associates at the Wisconsin Center on Organization and Restructuring of Schools. Cooperative structures do not give all the necessary nutrients for these blooming schools of thought and their budding pedagogy, but they can help nourish them.

One important source of meaning for Newmann (1993) and others is the experiences and ideas of students themselves. Both young and adult learners already have developed some understanding of most topics in social studies; and these understandings or "scripts" can be a powerful influence on how they learn our subject. On one hand, scripts can be helpful. For example, students certainly know a lot when asked about what makes a group work well, which can make a good introduction to cooperative learning. Building on student knowledge gives value to their experiences. Moreover, new knowledge may be more easily retained and have a stronger interest for the students if it builds on what students already know.

On the other hand, student scripts can be a hindrance. They may be naive, stereotypical or mistaken and can interfere with learning academic content or developing responsible citizenship. For example, Howard Gardner (1993) of Project Zero talks about the Star Wars script: the good guys look like you, the bad guys look different, the two gangs struggle, and in the end, the good guys win.

If we want to guide students to a sounder and deeper understanding of culture and cross-cultural perceptions, and not just paint over racial stereotypes (or any other mistaken understanding about social studies topics), we need to access those scripts. As teams this can be done with Reaction Wheel or Three-Step Interview and as a class with Find-Someone-Who. The narrative Images of the World for the Mystery Game structure offers an example of how to begin to reconstruct a stereotypical script that young and old often hold about Third World countries.

Another approach to seeking meaning and acquiring social studies knowledge is to generate data, for example, through surveys, interviews, or document analysis, categorize the data, and interpret them. The Sort and Sequencing structures are two ways to do this cooperatively. The narrative for the Sort, for example, describes an activity that uses the data from a field study of the school parking lot to look at larger issues of trade and consumption. The ideas and narratives of Corners, Formations, Team Statement, Team Web and the Sketch-Pair-Write-Pair-Share variation also give ways for students to interpret knowledge in different forms using multiple intelligences.

To seek meaning also means dialogue. To have quality dialogue means good skills and habits in reasoning and communicating. There are many cooperative structures to encourage such dialogue including Three-Step Interview, Mystery Game, and Corners with Paraphrase Passport. Analyzing Arguments on Women's Role is one of several narratives that features critical thinking.

Meaning can not be constructed just in short activities, however sweet and neat. Social studies sometimes needs to be as messy and tentative as the world it studies. Students should investigate important, complex topics and issues, and follow their own interests with projects using Co-op Co-op or Creative Controversy.

Let us note, as well, that acquiring knowledge and constructing meaning are interrelated. When engaged in a Creative Controversy, a Co-op Co-op project, a Sort or Sequencing, students also learn factual knowledge and skills.

Developing Responsible Citizens

Social Studies is about good people as well as good learners. And in developing the values of good people or responsible citizens—values like caring, respect, and a commitment to rational discussion—cooperative structures have a vital role.

A well planned cooperative lesson can give students an opportunity to express and reflect on what the NCSS calls civic competence. For example, when the teacher establishes the rationale for a structure like RoundRobin, students are quick to recognize the fairness of taking turns, as well as the likelihood that this will generate more and better ideas. When reflecting on group process, most students will also dedicate considerable energy trying to make their teams ones where participation is widespread, where everyone is respectful, and where all team members pull their own weight. This effort may mean conflict. It may feel uncomfortable. And it will take time. There is no fast track to good cooperation and good citizenship. Just as students are constructive learners in the intellectual domain, students need lots of opportunities to construct meaning in the ethical and social domain.

Democratic values, such as the caring for the learning of classmates, are prerequisites for academic achievement in cooperative learning, as well as values for good citizenship. Throughout Part Two of *Cooperative Learning and Social Studies* there are references to teambuilding and classbuilding activities that can help build caring for others. Team Projects, Three-Step Interview, and Find-Someone-Who are perhaps the most commonly used structures for this purpose. The teaching of social skills discussed in the next chapter also helps to build a caring classroom.

Another value of a responsible citizen, especially in a culturally diverse society, is respect for differences. Since its early years, cooperative learning has been closely linked with the improvement of mutual respect and liking whether students differed because of intellectual ability, ethnicity, race, gender, handicapping conditions, social class or gender. It does this by encouraging students to develop an appreciation for their own background and that of others, a strong superordinate national identity, and a set of pluralistic values about democracy, individual rights, civic responsibilities, freedom, justice, and equality (Johnson and Johnson, 1992). The narratives Assimilation with Find My Rule, Globingo and Lobingo with Find Someone Who, and Personal and Political Change with Three-Step Interview are a few of several model lessons in *Cooperative Learning and Social Studies* that encourage respect for differences.

Most social studies teachers would also expand the goal of respect to include non-human species. A good citizen is a global citizen, a steward of the planet. The theme of interdependence resonates through cooperative learning and parallels environmental interdependence. The narratives Land and Logging with Pairs Compare and Forest Ecology with Sequencing are examples of using cooperative structures to teach an appreciation of our natural environment.

A responsible citizen in a democracy is also one who engages in principled discussion, like that described in the procedure of Creative Controversy. Power in a democracy comes from production of ideas not just consumption and students need to exercise that power. Unfortunately, too many classrooms are built for silence. Australian educator Garth Boomer has even said that schools that value silence are a menace to democracy.

Moreover, when the discussion is about controversial issues, students can acquire knowledge and construct meaning from challenging other perspectives and from having their own views challenged. Although in a traditional competitive debate students often focus more on winning than determining truth or the best answer, when discussion of a controversy is cooperatively structured, students can deepen their thinking at the same time they develop open-mindedness and fair-mindedness. Creative Controversy, Corners, Value Lines, Role Play Inside-Outside Circle, Jigsaw and Think-Pair-Share, especially the methodological belief adaption, are structures that are well suited to the study of controversial questions.

Social studies, with its melange of disciplines and long lists of outcomes, may seem demanding, diffuse and maybe doomed, but with cooperative structures to help students acquire and construct knowledge and use that knowledge for being good citizens, social studies can be an interesting subject for interesting times.

Notes

Chapter 3
Crossing the Implementation Dip—How Do I Get Started?

> **Chapter at a Glance**
>
> Chapter 3 on implementation suggests several ways to begin using cooperative structures in middle school and secondary social studies. It gives ideas for managing the hurly burly of small group learning and developing cooperative skills and norms.

Start a conversation on cooperative learning in the first few months of implementation and you might hear comments like these:

"Not everyone wants to work in a group."

"Some of my students don't have the skills for effective group work."

"The groups never get down to work."

"The noise level of my groups is deafening."

"Some groups finish early and get restless."

"When I want the group work to end, I find I have to shout to get their attention."

> **Key Concepts**
>
> - Start With the Right Structure
> - Establish Management Routines
> - Encourage Cooperative Norms
> - Teach Cooperative Skills
> - Teach the Structure

In the long run, cooperation works. In the short run, changing your class to a cooperative one can be hard. While some of us sprint from the starting gate with cooperative learning, others stumble in the first few meters or tire in a later lap. In the staff room, those who see problems only as impassable mountains may be the most passionate and convince the tired to join them on the sidelines.

Educational research on the implementation of new instructional models confirms common teacher knowledge: when we try new skills or behaviors that are significantly different, things often get worse before they get better. Our practice may be clumsy, then mechanical and, only if we stick with it long enough, fluid. Michael Fullan has called this process of changing our teaching practice the "implementation dip."

This chapter has suggestions on how to keep on your feet and move forward, slowly and steadily, past the dip, until cooperative structures do become a fluid gait. It will also suggest ideas for teaching social skills and building a spirit of togetherness that will help push learning teams to greater performance.

STARTING WITH THE RIGHT STRUCTURE

Short and simple structures: The content demands of social studies worry some teachers who want to make that first step into cooperative learning. Others are unsure if their students know enough to learn on their own. So one good answer to the question of where to start is with a short and simple structure. For example, a Scavenger Hunt, in which students skim for simple answers in a textbook and then team members copy them down, runs less risk than a Jigsaw which involves the acquisition and synthesizing of what might be difficult content, and then teaching it to other students. In our experience, many social studies teachers have rushed too quickly into a lengthy Jigsaw and students have performed poorly.

Pairs Work: Simultaneous interaction and individual accountability are high in most pairs activities. It is hard to get left out of a pair. Our students especially appreciate the chance to talk about what they are reading as they do in Pairs Read. Pairs Check, Pairs Compare, Inside-Outside Circle and Values Line also rely on pairs.

Exploratory talk: Another answer about where to begin would be when you want students to learn through talking. Purposeful, quality talk turns passive reception of information into exploration, clarification, shaping and reshaping of ideas. To reduce the risk of off-task talking, you can include some written or visual product that is easy to monitor, for example, a Write-Pair-Share, a Pairs Compare, or a Team Web, especially when students discuss and write arrows showing relationships among the web's sub-topics.

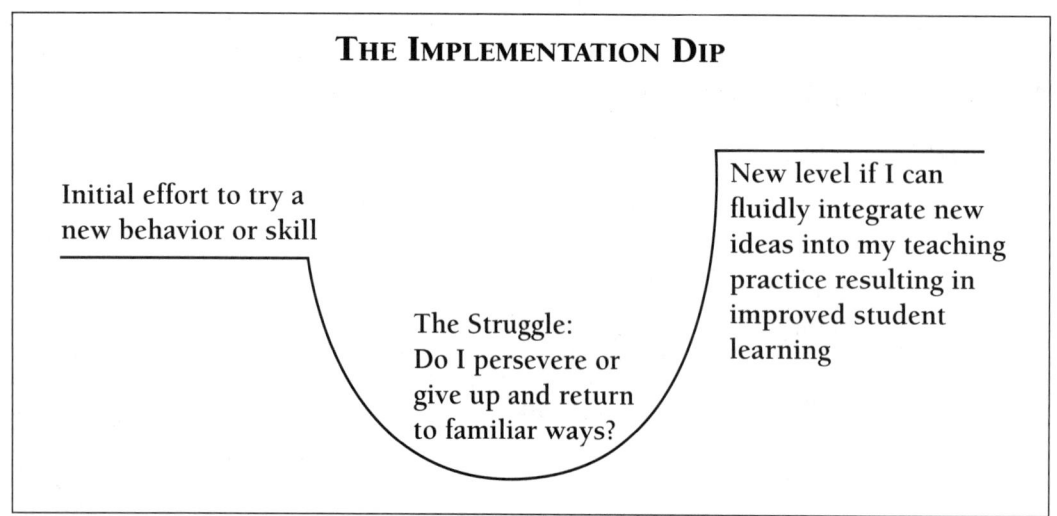

THE IMPLEMENTATION DIP

Initial effort to try a new behavior or skill

The Struggle: Do I persevere or give up and return to familiar ways?

New level if I can fluidly integrate new ideas into my teaching practice resulting in improved student learning

Problem solving or decision making: A fourth place to start is with activities that have a puzzle to solve or a decision to make. We have seen some very rowdy groups cooperate beautifully with the challenge of a Mystery Game or Sequencing.

Activities in which a variety of abilities are required: Different students will be able to bring their different talents and experiences to many of the Team Projects. Formations, Role Play Inside-Outside Circle, Sketch-Pair-Write-Share, and Team Graphics also require abilities beyond reading, talking and writing and increase the chances that a variety of students will participate fully.

Team and class building: If the initial cooperative activities are enjoyable, assured of success, and build norms of respect and trust, there is a great chance that the class will join a loop of continued fun, success, and positive norms. Team and class building are mentioned throughout Part Two. Line-Ups, Team Projects, Three-Step Interview, Find-Someone-Who and Color-Coded Co-op Cards are especially useful structures for these purposes.

Review: If you have relied on whole class instruction and individual seatwork in the initial teaching of a topic, team review offers variety. Numbered Heads Together, Stir-The-Class, Team Web or the RoundTable preparation of a practice test are examples of useful structures for review. Color-Coded Co-op Cards is built on repetitive review with flashcards.

Establish Management Routines

Teaching with the structural approach does not mean a teacher crosses through a worm hole to emerge in a new dimension where different management rules apply. Teachers still need down-to-earth class rules, respect for the student and well planned lessons that keep the students engaged and, thus, unlikely to be disruptive. Moreover, the discussion in Chapter One which compared Whole-Class View Question-Answer to Pairs View demonstrated how a cooperative structure alone can promote increased engagement and thus, less chance of disruption. Nonetheless, cooperative learning has a certain hurly-burly that can be lessened by careful management of grouping, seating, and quieting.

One of the features of most models of cooperative learning is the use of heterogeneous groups, that is, groups that are mixed according to academic level, ethnicity, gender, and social-economic status. Compatibility is another ingredient in the mix. Considerable research and teacher experience says that if we want the most academic achievement for all and the greatest sense of class cohesiveness, heterogeneous groups are essential.

Students who are not used to cooperative learning, on the other hand, often want to choose their own groups and want to choose only their friends. So there may be a tension when the teacher chooses the groups.

The teacher needs, therefore, to explain clearly why there is a need for mixed groups along the lines of the following:

- Social studies class is where we learn how to be good citizens and part of that is learning to work with others who may be different from us but with whom we share this classroom and share this planet.

- When we work, we do not choose our fellow employees and certainly not the customers; learning to work with others whom we do not know well is learning for life.

- Often we work better with those who are not our friends—there's a lot less social talk about sports or movies and the like.

- For some top academic students, when we explain something to someone, we help that person learn, but we also learn ourselves because we think through and organize our ideas.

- You will probably work with everyone in the class at some point during the year.

During the early part of the year until you know enough about the students' levels and compatibility to be able to choose effective groups, random selection is most appropriate. This can be done in several enjoyable ways: counting off the names of famous figures, counting off in a foreign language, distributing playing cards with the common cards sitting together, or with a Line-Up or Mix-N-Match.

As a class develops as a learning community, one that is inclusive by habit, you may wish them to choose their own teammates. Corners and Human Graph are structures with pairs chosen by the students. Co-op Co-op, as well, depends on student choice.

Group size is another decision. Foursomes are convenient because they can be divided into pairs for greater simultaneous interaction or kept as a foursome for more variety of ideas.

Whatever the group composition or size, we want students to move quickly and quietly to their group seating. This may mean that the teacher needs to set a time limit—"Let's see if we can move to our teams in one minute today (and eventually a half minute)." This may mean asking students to lift desks so as to make less noise. And certainly it will mean explaining how the teacher wants students to sit. Students need to sit close to their fellow group members. "Eye to eye and knee to knee," the Johnsons like to say. They also need to be seated so that they can easily face the teacher when the time comes to address the class as a whole. It is a truism, but worth repeating, that one pays attention to where one is facing, so we need to be sure that students are facing us when we talk to them.

If you have an overhead projector, a "template," like Figure 1 for groups of four can give students a clear idea of how they should sit: facing each other, but able to turn easily to face the front. You may also want to write the names of students on the template to be sure that they are clear about where to sit and with whom.

The third management routine is to have teams work quietly together and, when the teacher wants to talk to the class, complete silence and attention to the front. For quiet group work, students may need to be taught "quiet voices." Delta teacher John Maschak calls this "rhubarb voices" and tells his students the tasty tale of the origins of this term. The idea originally comes from theater. Sometimes a director wants supporting actors in a scene to make background noise behind the dialogue of the principle characters. Yet, the background conversation must not interfere with or detract from the main conversation. So the supporting actors repeat "rhubarb, rhubarb, rhubarb" over and over. It sounds like conversation without risking that a real background discussion might result in laughter or some lively comment which would spoil the main scene.

In his classroom John explains that he should not hear anyone beyond 30 centimetres or one foot, about the length of a rhubarb.

Spencer Kagan has also developed the "Quiet Captain" role for the group member whose job it is to ensure that discussion from her/his group does not distract a neighbouring group.

When it is time to discuss something as a whole class or receive further instructions from the teacher, quiet should mean total quiet, silence. Before doing this you may want to give the groups a two minute (or five or one) warning. Do this orally or, less disruptively, pass amongst the groups with a sign saying two minutes left.

When it is time for complete attention, most teachers also develop some kind of a silent signal, if for no other reason than to save their voice. When you give this signal,

Notes

FIGURE 1: SEATING ARRANGEMENT

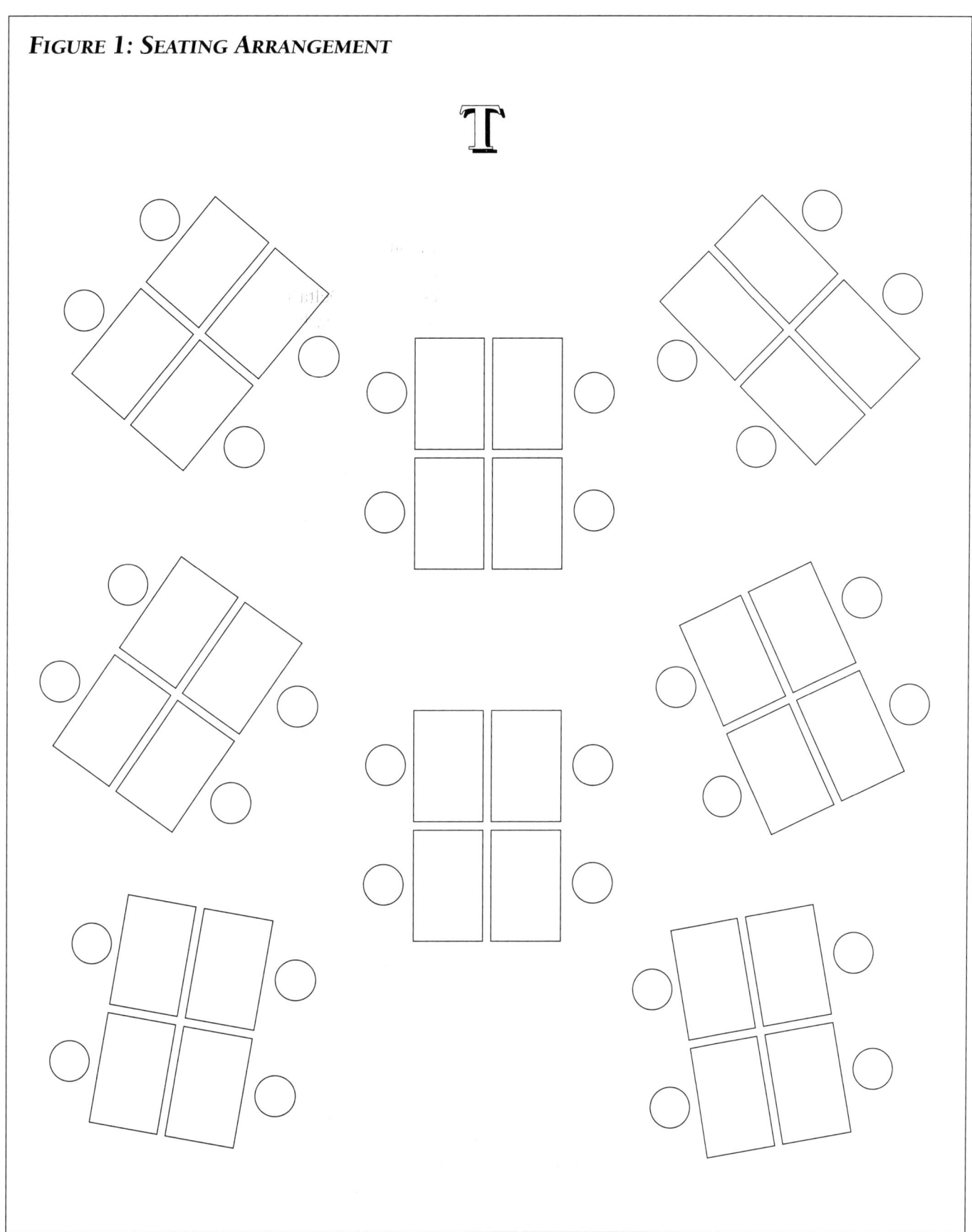

such as raising a hand or clapping your hands with some rhythm, students must

a. finish the sentence they are saying (if speaking),
b. alert all group members to the teacher's signal,
c. face the teacher,
d. return the signal,
e. cease talking until the teacher gives further instructions.

When you introduce students to this procedure, provide a rationale and give students an opportunity to practice. You may also give students a say in the nature of the signal to be given. With practice of this and all these routines should come specific, supportive feedback in which the stress is on praising improvement rather than criticizing.

Encourage Cooperative Norms

Routine means only habit. Management routines mean just those basic habits so that things don't fall apart, the center holds. We want, however, to go beyond just management and to encourage students to enter more fully into the spirit of learning together. We suggest that you discuss with your students what constitutes a good learning team and then work throughout the year to develop them. This means modeling, reflection, exhortation, and praise; class and team building; and bulletin boards with the positive messages about cooperation. (In a unit on propoganda or advertising, students can make their own posters.)

Math educator Marilyn Burns (1981) suggests three norms to make explicit for your class:

1. You are responsible for your work and behavior.
2. You must be willing to help any group member who asks.
3. You may ask for help from the teacher only when everyone in your group has the same question.

The third rule implies that students will develop more independence, leaving you free to help those who really need you, check for accountability, or monitor group process.

Morris (1977) offers these rules for cooperative problem solving:

1. Say your own ideas.
2. Listen to others; give everyone a chance to talk.
3. Ask others for their ideas.
4. Give reasons for your ideas and discuss many different ideas.

A norm that Elizabeth Cohen (1994) uses to create the expectation that everyone has something to contribute and should be valued is,

> *None of us is good at all the abilities needed for learning. Each one of us has some of the abilities.*

In our own classrooms we also spend time on the norm of "putting up" not "putting down." We ask students why a sports team does better on its home court (field, ice) than in away games. They often suggest that they know the court better or that they are less tired among other answers, but they also recognize that a cheering, supporting crowd is a major part of the home court advantage. This idea of home court becomes a norm for our classroom. Whenever they hear any put-downs, students should tell that person, "Home court!"

At the most succinct, a teacher should at least insist on the norms that "Everyone participates" and "Everyone helps."

Teach Cooperative Skills

What we have called routines, like moving quickly and quietly to groups or talking in quiet voices, might also be called beginning cooperative skills. However, to practice norms like participation and discussion of differences, and to move towards highly productive groups, students must practice more sophisticated skills. These include encouraging another team member to participate, taking turns, paraphrasing, or disagreeing respectfully. Most teachers new to cooperative learning do not teach these skills at the start, but they are key to moving to a higher level.

The old Bauhaus dictum for architecture that "less is more" applies to cooperative skills. It is best to focus on just a few skills like taking turns and checking and persist until the class has mastered their use. Spencer Kagan's Cooperative Learning (1992) and other books describe effective ways of teaching these skills. These incude the following:

- State the rationale for the skill.
- Describe or define it.
- Model the skill in front of the class with a student (students especially like to role play a negative model as well as a positive one).
- Give guided practice.
- Reflect with students on their use of the skill.
- Have students practice the skill independently.

Several of the structures depend on social skills. This means that the structure will reinforce the use of the skills; however, it also means that if the students fail to use the skill, the structure will not be effective.

Teach the Structure

The first Kagan structure I ever tried was Three-Step Interview and it failed miserably. Many students only did a perfunctory interview, many were off topic, and many just talked as a whole group. Today, as with social skills, I take the time to explain the rationale—it is a good way to review content, to learn active listening which is an important work-related skill, and a chance to show some caring towards a teammate. And I work through definition to modeling to guided practice, reflection and independent practice. Today, Three-Step Interview works.

An important feature of the structural approach is that you can ease into cooperative learning by teaching and using one structure at a time. Many teachers set themselves on a "structure a month" schedule. Thus, after two years of gradual implementation, they find themselves quite comfortable with up to two dozen cooperative structures. This gradual approach keeps the implementation dip from becoming an chasm.

The narrative "Personal and Political Change" that illustrates Three-Step Interview in Structure 23, p. 202, gives a description of how a teacher might go about implementing a structure a month. In this case the teacher explains the rationale as well as the procedure, reflects with the students on how well it worked, and uses it several times over the month.

What we have not discussed in this chapter is that key part of implementation that is beyond this book: the support and help of your colleagues. What applies to students applies to teachers as well: we need each other for encouragement and help in solving problems and sharing good ideas. Whatever you can do to develop a professional support team, and nurture the support of your administration, will eventually help you and all the students in your school.

Chapter 4
EVALUATION

> **Chapter at a Glance**
>
> Chapter 4, Evaluation, discusses the role of cooperative structures in traditional exams and in alternative evaluation such as projects and presentations. It explains how students can reflect on their thinking and on their group process. Several examples and forms for reflection are included here and throughout Section Two.

Evaluation is so often "the tail that wags the dog." Though teachers may aspire to noble goals like quality thinking and responsible citizenship, so often what counts is their answer to the question, "Is this for a grade?"

Key Concepts

- Traditional summative evaluation

- Alternative summative evaluation

- Reflection on thinking

- Reflection on group process

Teachers still want to encourage students to see those higher goals and nurture their intrinsic motivation, but they also need to answer, at least for themselves, what part of the cooperative activity is the "keeper" for the grade book, and what should be evaluated in different ways other than giving a grade. Above all, teachers want to have evaluation and the goals of social studies to work together; the dog and the tail can wag together.

There are no definitive answers to the questions of evaluation that are inherent to cooperative learning, but there are several guidelines consistent with its spirit. This chapter will consider first summative evaluation, that is, final judgements about a student's performance in knowledge or skills. It will also offer some ideas for alternatives for assessment and evaluation, that is, ways of gathering data and judging a student's achievement. It will also consider formative evaluation, reflection on how students go about thinking and learning and reflection on how the group works as a team.

Cooperative Learning and Social Studies: Towards Excellence and Equity by Tom Morton
Kagan Publishing • 1(800) 933-2667 • www.KaganOnline.com

Traditional Summative Evaluation

Most social studies teachers at some point use traditional tests of knowledge and skills such as multiple choice questions or essay tests. The role of cooperative structures in such cases is to prepare the students for the test. Three-Step Interview, Numbered Heads Together, Mix-N-Match, Stir-The-Class, Pairs Compare or a Team Web are effective ways to review knowledge. Color-Coded Co-op Cards is built on repeated drill of factual knowledge. Pairs Check is intended for mastery of skills.

One way to prepare students that we particularly like is having teams prepare practice tests and answer sheets using a RoundTable. Each team passes the test to a neighbor team, who answers it together using RoundTable again, and then passes it back to the team that created the test for grading. The teacher may also take a sample of the questions from each team to make up the final test.

The answer to the question "Is this for grades?" in these activities might be, "I don't think you are ready yet for the final test. Let's have a practice test first."

Although the preparation for the test is as a group, the test itself is written by the individual and the grade obtained is an individual one. Some teachers have tried to use group grades for positive interdependence in order to motivate students to co-operate; however, group grades can be criticized on a number of grounds (see Kagan, 1995); and they are unnecessary as there are so many other ways to encourage cooperation.

Alternative Summative Evaluation

The term "evaluation" is often used as a synonym for "testing", but there are many alternative tools for gathering information about the learning of students. Student presentations, portfolios, projects, field study, and writing can let the teacher view both process and product. Structures like Formation, Team Graphics, Team Projects, and above all, Co-op Co-op fit especially well with alternative assessment and evaluation.

Alternative assessment will be most consistent with the spirit of cooperative learning if the teacher does the following:

- Creates the criteria and marking scale for the assignment with the students well before the presentation or project due date;

- Includes self evaluation of the assignment at various stages so as to promote the students' critical awareness of themselves as learners and to help them take some control over their learning;

- Includes peer evaluation to give students more responsibility and to give you a wide source of assessment information;

- Evaluates at different stages (formative evaluation) before the summative one so that students may re-think and refine their work in order to produce their best effort;

- Uses assessment tools that allow students to use a wide range of intelligences following Gardiner's and Cohen's (1994) ideas about intelligences and cooperative learning;

- Evaluates in a manner that is constructive and supportive and promotes self-esteem;

- Encourages student responsibility, but accepts that the teacher is the major decision maker and is ultimately responsible. (For example, status differences may mean students mark some classmates harder than others.)

Figure 1 gives an example of an evaluation form for a team metaphor. After reading the assignment, the class develops criteria and standards for the written and visual components of the Visual Metaphor. These might include accuracy of information, detailed explanation of the metaphor, clear answer to the focus question, correct writing mechanics, bold and colourful illustrations, and neatness.

In a cooperative project that lasts over several periods and involves complex tasks as it might with Team Projects or Co-op Co-op, it may be difficult for the teacher alone to judge the work of each individual member unless there have been several points along the way to assess performance and individual contributions. In cases where you do not feel that you have enough information to be sure how to divide credit for a final project among the group members, peer and self evaluations will take on even more importance.

So for alternative evaluation the answer to "Is this for grades?" might be at a formative stage, "A small grade just to give you credit for having completed your first draft" or "No, not yet." At the summative stage it might be, "As we discussed last class (and before that), yes this is for grades. Please evaluate yourself and your team mates according to the standards that we set and then I will."

Figure 2 provides a performance rubric for a visual metaphor. Students may help construct the standards, evaluate themselves, and evaluate their peers.

REFLECTION ON THINKING

We should not expect students to arrive without having travelled. (Douglas Barnes)

Cooperative learning has often been allied with teaching for thinking. Ideas are often formed at the point of utterance and in cooperative groups students have much more opportunity to talk and thus form ideas than in traditional direct instruction. Teams, moreover, generate more varied ideas and refine them further than do individuals. Listening to different perspectives on problems or public issues can expand and deepen thinking on values questions as well.

Supportive, constructive evaluation is essential to the development of thinking and cooperative structures can help with this evaluation. The structures can provide windows into the minds of the learners while they are learning so that the teacher and learners may reflect on their progress and plan improvement.

"Is it for a grade?" "No, now is the time for exploring and discovering what is important and interesting. I want to hear what you think, not always sit in judgement over you. However, over time these activities will improve learning and eventually grades."

Five structures especially, Sort, Find My Rule, Mystery Game, Creative Controversy and Co-op Co-op, emphasize the thinking process. They include frequent assessment and feedback as students develop, apply and extend concepts and complex knowledge.

Other structures are useful in opening that window into the learner's mind: a Reaction Wheel can give the teacher an assessment of student ideas and feelings on a topic and give the student feedback from other team members. Pairs Compare, Team Web, and several of the Simultaneous Sharing structures also can assess student learning in a graphic or written form that is easy for the teacher or other students to reflect on.

Other structures like Think-Pair-Share, Corners, Line-Ups, Spectrum, and Creative Controversy can reveal thinking about controversial issues.

An example of how these structures might work in an activity would be with K-W-L (Know, Want to Know, Learned). Prior to a unit, students can use Think-Pair-Share to establish a knowledge base and a RoundTable brainstorm to generate questions for study from which individual students may chose ones on which they wish to focus. When reflecting on what they have learned, students could answer and then share in a RallyRobin, RoundRobin, or Three-Step Interview their answers to questions like these:

FIGURE 1: EXAMPLE OF ALTERNATIVE ASSESSMENT

GEOGRAPHY PROJECT:
A Metaphor for the World

(Based on Bower, Lobdell, and Swenson, *History Alive*, Addison-Wesley, 1994)

Your project will be to create a poster of a metaphor for the world. Your poster should answer the question, "In what ways is the world interdependent?" for at least three topics: the physical world, the biological world, and the economic world. You may also wish to include a fourth category such as public attitudes or communication. Each category should include a visual that illustrates your metaphor and a paragraph that explains and supports your interpretation.

Directions

1. With your partner choose one of the following metaphors. If you wish to choose a different metaphor, discuss your choice with me.
   The world can be thought of as a global village, a spider's web, a mother, or a teacher.

2. Take notes on how your metaphor is similar to the following three domains:
   - the physical world
   - the biological world
   - the economic world

   These notes could be in the form of a chart with the following titles:

Characteristics of Physical World	Similarity with	Characteristics of Village

3. Divide your poster into three sections, one for each topic. For each section, create a visual that shows how your metaphor explains one of the three worlds. You may use diagrams, drawings, cutouts, photographs, and photocopies to show the similarities between your metaphor and the topic.

4. Write a paragraph of explanation below each of your visuals, using examples and explanations from geography to support your interpretation.

5. Write another paragraph which states your opinion as to whether the trend towards a more interdependent world is good or bad giving reasons for your point of view.

6. Include a bold title on your poster.

7. On a separate sheet of paper give a description of what each of you contributed to your project.

8. Evaluate your poster according to the performance rubric and give reasons for your rating.

FIGURE 2

Performance Rubric for a Visual Metaphor

Students may help construct the standards, evaluate themselves, and evaluate their peers.

The visual metaphor has

4
- all of the required sections;
- attractive and bold visuals that support the metaphor;
- paragraphs that explain in depth the parts of the metaphor;
- ample and accurate evidence or examples to support each explanation of the metaphor, some of which are original;
- correct grammar;
- neat printing.

3
- all of the requirements;
- attractive visuals that support the metaphor;
- paragraphs that explain the metaphor;
- an accurate example or some other evidence to support each explanation of the metaphor;
- correct grammar with only minor errors;
- neat printing.

2
- most of the requirements complete; one may be missing;
- attractive visuals but they may not necessarily support the metaphor;
- some explanation of the metaphor;
- some supporting examples or evidence taken from the textbook or material given in class;
- perhaps some errors in grammar;
- neat, though there may be some messy sections.

1
- some requirements missing;
- visuals that are not necessarily related to the metaphor;
- explanations that are brief and use the same wording as the textbook;
- there may be some inaccurate statements;
- little if any supporting evidence;
- some errors in grammar;
- some messy printing.

- What did you learn that surprised you the most?
- Which of your original questions are you still curious about?
- What new questions do you want to find out about?
- Where did you think you would find the answers to your questions?
- Where did you find the answers?
- Was it difficult to find information? If so, what did you do?
- How did you link the new information that you learned to something you or others know?

REFLECTION ON GROUP PROCESS

A learning team engages in reflection on group process when team members discuss how well they are working together and how they might improve. Most of the time this will be done as a group, but the teacher, individuals and whole class also have a role.

Reflection or processing is important because students can learn about themselves and group behavior; they can prevent problems in cooperating; improve their social skills; and maintain good group relationships.

Our answer to "Is it for grades?" is similar to that for reflection on thinking: "No, this is learning for living. But one of the reasons for building good relationships and social skills and for preventing problems is so that group work will really improve learning and this means grades."

Some of our colleagues do give grades for reflection on process. Their students must keep records of specific behaviors and thoughtful plans for improvement that they actually attempt to complete. To do this fairly requires considerable observation and record keeping by the teacher as well.

Although the reflection is about group process, process and product go together. In an airplane plant we want workers who share and smile but also remember to rivet the wing to the plane. Similarly, we want students to work as a team in order to achieve excellence. We do not want them to leave the room, self esteem high, happy with their team, and then wonder, "Didn't Mr. Morton want us to do something this class?"

Reflection may mean looking back, but the first of a three-step sequence starts at the beginning of the class and the final step has students look forward to the next class:

1. The teacher or teacher and students together decide what specific social skills are required for the task;

2. The teacher or a student observer gathers information during the lesson on what the groups are doing; and

3. The teacher sets aside time during the lesson or at the end for groups to consider how well they have been cooperating and plan improvement. If there is little time, the teacher may be the one to reflect on how the class worked, although ideally it should be the students themselves.

"What is unsought will go undetected" (Sophocles) so the teacher needs to be clear in the first step about what constitutes a skill like encouraging participation or checking for understanding and be clear in step 2 how to gather data. There are several ways to gather them:

1. A tally sheet completed by the teacher
2. A tally sheet completed by a student observer
3. Anecdotal comments by the teacher, preferably with words written verbatim
4. Information from group members

Figure 3 gives an example of a tally sheet. Each time that a student does one of the behaviors listed, the observer makes a

FIGURE 3: TALLY SHEET FOR THE OBSERVATION OF GROUP PROCESS

Social Skills	Ernesto	Yee Wah	Doug	Susan
1. Giving ideas or information	|||| ||	|||| ||	||	|||| ||||
2. Encouraging participation		||		||
3. Checking for understanding and agreement			||			
4. Other				||	|||

mark. He or she does not speak. "I'm not here," is what we say to groups when we are observing.

For student observers, limit the number of skills that they are asked to identify and monitor carefully their observation. After five to twenty minutes, the observer—teacher or student—shares the data with the group and asks them to interpret it.

Feedback to other students should be supportive. As an observer, catch them doing something good. It should also be specific and descriptive, allowing the group to interpret. For example, you might show your tally sheet to the group and then ask them, "What does this tell you about how you have been working as a group?"

The teacher may offer his or her own anecdotal comments and ask students to recollect what behaviors they noticed while working together.

In stage three, students reflect on what behaviors were helpful or unhelpful. This might be done by asking them to answer, "Name three things that your group did well." and "Name one thing that you could do better next time." Forms like Figures 4, 5 and 6 often produce more detailed reflection. Co-op Co-op, Creative Controversy and Jigsaw have specific forms that are included in the description of their procedures. Students can also keep a group or individual journal in which they write answers to questions like these, or a folder of processing forms.

In reflecting, the teacher may want students to use structures like RoundTable, RoundRobin, or Team Discussion. They might also make a Team Word Web that illustrates the secrets of success of their team (Bennett, B, Rolheiser-Bennett, C. Stevahn, L, 1991).

It may be useful, as well, to make public to the whole class a good example of the use of a social skill to serve as a model for others to follow. For example, if a class is being very quiet and discussing little, the teacher might take note of someone asking another, "What have you got for number 3?" and then share the verbatim words with the whole class as a model of encouraging participation and an incentive for others to discuss. In Corners with Passport Paraphrase the feedback on the use of paraphrasing is immediate and in front of the whole class.

The Johnson brothers and their sister, Edythe Holubec (1994), list some potential pitfalls of processing and offer possible solutions:

There is not enough time in the lesson. This is a common situation for so many of us who are task oriented. However, we can decide that the lesson content can be continued the next day. Teachers may also decide to process rapidly, by making comments themselves or asking for a show of hands response to a question like, "Who felt they were able to paraphrase at least once this class?" Moreover, the teacher need not wait until the end of class when everything seems rushed. A brief class discussion or teacher observation part way into a lesson can focus student thoughts on the use of social skills.

Processing is vague. Be explicit in introducing the required social skills and in introducing the reflection time. Use observers too.

Students are uninvolved. Use a reflection form or ask the most uninvolved student to lead the team discussion. The forms can also be part of an individual or group portfolio.

After a game, you can't stop athletes from reflecting. I remember vividly hockey games from 25 years ago. In time, reflecting on thinking and group process, even reflecting on summative tests, can become as natural a routine for social studies students as it is for hockey old-timers.

FIGURE 4: REFLECTION ON GROUP PROCESS

Participation Pie

Divide the pie to illustrate how much each member of the group is participating in the task. Write down reasons why you divided up the pie as you did and suggest ways that you might improve the effectiveness of your group.

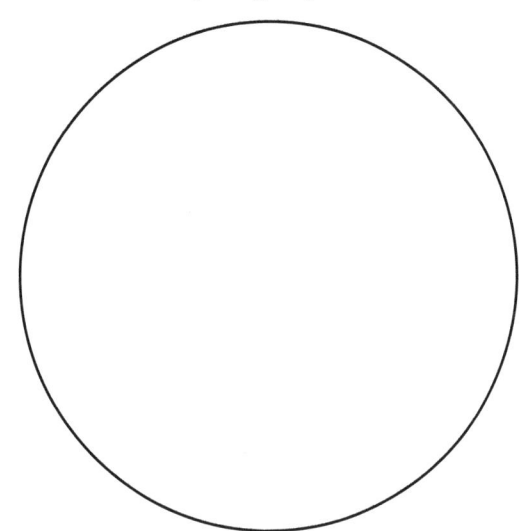

Reasons: _____

_____

Ideas for Improvement: _____

_____

(Adapted from *Cooperative Learning: Where Heart Meets Mind* (1991) B. Bennett, C. Rolheiser, L. Stevahn, p. 154.)

FIGURE 5

Individual Reflection on Work in Pairs

Name:	Seldom				Always
1. I made certain we both understood the material we were studying.	1	2	3	4	5
2. I listened to the contributions of my partner.	1	2	3	4	5
3. I felt that my partner listened to me.	1	2	3	4	5
4. I took thorough notes.	1	2	3	4	5
5. My partner took thorough notes.	1	2	3	4	5

FIGURE 6: REFLECTION ON GROUP PROCESS

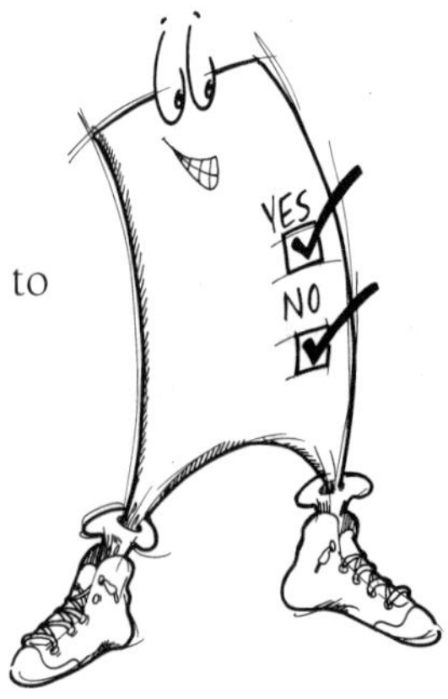

Group Evaluation Form

Please fill out this form together. Ask one team member to chair the discussion and another to record your evaluation.

1. Circle one

Our group	did not get started	got started pretty soon	got started immediately
Our group	did not stay on topic	stayed on topic to some extent	stayed on topic well
Our group	did not cooperate	worked together to some extent	worked together quite well

2. Circle one

Everyone in our group contributed ideas.	Yes	No
Everyone in our group listened carefully to each other	Yes	No
Everyone in our group tried to help others contribute thoughts and feelings	Yes	No

3. One thing we could do differently next time to improve how we work as a team: _____

_____

_____

_____

_____

_____

(Adapted from *Together We Learn*, Clark, J. et al. Reproduced with permission of Prentice-Hall, Canada, Inc. 1990)

Structure 1
COLOR-CODED CO-OP CARDS

Steps at a Glance

❶ Class takes a pretest.
❷ Pairs create team names and team handshakes
❸ Students create Color-Coded Co-op Cards
❹ Students play the Flashcard Game
❺ Class takes a practice test.
❻ Students post their improvement scores.
❼ Students study missed items.
❽ Class takes the final test and calculates improvement scores.
❾ Teacher and class recognize individual, team and class improvement.
❿ Reflection

Students make flashcards based on items missed on a pretest, then work in pairs to help each other master the material for a post-test. Students can master factual material while building team and class spirit.

Social Skills
- Helping
- Praising

Ideally, the curriculum represents what Matthew Arnold called "the best that is known and thought" and ideally, there would be little question that students should master it. And there is general agreement that our students should know facts like who Abraham Lincoln was or skills like how to use an atlas so that they have a firm base in order to participate in civic culture and to think at a higher level.

Beyond this basic general agreement, however, there is much questioning. Some say why include so much on Lincoln and not on Harriet Tubman? And why so many famous figures anyway? Why not more social history? This would be more in keeping with contemporary historical research.

In many of our curriculum guides and textbooks the answer to this debate over inclusion is to include everything. The course content becomes a mile wide and an inch deep. It is not a coincidence that the very word, curriculum, comes from a Latin origin meaning a race course; racing is the only way to teach everything that social studies teachers are asked to. This side of the debate is more involved than can be considered here, but we introduce it to explain in part why we often do such a poor job of helping students master key skills and knowledge.

Unfortunately, because of race course teaching, strategies for mastery like drilling have received a bad reputation. However, students can drill important knowledge and skills in positive, progressive ways that have active involvement, mutual support and team spirit. Color Coded Co-op Cards is a series of structures that can help the teacher give drill a positive rep.

STEPS

❶ CLASS TAKES A PRETEST
Give all students a pretest on the facts to be mastered, such as vocabulary words, key dates, historical figures or location of countries. Twenty to twenty-five items is a workable number for most students.

❷ PAIRS CREATE TEAM NAMES AND TEAM HANDSHAKES
Based on the results of the tests, create heterogeneous teams of four. Each team should first create a team name. This can be done based on similarities found during an exercise like Windows (Kagan, 1992) or teams can create one without any preliminaries. There are three rules for making a name: (1) All team members should have a say; (2) Everyone must agree with the name; and (3) The name should be positive (not rude, sexist, racist, etc.). Set a time limit and if teams are slow to choose, say that you will choose a name for them and all your favourite names are wimpy.

Team handshakes and team hugs are common in team sports. The hug may not be appropriate for the class room, but certainly a team handshake can be. Ask your teams to create one. (See the Team Project structure for other ideas for team building.)

Combine the scores of the members of the team and post them next to their team name. Although each student will receive an individual mark according to his final test, the teacher publicly recognizes the improvement of the teams from pretest to practice test to final.

❸ STUDENTS CREATE COLOR-CODED CO-OP CARDS
Distribute rectangles of different colored paper to each team member and ask them to make a set of flash cards on the items that he or she missed on the test. Letter sized paper, 8½" x 11", can be cut into quarters and with careful centering of the hole punch each card can have two holes in it and be kept in a binder.

❹ STUDENTS PLAY THE FLASHCARD GAME
Round 1. Maximum Cues. Once the cards are make up, teams divide into

pairs. One student in the pair becomes the tutee and hands five of so of his or her cards to the other student who will be the tutor. The tutor holds up one card, shows and reads the tutee the front of the card (question or cue) and then shows and reads the back (answer). For young children or kinesthetic learners, the tutee may trace the answer or write the answer. The tutor then turns around the card again, showing the front, and asks for the answer from short term memory. The tutee attempts an answer. If the answer is correct, the tutor gives an exaggerated praise, such as, "You are a fabulous learner," "Super fantastic job," and the card is "won back" (returned to) the tutee.

At this point, 90% or more of all answers should be correct, because the student has been told and shown the answer immediately before being asked for it. If, however, the tutee fails to answer correctly, he or she receives a "helper" rather than a "praiser." Helpers might be hints, showing and telling the card again, an opportunity to trace or write the right answer, reminders, and the joint creation by tutor and tutee of fantastic visual images which are difficult to forget. If a "helper" is given, the card is not won back, but rather placed back in the stack of cards the tutor holds, so that it is repeated. Note: this method insures time-on-needed-task, as the easy items are quickly returned to the tutee and the more difficult items are repeated as needed. When the tutee wins back all of his cards, the tutor and tutee switch roles.

Round 2. Few Cues. After both students have won back all of their cards on round 1, they progress to round 2. In round 2 the same basic procedure is followed, but this time fewer cues are given, and students move from short to long-term memory.

Thus, for example, the tutor shows the tutee the front and asks for the back from memory. Not having just seen the back, the student must produce the information on the back from long-term memory. The same rules prevail: a correct answer produces an exaggerated praise and the card is returned to its maker; a slow or false answer produces a helper, and the card is placed back in the stack of items to master.

To keep the game fresh, for both the tutor and tutee, each time a card is won the tutor should make a different, unexpected praise. Students are encouraged to be creative about the praises, so as the teacher circulates he/she might hear things like,..."Our team will always be a winner with you," "You are extraordinarily intelligent."

Round 3. No Cues. Again, after both students win back their set of cards, they move up a round. On the third round, no cues are allowed. So, for example, the tutor might... say the vocabulary word without even showing the tutee the card. As in the other rounds, a correct response receives the card as a token of success accompanied by a praiser; a hesitant or false response receives help and repeated work.

❺ **CLASS TAKES A PRACTICE TEST**

❻ **STUDENTS POST THEIR IMPROVEMENT SCORES**
After the test has been marked, each student should calculate his or her improvement over the pretest and then add it to that of his or her group members to give a team improvement score. This should be posted next to the team names and then all scores should be added to give the class improvement score.

❼ **STUDENTS STUDY MISSED ITEMS**
Students now drill each other on any items that they have missed on the

Structure 1   COLOR-CODED CO-OP CARDS

practice test. These may be items that they initially had correct on the pretest and new flash cards will have to be made. If some students did so well on the test that they have fewer than five cards to study, then supply those students with more items (vocabulary words, countries, etc.) so that they have a minimum of five for drill.

Teacher Tip: Do not count these extras for any kind of grades or students who have yet to master the core material will try to study the extras as well and master neither.

⑧ CLASS TAKES THE FINAL TEST AND CALCULATES IMPROVEMENT SCORES

⑨ TEACHER AND CLASS RECOGNIZE INDIVIDUAL, TEAM AND CLASS IMPROVEMENT

Individuals: All students who improved their scores from the pretest should stand up and take a bow.

Teams: Teams should should take turns coming up to post their improvement scores and demonstrating their team handshake.

Class: Once all improvement scores have been posted the teacher should calculate how much the class has improved and ask them to give an energizer, like a round of applause or a "Yes! Yes! Yes!"

⑩ REFLECTION

Because there is so much consistent helping in this model, this makes a good opportunity for groups and the class to reflect on what kind of help they found most useful. They might suggest teaching techniques such as diagrams, key words, or mnemonic devices or they might suggest qualities such as patience or encouragement. If this reflection is done well and built upon, students will become better helpers.

IDEAS FOR USING COLOR-CODED CO-OP CARDS IN SOCIAL STUDIES

- **Vocabulary**
  The term is on one side; the definition or examples are on the other.

- **Location of Places**
  The name of a city, country, or river is on one side; a mini-map with its location is on the other.

- **Landform**
  The name of the landform is on one side; a drawing of it is on the other.

- **Map Symbols**
  The symbols on one side; the meaning on the other.

- **Capital Cities**
  Capitals on one side; the state or country on the other.

- **Key Dates**
  Dates on one side; event on the other.

- **Key Events**
  Name of event on one side; explanation on the other.

- **Key Historical Figures**
  Description of person one one side; name on the other.

- **American Bill of Rights**
  Ken Attebury from ABC School District has students put the number of the amendment to the Bill of Rights on one side and the principle feature of the amendment on the other side.

Notes

NARRATIVE OF A LESSON USING COLOR CODED CO-OP CARDS

Geoflash on Europe

Themes
- People, places, and the environment

"No more England in the Mediterranean, no more Spain between Russia and Germany," thought Pat Koh. He had adapted Color Coded Co-op Cards to make a game he called "Geoflash." It was early in the year and he wanted his students to have a sound sense of location before teaching them the evolution of the European Economic Community in his unit on International Co-operation. To prepare for Geoflash he used MacGlobe and SuperPaint software to put 4 outline maps of European countries on a single letter sized page. These were his Co-op Cards. (A page of 4 mini-maps is reproduced here on page 37.)

The students took a pretest that asked them to locate 25 countries in Europe which Pat corrected. He used the results to set up heterogeneous teams and asked them to decide on a team name: "I don't want to say the Gary, Carolina, Deep, and Syed team. Let's have something more catchy. Remember that you all must agree to the name and it needs to be positive."

He also added together the test scores for each student to give a baseline that he posted on the blackboard next to the team names. Although students would receive their individual score as the final evaluation, the team totals were the ones posted after each subsequent test and the totals that received praise from Pat.

When he gave back the pretest, each student noted only the countries that were wrong and took a Geoflash card for each of these wrong answers. On one side of each 4" x 5¼" card was a blank outline map of Europe which Pat Koh had cut out and hole punched. On this the student outlined the boundaries of one of the countries that he or she needed to study and wrote the name on the other side of the paper to make a card.

Pat wrote the rules for the game on the board and monitored the students. He publicly complemented students who used effective helping strategies and imaginative or especially enthusiastic praise.

After the first practice test, students worked only with those locations which they had wrong. For those who had them almost all correct Pat gave the names of several more countries so that each student always had at least 5 to work with.

He did not, however, give any extra marks for these on the final test. Instead, he used this as an opportunity to give his favorite speech on the value of intrinsic over extrinsic motivation. "You will never enjoy work, if you only work for a pay check and you'll never enjoy learning if you just study for grades," Pat would say.

Although several of the top students wished that they could have more extrinsic motivation, they still accepted Pat's intrinsic argument enough to study the extra countries.

Structure 1 COLOR-CODED CO-OP CARDS

FIGURE 1: MINI-MAPS OF EUROPE

Cooperative Learning and Social Studies: Towards Excellence and Equity by Tom Morton
Kagan Publishing • 1(800) 933-2667 • www.KaganOnline.com

Structure 2
CO-OP CO-OP

Steps at a Glance

1. Teacher presents a broad topic and students discuss subtopics of interest.
2. Students choose a sub-topic and form teams.
3. Students complete a team building activity.
4. Teams refine their subtopic.
5. Individual team members choose a mini-topic.
6. Individuals research their mini-topic.
7. Individuals present their research to their teams.
8. Teams prepare their presentations.
9. Teams present to the class.
10. Everyone evaluates.

Students form groups with others who share an interest in a topic, research a part of that topic, then pool their knowledge to prepare a class presentation. Students have an opportunity to pursue their own interests while having the support of a group in researching and presenting a topic.

Social Skills

- Checking for agreement
- Checking for understanding
- Helping
- Long term projects will need numerous other social skills

In Co-op Co-op student teams explore a topic of interest to them and then teach it to the class as a whole. They cooperate as a team in order to cooperate with the whole class in their joint study of the topic, hence the name.

Spencer Kagan (1992) has written that Co-op Co-op "provides conditions so that the natural curiosity, intelligence, and expressiveness of students will emerge, develop, and guide learning." It gives students an opportunity for self-direction; they negotiate their own learning with the teacher and classmates. In addition, Co-op Co-op can integrate subject matter and integrate skills such as organizing as a group, researching, creative writing, and speaking.

The Procedure gives ten steps but they are not strictly linear nor are they clear and discrete. Students, for example, may have to replan and rethink their sub-topic as they find or fail to find information. Assessment and evaluation, moreover, should occur throughout Co-op Co-op, not just at the end.

A Mini Co-op Co-op may be as brief as one class period; however, more elaborate research topics can take a week, a month or even a term.

STEPS

❶ TEACHER PRESENTS A BROAD TOPIC AND STUDENTS DISCUSS SUBTOPICS OF INTEREST

The teacher should begin with activities to spark students' interest and provide an understanding of the overall topic and its components.

If the students are not interested or engaged, the purpose of Co-op Co-op to have students follow their curiosity is lost. If the students lack prior knowledge, they may not be able to define subtopics and the interrelationships among them.

After the teacher's introduction, the class discussion must be student-centered. Through brainstorming in groups and reporting to the class or brainstorming as a whole class, the students should generate a list of subtopics related to the overall topic. After they have done so, the teacher may help them to chose the subtopics that appear significant and relevant.

If the results of the brainstorming session are recorded on newsprint, they may be displayed and referred to during the unit.

❷ STUDENTS CHOOSE A SUB-TOPIC AND FORM TEAMS

A strength of Co-op Co-op is that students can follow their own interests with the support of those students with a similar curiosity. However, the teacher should reserve the right to adjust groups so that teams are of a manageable size and roughly equal in numbers, that they are based on mutual interest and not just friendships, and that they are heterogeneous. The teacher needs to decide how to balance student choice with his or her judgement of what is needed for good group learning.

The team selection might be done by having students submit a list of their top three preferences to the teacher who then chooses the groups, by putting their names on a newsprint sheet on which the subtopic is written, or by moving to a designated place in the room that represents a subtopic.

This negotiation of team membership may be messy, but it is necessary to ensure student commitment and a group composition that has a reasonable chance of success.

❸ STUDENTS COMPLETE A TEAM BUILDING ACTIVITY

Much more than short term structures, Co-op Co-op requires students who have trust in each other and the social skills to work as a team. Several of the activities listed under Team Projects, such as creating a team name and handshake, would be useful at this initial stage. After one of these the team can create a Team Web to show the qualities that helped them be a successful group.

❹ TEAMS REFINE THEIR SUBTOPIC

The teams need to define and elaborate upon their subtopic. This might begin with a Three-Step Interview on their knowledge of the topic and their reasons for choosing the subtopic. The students may need to look again at the brainstormed list of subtopics and they may even decide to change their choice. The teacher needs to monitor and co-ordinate any substantial changes so that there is no overlap with another group. This step ends when each group has a clear subtopic that they believe is important and interesting.

❺ INDIVIDUAL TEAM MEMBERS CHOSE A MINI-TOPIC

Each team member chooses one aspect of the team's subtopic to research and prepare for presentation. This may mean that the team has to brainstorm different aspects of their subtopic as they did in the whole class discussion of Step 1 before deciding who researches what. Framing the mini-topics in the form of a question can help students to define clearly what they want to research. The mini-topics need to be subject to the teacher's approval to be sure they are of significance for the understanding of the topic as a whole and are feasible in the time allocated.

Before the next step, the group could also suggest possible sources of information to each other such as people for an interview or a good magazine to read. Figure 1 gives a planning guide for this stage. This is also a good point at which to discuss assessment and evaluation.

❻ INDIVIDUALS RESEARCH THEIR MINI-TOPIC

Team members individually research their mini-topic and prepare a presentation to their team. The research can be done through a variety of means such as library research, surveys, or interviews. (Students may neglect to consider interviewing an expert as a source of information.) Explain to students that they may want to change their research question as they learn more about the topic. This is normal, but it should be done in consultation with you and the team.

The presentation, usually about five to seven minutes long, may be given with graphs, pictures or other teaching aid.

Although this stage is individual, team members are encouraged to help each other as needed.

❼ INDIVIDUALS PRESENT THEIR RESEARCH TO THEIR TEAMS

Each student in turn now shares his or her information while the others listen, support, and try to draw connections so that the pieces of their subtopic make sense as a whole. The team members who are not presenting may play roles such as Praiser, Question Commander (who checks to see if any one has any questions to ask), Recorder, Taskmaster, or Cheerleader. Time limitations need to be followed.

Figure 2 offers a form for evaluation at this stage.

⑧ Teams Prepare Their Presentations

Teams first need to decide what are the top ten (or less) ideas or pieces of information that are essential for understanding their subtopic. If the class forgot everything else from their presentation, what are the ten essential things they should remember?

Secondly, they need to decide on the most dynamic way possible to teach that information. This may include a diorama, dramatization, slide show, radio advertisement, soap opera, tv news format, game show, newspaper, model, or mural. Derek Sankey of Vancouver, for example, often has students prepare thesis statements on a poster with supporting visual and written information and then has the presentations done by Carousel Sharing (Structure 18, p. 168).

Criteria for evaluation should also be discussed. These may include involvement of all group members, clear communication of main ideas, support for the main ideas, involvement of other members of the class, and general interest.

⑨ Teams Present to the Class

Each team should be responsible for gathering their own resources like a slide projector and timing themselves. Some teachers have a feedback session from the class immediately after each presentation.

⑩ Everyone Evaluates

Evaluation is at three stages: (1) by teammates after the mini-topic presentation; (2) a combination of peer, self, and teacher evaluations after the team presentation; and (3) any additional test, essay or project evaluation by the teacher and student. All of the criteria and procedures should have been made clear during the first half of the steps of this procedure. Figure 2 gives a variety of evaluation forms.

Ideas for Using Co-op Co-op in Social Studies

Mini-Co-op Co-op can work in as little time as one or two periods if students have the resources readily available. In addition to the textbook, students may do the following:

- Analyze newspapers for different themes that relate to national or international politics;
- Search copies of magazines for persuasion techniques, images of men and women, or the probable audience;
- Use atlases, almanacs, yearbooks, or computer data bases to prepare a presentation on the geography of a country.

Full blown Co-op Co-op can be applied to any social studies topic that has some complexity and can spark student interest. In history, it could be a historical period like the Cold War; in geography it could be an issue of local pollution; in economics, unemployment or the manufacturing industry; in integrated subjects it could be a novel study combined with historical background.

One way to give a focus to the project is to have a culminating performance such as the following:

- A museum for which students need to create a display (see the assignment sheet),

Structure 2 CO-OP-CO-OP

- A medieval village,
- A press conference on a public issue with students as lobby groups,
- A re-enactment of a United Nations Conference, for example, on population,
- A re-enacted historical conference like Versailles,
- A real conference on the environment or international human rights which other classes may attend.

FIGURE 1: PLANNING GUIDE

Co-op Co-op Planning Guide

Whole class topic: _____

Team topic: _____

TEAM MEMBER	TASK FOR DAY 1	TASK FOR DAY 2	TASK FOR DAY 3
1.			
2.			
3.			
4.			

Resources

A. Books and documents:

B. People:

C. Other (e.g., videos, locations):

Cooperative Learning and Social Studies: Towards Excellence and Equity by Tom Morton
Kagan Publishing • 1(800) 933-2667 • www.KaganOnline.com

Structure 2   CO-OP-CO-OP

FIGURE 2: SAMPLE EVALUATION FORMS

SELF EVALUATION FORM
STAGE 1: RESEARCH

Name: _____
My role in this stage was: _____

	YES	NO	PARTIALLY
1. Did I complete my task?	___	___	___
2. Is a neat copy of my written work in the folder?	___	___	___
3. Did I help others in my group who were having problems?	___	___	___
4. Did I help organize the finished product?	___	___	___
5. Did I make the best use of time?	___	___	___

I believe I should receive the mark of:
　　less than 5　　5-6　　6-7　　7-8　　more (state)
for my contribution to the research stage.

My reasons for this mark are: (state specific things you YOU did) _____
_____
_____

Signature: _____

SELF EVALUATION FORM
STAGE 2: WRITTEN WORK

Name: _____
My role in this stage was: _____

	YES	NO	PARTIALLY
1. Did I complete my task?	___	___	___
2. Did I help others in my group who were having problems?	___	___	___
3. Did I help organize the finished product?	___	___	___
4. Did I make the best use of time?	___	___	___
5. Was I present in class every day our group met?	___	___	___

I believe I should receive the mark of:
　　less than 5　　5-6　　6-7　　7-8　　more (state)
for my contribution to the writing stage.

My reasons for this mark are: (state specific things you YOU did) _____
_____
_____

Signature: _____

SELF EVALUATION OF GROUP PRESENTATION

Name: _____ Date: _____
My role in this presentation: _____

Did I?:

	ALWAYS	SOMETIMES	NEVER
• make useful suggestions;	___	___	___
• share information and ideas;	___	___	___
• listen to others' points of view;	___	___	___
• make the best use of time;	___	___	___
• check for accuracy;	___	___	___
• complete my assigned work;	___	___	___

Circle the word(s) which best describe your overall contribution to the group activity:
　　COULD BE BETTER　　OK
　　PRETTY GOOD　　EXCELLENT

On the basis of the above, I believe that I deserve:
　　no more than 5　　5-6　　6-7　　7-8　　more (state)
for this assignment.

My justifications for this mark are (state specific things you did): _____
_____
_____

PEER EVALUATION FORM:
GROUP WORK

Name: _____
Group: _____

1. Please rate each member of your group according to the following criteria:
　　4 = always, excellent effort
　　3 = most of the time, quite good effort
　　2 = some of the time, could have been more helpful
　　1 = rarely, effort was not satisfactory
2. Rate yourself in the last column.

Factors	Names of group members here		
1. Completed assigned tasks in a satisfactory way			
2. Helped other members to organize and complete finished product			
3. Made the best use of time during library research			
4. Contributed usefully to group activity—gave good suggestions			
5. Was present for every class assigned for project			

Total = 20

Signature: _____

By Jackie Dippong, *Cooperative Learning*, Vol. 13, No. 1

Co-op Co-op Student Handout

Museum Project on Immigration

Project Focus
Why do people immigrate to the United States? What is it like to immigrate? How do immigrants influence this country? How do we influence them?

1. Your project is to create a theme exhibit that would educate museum visitors about what life is like for immigrants in their own country, en-route to this country, and in the USA. Your sub-topics could include culture like schools, food and entertainment here and there, economics, politics, history and geography. After looking through the resources, the class will decide on the topics to explore and we will chose groups.

2. The final exhibit prepared by your group should use at least two of the following:
   - food
   - music
   - artifact (replica)
   - model
   - drawing
   - collage
   - game
   - dance

3. Each section of the exhibit must also have a written plaque that describes the display for museum goers and explains its importance. Each should be one to two paragraphs in length.

4. Each group member is responsible for planning, researching, presenting the results of your research to the group, designing the exhibit, and acting as a docent (a trained guide).

Evaluation
Your final project will be judged on the following:
- how well the exhibit answers the focus questions
- the visual appeal
- the accuracy of the historical information
- consistent and purposeful group work
- the use of cooperative skills such as giving ideas, listening to others, encouragement, and "home ice" (praising).

NARRATIVE OF LESSONS USING CO-OP CO-OP

Immigration from Latin America

Themes
- Global connections
- People, places, and the environment

Skills
- Reference and information-search
- Classifying information
- Interpreting information
- Analyzing information
- Synthesizing information

Maria Wright teaches in a school with a high immigrant population predominantly Latin American. Her course on American history spends quite a bit of time on the role of immigrants considering questions like why they left their countries of origin, what it was like to move to a new land, how they influenced their new country, and how they were in turn influenced by America. For the last three weeks of the unit she wanted her students to study the topic in depth and have a chance to spread their wings. There was also a school open house coming and she thought that the parents might make a good audience for the students' projects.

Up to this time, the immigrant groups mentioned in the text and other resources had not included those from Latin American countries. When she introduced the Co-op Co-op project and the idea of focusing on Latin America, Ms. Wright still offered the students the choice of studying a different source of immigration. She was concerned that some students might feel neglected if their country of origin was not possible to study. In the end, Haiti, which had been in the news, was the only other country that became a subtopic.

Ms. Wright began with a brief overview of Latin American geography and politics and played two songs, "El Lavaplatos" (The Dishwasher) and "La Cucaracha Mojada" (The Wetback Cockroach) about Mexican immigration to spark student interest. (Songs and other useful resources can be found in Nuñez, 1993.)

The whole class then brainstormed a list of topics: countries like Mexico, El Salvador, Guatlemala, Cuba, and Haiti; people like Castro and Aristide; the war in El Salvador; the US occupation of Haiti; illegal immigration; the Sanctuary Movement; and NAFTA. When they winnowed the topics for research, the class decided on countries as the sub-topics. They also agreed with Ms. Wright's suggestion that the immigrant communities from those countries could be part of their research. She wanted the students to appreciate that they had good sources of information in their own city, maybe in their own family.

Ms. Wright let students chose their groups initially by writing their names on poster paper. However, once the groups started to refine what they wanted to study about their countries, several of the students wanted to change groups. She suspected that this was to avoid working with one particular girl, so she took charge of the reshuffling and convinced the girl to join a group that Ms. Wright felt would be compatible and supportive.

She wanted the students to be conscious of the parents as an audience so she created the idea that the final presentation was to be a museum exhibit. There information would be presented to the class, but it also had to be bold and appealing enough to attract a walk through crowd. A handout that describes the project is included here. The class and Ms. Wright fleshed out the criteria and standards in more detail.

The class had three library research periods over two weeks during which Ms. Wright taught lessons on different topics. There were also two and a half periods for the mini-presentations and preparation for the class presentation. During that time Ms. Wright was busy monitoring, helping and exhorting—a very active guide on the side.

The class presentations included tv news format, game shows, and a skit of a classroom with a hilarious take-off on Ms. Wright. The open house was more sedate, relying on posters and a videotape of the class presentations, but many of the students showed up to show their work to their parents.

Structure 3
CORNERS

Steps at a Glance

1. The teacher poses a question and offers three or four possible answers.
2. Students move to the corner that represents their choice and pair up to explain their reasons.
3. The teacher calls on students in one corner to give their responses.
4. Continue with other corners reporting followed by pairs paraphrasing.

The teacher poses a question that has three or four possible answers and designates corners of the room to represent those answers. Students choose a corner and move to it to discuss their reasons for their choice with a partner and the class. Corners is an energizing structure that can give an anticipatory set or synthesize material already covered.

Social Skills
- Paraphrasing

Corners is an old and popular structure in adult education, but considering its many strengths, it seems underused in the middle and high school. In Corners, students are active in choosing and moving, and the teacher can easily monitor comprehension because students must paraphrase to the class what their classmates say. As the suggested ideas and the narrative show, Corners can lead students to consider values questions and to reason with metaphors.

Structure 3 CORNERS

STEPS

❶ TEACHER POSES A QUESTION AND OFFERS THREE OR FOUR POSSIBLE ANSWERS

Announce the corners which will represent the choices. If possible, post a work or visual symbol in each corner. Usually there are four corners, but three or five may also be appropriate.

Teacher Tip: Give students the choices along with some time to think about which one they prefer. It is best for them to write their selection. This avoids some students just waiting to see where the class leader goes.

❷ STUDENTS MOVE TO CORNER THAT REPRESENTS THEIR CHOICE AND PAIR UP TO EXPLAIN THEIR REASONS

Ask them to paraphrase their partner while discussing.

❸ TEACHER CALLS ON STUDENTS IN ONE CORNER TO GIVE THEIR RESPONSES

The teacher then asks the pairs to take turns paraphrasing to each other the answers just given to the class.

❹ CONTINUE WITH OTHER CORNERS REPORTING FOLLOWED BY PAIRS PARAPHRASING

IDEAS FOR USING CORNERS IN SOCIAL STUDIES

- **Place to Visit**
  Cairo, Rome, Beijing, Mecca, Machu Pichu, Rio de Janeiro, New York, Tokyo

- **Historical Place and Time to Visit**
  Empire of Mali, Inca Empire, Medieval England, pre-contact Haida, Classical Greece, Ming Dynasty, New France, Court of Genghis Khan, 19th century American West

- **Decade of the Twentieth Century to Visit**
  Twenties, thirties, forties, fifties, sixties

- **Job that Requires the Most Social Skills (or Creativity, Intelligence, among others)**
  Carpenter, mechanic, lawyer, writer, manager, business person, secretary, farmer

- **Preferred Political Position**
  Queen (or king) of England, prime minister of Canada, president of the United States, mayor, head of the school board, secretary-general of the United Nations

- **Preferred Historical Character**
  Types like medieval pope, lord, bishop, knight, inn keeper, merchant, peasant, vassal, priest or people like Abraham Lincoln, Harriet Tubman, and Robert E. Lee or Winston Churchill, Mahatma Gandhi, and Mao Tse Tung

- **Most Powerful Dream**
  Excellence in some field like sports or art; a family; success in a career; contributing to a better world in some way

Notes

- **Most Influential Invention**
  Cotton gin, spinning wheel, and steam engine or radio, telephone, television, and computer or boat, bicycle, car, and airplane

- **Endangered Species that Interests You the Most**
  Panda, blue whale, trumpeter swan, orangutan, spotted owl, condor, Indian elephant

- **Tree that the Topic of Study Resembles the Most**
  Apple, maple, oak, fir, pine, dogwood, monkey puzzle, birch

- **Physical Landform that the Topic of Study Resembles the Most**
  Glacier, volcano, coral reef, desert, prairie, muskeg, river valley, river delta

- **Most Important Influence on the Weather**
  Latitude, elevation, wind direction, surrounding landforms, distance from the sea

- **Most Important Institution**
  School, hospital, police, local government

- **Metaphor that You Prefer**
  For the world: global village, spider web, mother

  For a multi-cultural society: melting pot, mosaic, orchestra, pressure cooker, county fair

  For an effective leader: captain of a ship, father or mother, general, teacher, shepherd

- **Best Definition of a Patriot**
  Someone who supports the country's leader all the way all the time; someone who tries to tell the country the truth though all may disagree; someone who does what the people want all the way all the time; someone who fights for the country against all enemies.

- **The Most Important Quality**
  In battle: Courage, strength, intelligence, belief in the cause, luck

  For a learning team: Giving good ideas, encouraging others, helping teammates, organizing the work, being positive, trying hard

- **Best Source of Historical Evidence**
  A secondary written source (textbook account, teacher's lecture, etc.), a primary written source (diaries, letters, etc.), primary visual source (paintings, photos, etc.), primary music (songs and dance)

- **Most Important Cause of Conflict**
  Political, economic, religious, racial/ethnic, psychological/human nature

NARRATIVE OF LESSONS USING CORNERS

Multiple Intelligences and Metaphors

Themes
- Time, continuity, and change

Values
- Respect for the contributions of others
- Concern for the common good

Skills
- Synthesizing information
- Decision making

The social studies department of a local Vancouver high school has been trying for the past few years to teach using the multiple intelligences of all its students. Teachers spend considerable time in September building class and team unity and explaining Multiple Intelligences to their new classes. A part of this introduction uses Corners.

Teachers ask their students to choose one of four choices to the question "What makes a good student?"

1. Someone who memorizes all the material presented by the text and teacher;
2. Someone who always tries to contribute his or her special talents to the learning task;
3. Someone who helps others to learn and enjoy being here;
4. Someone who understands deeply the main ideas and can apply them to new situations.

Although often the students overwhelmingly chose one or two corners over the others, there are usually enough thoughtful student responses from each one for the teachers to elaborate on as they explain that all four ways are valuable and all four form part of social studies.

As part of the multiple intelligence approach students frequently write and draw visual metaphors. They often consider questions like "Which metaphor best represents the Americas in the eyes of the Europeans: harvest, treasure chest, magnet, or magic lamp?" or "You've seen a film about Nelson Mandela. Now brainstorm metaphors to represent him.... Which metaphor is the best and why?"

Corners is one of the structures used to discuss these metaphors. For example, after reading about the history of the first few decades of the 20th century students were asked to chose the metaphor and its corner that best represented the 1920s:

Rose bush: beautiful flower and perfume, but watch for the thorns;
Cactus: prickly, survives in tough times, has a beautiful flower;
Apple tree: beautiful blossoms in the spring, bear fruit in the summer and fall;
Dandelion: most consider it a weed, but its flower is pretty and its leaves make a delicious salad and wine.

After discussion and paraphrasing of the reasons for choosing their metaphor students were asked to move again to the plant corner which best represented the 1930s to repeat the structure.

Processing in Corners focuses on paraphrasing and is usually done in one of two ways. First, when the teacher calls on a student to paraphrase in front of the class, the teacher will also ask the student who gave the original response if the paraphrase is accurate. Secondly, the teacher often asks students at the end of the structure to write down all the ideas given. This is both good review and a way to get some feedback on the quality of listening.

Structure 4
Creative Controversy

Steps at a Glance

1. Teacher presents the controversy.
2. Teacher teaches Guidelines for a Good Argument and Social Skills
3. Pairs prepare their position.
4. Pairs meet with others with the same position.
5. Pairs return to their original teams to present their positions.
6. Teams advocate and refute arguments
7. Teams reverse their perspectives.
8. Teams try to reach a decision,
9. Teams report to the class.
10. Teams reflect on their group process.
11. Students and the teacher evaluate thinking and knowledge.

Two pairs argue different sides of a controversial issue, switch roles to argue the other side, then work as a team to find a common position. This is an advanced structure for the study of public issues that encourages quality-thinking and open-mindedness.

Social Skills
- Disagreeing respectfully
- Listening
- Asking for justification
- Encouraging

A few years ago the management of Tiger stadium in Detroit closed the bleachers. It seems that two groups of fans had started to pursue the debate featured in a popular advertisement on the reasons for choosing a particular beer. Many may still recall the two opposing arguments "Tastes great!" and "Less filling!" shouted by various retired athletes on TV. The Tiger stadium partisans of this controversy began to embellish these already compelling arguments with references to various body parts and sexual practices. These became more and more explicit in word and gesture until fights broke out and the stands were closed. Clearly these were fans unskilled at resolving controversies!

In social studies we want better for our students. We want students to reach reasoned judgements about what to believe or how to act. We want them to think critically when faced with public issues or problematic situations of much greater complexity than a choice of beer. This means, among other features, that students should practice the habits of mind for a careful and conscientious thinker and understand the principles of quality thinking.

Good habits of mind include open-mindedness—willingness to withhold judgement and seek new evidence or alternative points of view and willingness to change one's mind if the evidence convinces one to do so—and fair-mindedness—acceptance of the duty to respect all points of view and honor the most persuasive as well as commitment to open and critical discussion. Principles of quality thinking include searching for accurate and unbiased information sources and assessing an argument for evidence and reasons, not accepting emotional appeals alone.

The series of structures called Creative Controversy, developed by David and Roger Johnson, can foster these habits of mind and the practice of quality thinking.

STEPS

❶ TEACHER PRESENTS THE CONTROVERSY (5–15 MIN.)

To heighten interest the teacher presents the controversy in a challenging and thought provoking manner. It will also smooth and shorten the initial steps in learning if students begin with a common base of background information and prerequisite vocabulary.

❷ TEACHER TEACHES GUIDELINES FOR A GOOD ARGUMENT AND SOCIAL SKILLS (5–30 MIN.)

The teacher gives the procedure for the classes to follow and the Guidelines that students are expected to follow. The ones suggested here emphasize social skills and habits of mind, but can be altered to emphasize more quality thinking.

If students are unfamiliar with such essential behaviors as criticizing ideas, not people, the teacher needs to teach these or call on students to give examples. Less is more with social and thinking skills, so limit instruction to just one of these guidelines for any one controversy and discuss only briefly the others.

❸ PAIRS PREPARE THEIR POSITIONS (ABOUT 15 MIN.)

Divide the class into groups of 4 and these in turn into pairs, each pair of roughly equal academic ability to the other pair. If the number of students in the class is not divisible by 4, then there can be groups of 5 divided into a twosome and threesome. (One variation from the use of a base group of four is to divide the class into pairs only and use Inside-Outside Circle for steps 5 to 11 with the pairs of the two sides of the argument in different circles.)

Each pair takes a different position on the controversy. They can either receive arguments prepared by the teacher, "position papers", or research the topic and prepare their own arguments. The following description will assume that students are given prepared arguments.

The students' goal at this stage is to master the material and plan how to argue it persuasively. Using Pairs Read younger students should read for comprehension with each partner alternately summarizing the main idea and giving supporting details. More advanced students might read to identify opinion, facts and definitions or reasoning and assumptions.

Teacher Tip: If you are concerned that one member of the pair may be reluctant to argue later in the lesson, then you might ask the pairs to assign different points to each member, each partner responsible for explaining an equal number of points.

❹ PAIRS MEET WITH OTHERS WITH SAME POSITION (10 MIN.)

This is similar step to when different expert groups meet in Jigsaw II. Pairs that have the same position on the controversy meet to form a group of 4 (up to 6 if numbers work that way). They share their main ideas in Roundrobin fashion. If time permits, they could alternatively use the Spectrum structure and take turns placing the different arguments on a scale from most persuasive to least persuasive. More advanced students can be asked to anticipate arguments from the other side.

❺ PAIRS RETURN TO THEIR ORIGINAL TEAMS TO PRESENT THEIR POSITIONS (5 MIN.)

Use Pairs Compare or RoundRobin to have each pair present their arguments. The other pair at this point should listen or ask questions for clarification, not criticize.

❻ TEAMS ADVOCATE AND REFUTE ARGUMENTS (15–30 MIN.)

Remind students of their purpose to reach the best decision for a group report and then invite them to begin arguing forcefully their positions using Team Discussion. Monitor for good examples of the use of the guidelines.

❼ TEAMS REVERSE THEIR PERSPECTIVES (10 MIN.)

Continue with Team Discussion but ask the two sides to reverse their positions, that is, to argue for the position that they were previously criticizing.

❽ TEAMS TRY TO REACH A DECISION (30 MIN.)

Ask students to drop their assigned points of view and try to reach a decision that all group members can agree with and explain. If it is the case that even after listening respectfully that not everyone agrees, then the group should be ready to report all viewpoints. Use Numbered Heads Together here explaining that any member may be called on randomly to explain both the majority decision and any dissenting opinions.

Alternatively, the group could begin with a Three-Step Interview on the students' opinions followed by the Team Discussion.

The group report may be in a written, oral, or graphic form.

❾ TEAMS REPORT TO CLASS (20–30 MIN.)

Use the procedures of Numbered Heads Together to have students report to the class and lead a whole class discussion.

❿ TEAMS REFLECT ON THEIR GROUP PROCESS

Ask students to complete individually the processing form in this section and then share their responses through a RoundRobin or Three-Step Interview.

Structure 4 CREATIVE CONTROVERSY

⓫ STUDENTS AND TEACHER EVALUATE THINKING AND KNOWLEDGE

In addition to the group reports that can be evaluated formatively, students should demonstrate their learning individually, for example, with an essay. Both the group report and individual work should be evaluated according to the following criteria:

- Multiple arguments in support of a position;
- Fair and convincing counter-arguments;
- A logical conclusion that recognizes different arguments.

For an essay the following "scaffolding" suggested by Parker, McDaniel, and Valencia (1991) can prompt students to continue to use the same quality thinking that was begun with the controversy discussion:

Write a four paragraph essay giving your point of view on the controversy. Each paragraph has a different purpose:

Paragraph 1: In this paragraph, you should briefly explain the conflict and give your position on it, but do not give any reasons yet.

Paragraph 2: In this paragraph, you should give your reasons for your position.

Paragraph 3: In this paragraph, you should give good reasons against your positon. Start this paragraph with some transition words like "On the other hand," or "Some people might say, however,…"

Paragraph 4: In this paragraph, you should come to a conclusion that refers back to the arguments in paragraphs 2 and 3.

Notes

STAGES IN A CREATIVE CONTROVERSY	POSSIBLE STRUCTURES
Preparing positions	Pairs Read, Team Discussion, Spectrum, Team Graphic of Arguments
Expert group sharing	RoundRobin, Spectrum
Presenting positions	Pairs Compare, Team Discussion, Inside-Outside Circle
Advocating and refuting	Team Discussion, Inside-Outside Circle, RoundRobin
Reversing perspectives	Team Discussion, Inside-Outside Circle, RoundRobin
Reaching a decision	Numbered Heads Together, Team Discussion, Three-Step Interview, Team Venn, Spectrum
Reporting to the class	Teams Tour, Team Inside-Outside Circle, Whole-Class Discussion
Processing	RoundRobin, Team Discussion, Team Statement

IDEAS FOR USING CREATIVE CONTROVERSIES IN SOCIAL STUDIES

The Johnsons' book *Creative Controversy* (1992) gives lesson plans and information sheets on the following:

- Who Should Get the Penicillin? In 1943 the U. S. Army had to decide whether to give a limited supply of the drug to soldiers who had contracted venereal disease or for the battle wounded.

- Should the Acadians be Deported? In 1755 the French speaking Acadians were in the middle of a war between the French and British and the British governor had to decide what to do.

- The Federalists Versus the Anti-Federalists. Different politicians held different views about what should be the form of the constitution for the new American state

- The Timber Wolf. Students consider whether the wolf should be preserved as a protected species or hunted to keep numbers down.

- What Makes Humans Human? Students discuss whether the impetus for humans to evolve was the use of weapons to kill or the development of higher levels of cooperation.

- There is an abundance of other questions that could form the basis of a controversy. Some examples would be

- Were the pyramids a good idea? (or the Crusades, French Revolution, Harper's Ferry, among others.)

- Who was right: American Patriots or British Loyalists?

- Who owns Canada (First Nations vs European land claims)?

- Should the Anne Frank family have stayed together or split up?

- What energy source is the best? (or means of transportation, country to live in, city to live in, political leader, and the like.)

- Is euthanasia justified?

- Is the use of violence to bring about change justified?

- Is advertising harmful?

- Should we have tracking in our school?

- Which will better prepare you for life outside school: cooperative or competitive skills?

STUDENT HANDOUT

Guidelines for a Good Argument

(Adapted from Johnson, D. and Johnson, R. (1992). *Creative Controversy*. Edina, MN: Interaction.)

1. Criticize ideas, not people.

2. Listen, even when you disagree.

3. Try to understand all sides of an issue.

4. Be willing to change your mind if the evidence convinces you to do so.

5. Go for the best decision, not victory.

STUDENT HANDOUT

Processing Questionnaire for after a CR8V Controversy

(From Johnson, D. and Johnson, R. (1992). *Creative Controversy*. Edina, MN: Interaction, p. 3:44)

1. To what extent did other members of the group listen to, and understand your ideas?

    (Not at all)   1   2   3   4   5   6   7   8   9   (Completely)

2. How much influence do you feel you had on the group's decision?

    (None at all)   1   2   3   4   5   6   7   8   9   (Complete)

3. To what extent do you feel committed to, and responsible for, the group's decision?

    (Not at all)   1   2   3   4   5   6   7   8   9   (Completely)

4. To what extent are you satisfied with your group's performance?

    (Very dissatisfied) 1   2   3   4   5   6   7   8   9   (Very satisfied)

5. How much did you learn about the issue under discussion?

    (Nothing at all) 1   2   3   4   5   6   7   8   9   (A great deal)

6. Write two adjectives describing the way you now feel.

Cooperative Learning and Social Studies: Towards Excellence and Equity by Tom Morton
Kagan Publishing • 1(800) 933-2667 • www.KaganOnline.com

NARRATIVE OF LESSONS USING A CREATIVE CONTROVERSY

Christopher Columbus: Was He a Great Man?

Theme
- Time, continuity, and change

Skills
- Study skills
- Interpreting information
- Analyzing information
- Decision-making

Recurring Question
- How do we know what happened in the past?

The quincentenary of Christopher Columbus' voyage to the New World was a boon for social studies teachers. It was a rare occasion when a historical event became front page news and, after all the debate and revisionism on Columbus and the meaning of his achievements, teaching about him would never look the same again. Long after the quincentenary had passed, lessons on Columbus would have implications for the teaching of Native Indians, the building of the American nation, the environment, and history itself.

It was during the sound and fury of the quincentenary that Dr. Peter Rothstein first decided to use the Creative Controversy method in his senior world history course to involve students in the debate and to help instill respect for differences of opinion and a quality argument. The topic of Columbus comes only a few weeks into his course so he needs to take some time to teach the guidelines of a good argument. For example, he invites some outgoing students to role play a bad argument in front of the class, which they usually do with great gusto. Then he invites the whole class to suggest what they could do to avoid a bad argument and what they needed to do for a good one. From this he constructs a "T-Chart" of what it would look like and sound like when someone disagrees nicely or criticizes ideas, not people.

In the first week of the term, the class has already discussed some central questions about history: how do we know what happened in the past? How do we know what or who is important? Does history ever change? Who writes history? Dr. Rothstein uses these focus

Structure 4 CREATIVE CONTROVERSY

questions again for the Columbus controversy.

Students start in groups of four who are divided into pairs. Dr. Rothstein shows some pictures of Columbus from textbooks and reference books (mindful not to say that there were no portraits of him while he lived and that these illustrations were mostly fanciful.) Students then write what they know about Columbus, discussing this with a partner and sharing with the class. Rarely has any student known much of the debate about Columbus's role in history and almost all have portrayed him as a great man, the discoverer of America.

After this, the whole class reads the introductory handout, "Columbus: Was He a Great Man?" Dr. Rothstein then gives different role descriptions, "Tainos" and "Children of Columbus", to the Pairs and asks them to use Pairs Read. The rest of the lesson follows the steps of the Creative Controversy. The procedure usually takes between two periods, but stretches to three if the discussion is especially rich. Last year, in between periods some students went to the Internet for more evidence (URL:gopher://marauder.millersv.edu:70/11/otherMU/columbus/data).

Once students have given their group report to the class and reflected on their group process, Dr. Rothstein uses a Think-Pair-Share to turn to questions about history:

"Since at least the beginning of the 1800s most histories have described Columbus as a great man just as you imagined him at the start of this unit, using many of the arguments that you read during the controversy. In the last few years, however, many people have started to criticize him with the reasons that you also heard in the controversy discussion. I want you to think about how opinions on Columbus have changed.

Who would have written this history in 1492? Who might write history today?

Should we celebrate the arrival of Columbus?

How do we know what happened in the past?"

(Although there are many reasons for the changing opinion, the questions are intended to lead students to consider the influence of voice or point of view. Until fairly recently, mainly Europeans and, later, Americans wrote the history of the Americas that we read in schools and universities. Except for the Mayans, Amerindians did not have written languages in 1492. Ronald Wright in *Stolen Continents* (1992) explains how the Spanish also destroyed the historical accounts of the time that were written by the Mayans or by the few Native Indians who became literate in Spanish. One Friar even forged documents to make it appear as if the conquered people praised their conquorers. Today, many Amerindians, like other groups, are telling their own version of history and trying to be heard.)

INTRODUCTION

Christopher Columbus: Was he a great man?

His voyage to the New World was called by Spanish historian Francisco Lopez de Gomara "the greatest event since the creation of the world." Five centuries later, there is one country named after him (Columbia), one major province (British Columbia), two national capitals (Colombo, Sri Lanka, and Washington, District of Columbia, USA), and one major river (Columbia). The United States, which has at times seen him as its national symbol, has a national holiday, Columbus Day. And there is also the famous ditty:

*In fourteen ninety-two,
Columbus sailed the ocean blue.*

Through much of the past 500 years, Columbus has been called great, the Admiral of the Ocean Sea, the stuff of legends. More recently, people have questioned our ideas about this sailor from Genoa, Italy. Some stories about him are clearly only legend. For example, there is the legend that he was a modern thinker who had concluded from his studies that the earth was round, while those who opposed him were close-minded religious fanatics who insisted that it was flat. This is false: it was generally accepted at the time that the earth was a globe. The Spanish commission that investigated his proposal to the King and Queen quite rightly doubted Columbus's estimate of the distance to Asia and rejected him based on this.

The debate over the real nature of Columbus is all the more difficult because there is so little known for certain about him. The only portraits were made years after his death. There is little written record of his early years in Genoa. We have the journals that he made on his voyages, but the original was lost. There is only what Bartolome de Las Casas partly copied and partly summarized in the 1530s, forty years after Columbus wrote them.

Even his name is controversial. He was born Cristoforo Colombo and was called Cristobal Colon in Spain. But he changed it often and at times referred to himself as Xpoual Colon, a Greek abbreviation for "Christ."

Your task is to try to learn as much as possible about this mysterious man and decide if he really was great. To do this you will play the roles of Tainos Indians and the children of Columbus. The Tainos were the first people whom Columbus met. They greeted him with great kindness by Columbus's own accounts, but later the Spanish and Tainos were to become enemies. On the other hand, Columbus' children always saw their father as a hero, even when he was strongly criticized later in his life.

The year is 1518 and you are speaking before an inquiry in Madrid, Spain. (There were, in fact, inquiries conducted by Spain about both Columbus and the Spanish treatment of the native people.) Later you will drop your roles and decide your own opinion about the character and achievements of Christopher Columbus.

Children of Columbus

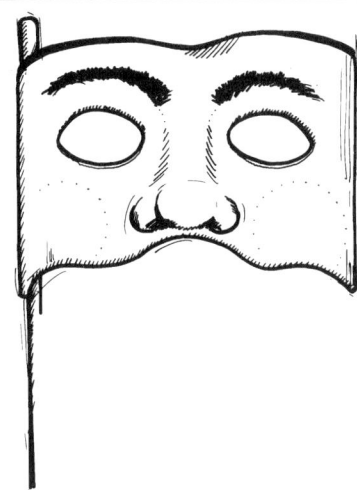

Instructions: You are to play the role of the sons or daughters of Christopher Columbus. Your position is that your father was a great man because he followed his dream and changed the history of the world. Despite many risks and many obstacles, he persisted and he succeeded. He was also a brilliant sailor and a deeply religious man.

Whether or not you agree with this position, play your role and give your arguments as strongly as you can. Below are some reasons that you should consider. Try to think of other arguments that make sense. Listen respectfully to the Taino Indians and learn their reasoning as well. Insist that they too have facts and logic to support their position. Determine where you both need more information.

1. Our father, Christopher Columbus, had a dream: that a ship could sail west from Europe to where no European had ever gone before, to lands where stories told of monsters, Cyclops, and wild men. He was a great man because he faced great opposition and great danger, but he persisted in following his dream of finding a sea route to Asia.

Our father could not afford to pay for an expedition by himself. So he travelled to Portugal to ask the King for support. He was refused. In 1485, poor and homeless, he moved to Spain to seek support from King Ferdinand and Queen Isabella. The King and Queen's experts said that his plans did not deserve support. Still he persisted, until in 1492 the Queen agreed to finance three ships.

2. Our father was a deeply religious man. He followed his dream in order to bring the benefits of Christianity to other people of the world. Faith guided him. He wrote to Ferdinand and Isabella that "no one should be afraid to undertake any project in the name of our Saviour (Jesus Christ)."

3. Columbus was a brilliant mariner. Michel de Cueno, who sailed with him, said that "by a single look at the night sky, he would know what route to follow or what weather to expect." He was able to plan the best possible way—sailing west from the Canary Islands and east on the latitude of the Bahamas—to travel to and return from the New World.

4. Columbus was a great man because he changed the course of history. Although he was not the discoverer of a new continent in the sense that he was the first to travel there, he was the first to announce what he had seen to a wide audience. As Las Casas said, "The Admiral (Columbus) was the first to open the gates of that ocean which had been closed for so many thousands of years before...He it was who gave the light by which all others might see how to discover." (*A look into the future: His voyages changed the lives of both Europeans and the people of the Americas: new plants and animals crossed the ocean, millions of people migrated, new empires rose and fell, new countries and cultures began.*)

5. The greatest tragedy of these voyages - the death of so many native Americans - was not the fault of our father or Spain. It was the unforeseen result of native people like the Tainos coming in contact for the first time with the diseases of Europe. The real conquerors of the Indian people were measles, malaria, pneumonia, typhoid, tuberculosis, and smallpox, especially smallpox.

Tainos

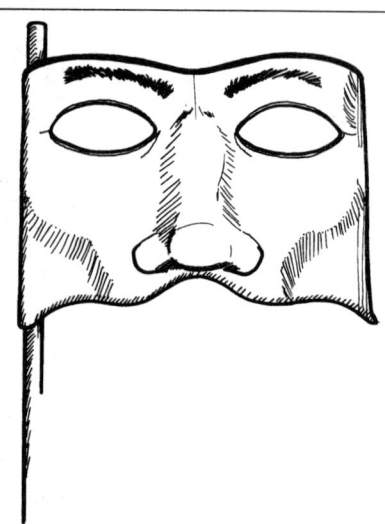

Instructions: You are to play the role of Taino Indians, the people who lived on the Caribbean island where Columbus first settled. Your opinion is that Chistopher Columbus was exceedingly greedy for gold. This drove him to horrible treatment of your people. Although he was the first European in centuries to reach the Americas, he thought he was in Asia and that we were Indians from India. This greed, cruelty, and ignorance do not make him a great man.

Whether or not you agree with this position, play your role and give your arguments as strongly as you can. Below are some reasons that you should consider. Try to think of other arguments that make sense. Listen respectfully to Columbus's children and learn their reasoning as well. Insist that they too have facts and logic to support their position. Determine where you both need more information.

1. Columbus was excessively greedy. He demanded from King Ferdinand and Queen Isabella 10 per cent of all the wealth returned to Spain from the new colony of Espanola, the title of Admiral of the Ocean Sea, governor and viceroy of all the territory he discovered. All these titles were to be inherited by his descendants.

He even stole the reward from the sailor who first sighted land, October 12, 1492. He had promised a prize of 10,000 maravedi a year (about $90 dollars in a time when the average sailor made about $100 in a good year.) Although Juan Rodriguez Bermejo was the first to cry, "Terra! Terra!" Columbus later claimed that he had seen a distant light hours earlier.

2. Columbus followed his dream, but he did not understand what he eventually found. He thought first of sailing to Asia and calculated that it was some 2,400 miles to the West. In truth, Asia is more than 10,000 miles from Spain. When he did sail and reached the Americas, he was sure he was in Asia. He called us Indians by mistake and the error stuck. Only later in his life did Columbus admit that he had found a new continent.

3. After his first voyage, Columbus was made governor of the new colony of Espanola (now the Dominican Republic and Haiti). However, he was a terrible leader. Many of the Spanish colonists mutinied against him. In 1500 the Spanish crown sent a new governor to arrest Columbus and send him back to Spain.

4. The saddest part of the story of Columbus was how he treated our people. Although he wrote in his journal that the Tainos "were the best people in the world and above all the most gentle" and elsewhere that we were intelligent and "without greed," he still took us as slaves. In 1495 he shipped 550 of our strongest men and women back to Spain.

Columbus also ordered every one of our people to bring him a hawk's bell (the size of a thimble) of gold every three months. Those that could not had their hands cut off and were left to bleed to death. However, there were no gold fields. The tiny bit of gold that there was had to be panned slowly from the streams. We could never satisfy his order.

In 1492 there were between 400,000 and 2 million of us, now in 1518 we are only 8,000. *(A look into the future: by 1550 the Taino people would be extinct.)*

Structure 5
FIND MY RULE
(AKA TWO-BOX INDUCTION AND CONCEPT ATTAINMENT)

Steps at a Glance

❶ As the teacher gives examples and non-examples of a concept, students try to find the rule.

❷ Students test the rule.

❸ The class reaches a consensus on a definition.

❹ Teams apply the rule to new items.

This structure is a kind of guessing game where the teacher gives various items, some of which are examples of a particular concept, and some of which are not. Groups try to determine the items that fit the concept and define its characteristics. Students learn key concepts from history, geography or the social sciences while they practice categorizing and defining.

Social Skills

- Checking for agreement
- Checking for understanding
- Asking for justification

Famed cellist Yo Yo Mah tells the story about how his father made learning music fun. He would play for Yo Yo a note, for example, A, then another note and another, asking his son after each one if it was an A or not.

This simple learning game is much like the Concept Attainment model developed by Jerome Bruner and adapted to cooperative learning as Find My Rule by Spencer Kagan. Just as a musician needs to distinguish notes to play an instrument, so students need key concepts like "revolution" to make sense of history or "region" to understand geography. Just as Yo Yo Mah's father would ask his son to pick out the common notes from a series, so social studies teachers can challenge students to find the similarities and differences in a set of photographs, national anthems, or occupations.

Structure 5 FIND MY RULE

Find My Rule is a structure, or a series of structures, for teaching thinking and for the mastery of intellectual concepts. It is especially suited to those ideas that are important to the social studies like primary and secondary documents or renewable and non-renewable resources but that students are unlikely to discover on their own.

It is similar to the Sort structure, but is more teacher directed. Moreover, the teacher needs to prepare numerous examples and non-examples before the lesson while in a Sort the students often generate the data.

STEPS

❶ AS THE TEACHER GIVES EXAMPLES AND NON-EXAMPLES OF A CONCEPT, STUDENTS TRY TO FIND THE RULE

Students work in groups of 4 divided into pairs. Give them items one at a time on the blackboard in one of two boxes. The items in Box 1 differ from Box 2 because they follow a certain pattern or rule that defines a concept. The students' task is to figure out the rule. Sometimes Box 1 is labeled Yes's because these are examples of the concept and Box 2 is No's because these are not examples.

If you want to emphasize the concept you can prompt students to focus on the particular attributes of the items, for example, by saying, "I want you to pay attention to the type of work the following people do." If your emphasis is more on the process, you may want to do no more than encourage participation and recognize the worth of the variety of answers.

Box 1	Box 2
secretary	*logger*

Use a Think-Pair-Share structure in asking for all the rules that could be used to distinguish Box 1 from Box 2.

Next, add one or two more items like the following example:

Box 1	Box 2
secretary	*logger*
day care worker	

Again ask students to think about how the two boxes differ, to share their answers in pairs, and then have a Team Discussion.

Now add another item.

Box 1	Box 2
secretary	*logger*
day care worker	*carpenter*

Ask students to Think-Write-Share. At this point you should write students' ideas about the rule or have students share them simultaneously on the blackboard. Here are some hypotheses that they may give:

Box 1	Box 2
work with	*work with*
people	*wood*
mostly women	*mostly men*
lower pay	*higher pay*
indoors	*outdoors*

Continue with more items and more cooperative structures.

Box 1	Box 2
secretary	*logger*
day care worker	*carpenter*
waitress	*farmer*
mechanic	*autoworker*
trucker	*baker*
teacher	*miner*

Teacher Tip: As the exercise continues, students may wish to give the name of the concept without taking the time to describe the attributes. As soon as they do that, thinking stops. The goals here, however, are for students to

Notes

68 *Cooperative Learning and Social Studies: Towards Excellence and Equity* by Tom Morton
Kagan Publishing • 1(800) 933-2667 • www.KaganOnline.com

Structure 5 **FIND MY RULE**

understand the attributes of the concept and to be aware of their thinking, so tell them that you are interested at this stage in explaining the rule and not naming it.

❷ **STUDENTS TEST THE RULE**
After several examples, begin to give items without assigning them to a box and ask the students to think where they should go, then share their thoughts in a Round-Robin or Team Discussion. Of course, vary the order of Yes's and No's in presenting items so students do not second guess you that left side will be followed by right side and so on.

Poll the class for their choices and once you have most groups choosing correctly, ask for an articulation of the rule, which is that the occupations on the left all involve a service while those on the right involve goods. Continue to test for the rule by asking the groups to come up with new items for Box 1 and 2.

❸ **CLASS REACHES A CONSENSUS ON A DEFINITION**
Once students are at ease with the concept, have them reach consensus on a statement of the rule being followed, in other words, the attributes of the concept. At this stage you could ask for the name of the concept: service or tertiary industry.

❹ **TEAMS APPLY THE RULE TO NEW ITEMS**
Finally, use a structure like Numbered Heads Together to check if students can apply the rule by providing them with some new examples to place in the boxes. For example, you could give them sales person (in a clothing store), the textile worker (who makes the clothes), a guitar maker, a guitarist, a concert promoter (for the musician), and a printer (of tickers for the concert).

Two other ways to apply the concept are (1) to ask students to change the description of an item in one box so that it would fit in the other box, e.g., what would a baker have to do to be in the service industry? and (2) if a concept is complicated and involved, like revolution for example, to use Pairs Check with a list of examples and non-examples for students to choose.

Teacher Tip: The Student Handout "Topics for Find My Rule" lists a number of important social studies concepts that could be taught with this structure. However, the list leaves out other important concepts, for example, "patriotism" because its attributes are so unclear that it is hard to teach using this structure. Though patriotism may be defined simply as "love of one's country," it would be hard to find a number of people who would agree as to what actions are patriotic. Concepts like "patriotism" and "justice" would be better taught using structures more suited to discussing controversies like a Values Line or Spectrum. Still other concepts like "democracy" or "culture" are less controversial but still too open ended for just Find My Rule. These could be better taught using a Team Web.

Cooperative Learning and Social Studies: Towards Excellence and Equity by Tom Morton

Structure 5 **FIND MY RULE**

Stages in Find My Rule	Appropriate Structures
Inducing the Rule	Think-Pair-Share (in the form of discussion, listing, webbing, or writing), Numbered Heads Together, Team Discussion, Simultaneous Sharing.
Testing the Rule	RoundRobin, Team Discussion, Think-Pair-Share (discussion, listing, webbing, or writing), People Sort
Class Consensus	Numbered Heads Together and Simultaneous Sharing with a Whole Class Discussion
Application to New Items	Numbered Heads Together, Teammates Consult, People Sort, Think-Pair-Share (discussion, listing, webbing or writing), Pairs Check

IDEAS FOR USING FIND MY RULE IN SOCIAL STUDIES

- **History**
  Primary and secondary documents (see the example on the following pages); fact, opinion, and argument; bias; revolution and reform; hot war and cold war; cause and effect

- **Geography**
  Various natural regions like rain forest, forest, and savanna; erosion; glaciation; cultural diffusion; industrialized countries; developed countries

- **Sociology**
  Roles, norms, cooperation, competition, prejudice

- **Anthropology**
  Assimilation, ethnocentrism, stereotyping, scapegoating

- **Politics and Government**
  Various ideologies like communism, socialism, free enterprise, fascism; propaganda and its various devices like loaded language, omission and distortion

- **Economics**
  Primary, secondary and tertiary industries; fiscal policy; monetary policy; free market, command, and traditional economies

- **Environmental Education**
  Environmental interdependence, recyclable products, renewable and non-renewable resources (see the example on the following pages), plant succession, bio-diversity

- **Global Education**
  Economic interdependence, developed and developing countries

---

Teacher Tip: In Find My Rule students actively learn the concept, but the lesson still can involve a good deal of preparation by the teacher. She or he needs to be sure of the critical attributes of the concept, those that define it, and the non-critical attributes, those characteristics that may be associated with the concept but are not essential. In addition, the teacher must collect at least six pairs of examples and non-examples for simple concepts, up to 25 or more pairs for complex ones. Below are examples of definitions and data sets for "renewable resource" and "secondary and primary source."

Notes

Renewable Resource: Example of a Definition and Data Set for Find My Rule

The various examples and non-examples could be given one at a time on the overhead or blackboard. As each item is presented, students will write it in one of the two boxes.

Concept   Renewable resource

Critical Attributes   It is a material that comes from something that can
(those characteristics   be grown or raised, that is, from a plant or animal.
that define the term)

Non-critical Attributes   Renewable resource is not defined by being recyclable.

Examples		Non-examples	
fish	wheat	gold	petroleum
paper	wood	plastic	coal
sisal (rope)	cotton	steel	rayon
milk	leather	glass	gasoline
pepper	silk	salt	polyester
ivory		electricity	

Primary and Secondary Sources: An Example of a Data Sheet for using Find My Rule

Another approach is to give students all of the items on a handout. The teacher or students read out one item at a time and write the item's number in one of two boxes representing the two concepts.

Concepts   Primary and secondary sources

Critical Attributes of   **a.** It is human-made such as a document, object, or
a Primary Source   oral account;

                                        b. It was produced by people who participated in, or were present at a historical event or time.

Critical Attributes of a   **a.** It is human-made such as a document, object, or oral
Secondary Source   account;

                                        b. It was produced by people who did not participate in or were not present at an event or time.

Non-critical Attributes   The source is not defined by its truthfulness or accuracy. (Students often assume that a primary source is truthful. One example to the contrary would be King George IV who convinced himself that he led a cavalry charge at the Battle of Waterloo, while in truth he never visited Waterloo until 1817, two years after the battle. There is also the celebrated photograph of Lenin giving a speech that had been altered to remove Trotsky standing nearby.)

Note: The definitions above are common ones, but the distinction between primary and secondary sources often depends on the context and purpose. For example, Denzel Washington's portrayal of Malcolm X on the following page could be a primary or secondary source, depending on how it is used. The first half on the list of items give that context, but the others need some further information supplied by the teacher or students to make it clear whether it is secondary or primary. There will be some debate.

Structure 5 FIND MY RULE

Student Handout

Topics for Find My Rule

1. Interview with a veteran of the Vietnam War about his participation in the war as part of research for a history paper
2. Discussion with high school students about their opinion of the Vietnam War as part of research for a history paper
3. A 19th century painting by a travelling artist of North American pioneer life as a source for learning about the pioneers
4. *A League of Their Own*, a Hollywood movie about an all-woman baseball league in the 1940's, for a social studies class on women's history
5. A chapter in a social studies textbook on the history of the forestry industry.
6. Hand saws and other tools from an early 20th century logger that a museum used to show visitors what logging was like in the past
7. Denzel Washington's portrayal of Malcolm X in the movie *Malcolm X* as part of a study of the civil rights movement
8. Denzel Washington's portrayal of Malcolm X in the movie *Malcolm X* as part of a study of Afro-American actors
9. *The Autobiography of Malcolm X* as part of a study of his life
10. Reading the diary of 15 year old Nelly Ptaschkina who fled the Russian Revolution to find out about life in Russia at that time
11. A lecture by your history teacher on the Russian Revolution
12. *Mein Kempf* by Adolph Hitler used by a historian to learn about Hitler
13. A book on Hitler by a historian
14. A *World Book Encyclopedia* article on Christopher Columbus
15. Using the *World Book Encyclopaedia* as part of a study of the resources in school libraries
16. The ship's log of Christopher Columbus
17. Heiroglyphs on a Mayan temple
18. A videotape of Arthur Kent reporting live on NBC from Saudi Arabia on the Gulf War
19. A census
20. Oliver Stone's film *JFK* about President Kennedy's assassination
21. Film footage of police raids and interviews during the October Crisis in Quebec in 1970
22. A class survey of the attitudes of the school's students towards the environment
23. A student essay on Napoleon Bonaparte
24. The transcripts from a court case
25. A map in the school atlas showing the route of Jacques Cartier's voyages
26. A family scrapbook
27. Lincoln's Gettysburg address
28. The Haida legend of the raven as told by Guufaaw, a medicine man of the Haida Gwaii
29. Clothes of French nobility from the 18th century
30. Castle ruins
31. A magazine article on the Canadian Bill of Rights

Cooperative Learning and Social Studies: Towards Excellence and Equity by Tom Morton
Kagan Publishing • 1(800) 933-2667 • www.KaganOnline.com

NARRATIVE OF LESSONS USING FIND MY RULE

Assimilation

Themes
- Culture
- Individual development and identity
- Individuals, groups and institutions

Skills
- Interpreting information
- Evaluating information

Janet Bibb teaches grades ten and eleven social studies to students who are primarily the sons and daughters of immigrants. Several have English as their second language. In an effort to help the students understand some of the personal choices facing immigrants in the past and today, she wants them to understand clearly the concept of assimilation and its implications.

This concept might be defined as the process by which a cultural group changes its traditions or values to those of another cultural group. Non-critical attributes would be the methods of assimilation—it could be by force or free choice—and the age of those who assimilate. The relative number and power of the groups is not essential either, although almost always it is a less powerful minority that assimilates to the traditions and values of a more powerful majority.

Since this is the first time students have played Find My Rule, Bibb introduces the structure with the old game "Slow Boat to China." It is similar to Find My Rule and is a game that she uses to amuse her own children on long car trips.

Students are in fours divided into pairs. Bibb then draws two boxes on the overhead and tells them that she is planning to take a slow boat to China and she is going to take luggage and writes the word in Box 1, but she can't take a suitcase which she writes in Box 2. She wants to read so she will take a book (Box 1) but not a magazine (Box 2). All the objects in Box 1 have some characteristic in common, she explains, which those in Box 2 do not have. To come to China on this luxury cruise the students have to guess what they can take. Can you take your pet dog? (No.) A parrot? (Yes.) After this she asks students to think if she can take an apple to eat, has them share with their partner, and then raise their hands if yes. (Yes, they could.) Again, a Think-Pair-Vote to consider cookie (Yes) and then a Team Discussion to consider an orange (No) and more items. Eventually, students suggest their own things to take and the rule emerges: all those items in Box 1 have double letters and those in Box 2 do not.

Now she instructs students to make two boxes in their paper and distributes the handout "Find My Rule" with brief paragraphs which describe assimilation or describe some other phenomena. The class follows the steps of Find My Rule with Bibb mixing the order of the descriptions and the structures as she did with the Slow Boat to China.

Janet Bibb also wants her students to consider the effects of assimilating or preserving one's culture of origin. She starts with Think-Pair-Share and Peter Elbow's Methodological Belief described in Structure 22, p. 195. She doesn't use Elbow's fancy sounding term, but she uses his approach when she asks students to put aside their feelings and consider why some people come to this country and decide to assimilate completely, to drop all of their former culture. Students think, share with their partner and then with the class. Bibb then poses the opposite: why would someone decide to hold fast to their religion, language, and the like and not adapt to North American ways.

The groups of four then use Pairs Compare to fill out a grid of arguments for and against assimilation.

Later, Bibb extends thinking on similarities and differences with questions like the following:

In your cooperative teams what are some advantages to being the same (ideas, background, attitude)? What are some good things about diversity, having different opinions or different backgrounds?

Whether people are the same or not, why is it important to help everyone feel comfortable in a group? in the country?

What could you do in your groups to help people feel welcome?

What could the school do to help minorities feel accepted and recognized?

Bibb also uses Corners to consider how students see the diversity at their school. Do they see the school and its many cultures like a melting pot, a county fair, a jigsaw puzzle or a pyramid? The idea of a pyramid with some people on top is a difficult choice to discuss, but Bibb has been able to guide discussion to a positive resolution.

STUDENT HANDOUT

Find My Rule

1. Immigrant children spend much of their day in English. Many of them slowly lose their mother tongue.

2. Some immigrants, especially older people who lack the opportunity to attend language classes, do not learn English.

3. Some Chinese speaking students, on entering school, take on an English name in order to be similar to the other students or to avoid the embarrassment of their Chinese name being mispronounced.

4. Many North American cities have several ethnic community centres which hold events of particular interest to their communities.

5. Mounties, members of the Royal Canadian Mounted Police, who are Sikhs may wear a turban instead of the traditional RCMP hat.

6. In some schools teasing by classmates has led Sikh boys to abandon the wearing of the turban.

7. Advertising and peer pressure encourage young people to wear certain kinds of clothing like baseball caps or jeans. Few children of immigrants wear traditional clothing from the country of their parents.

8. Most North American cities have temples, churches, mosques, and synagogues of various religions. There is no required religion in the United States and Canada. The constitutions of the two countries protect the freedom to practice the religion of choice.

9. Navaho Indians run their own judicial system including native police on their own reserve.

10. In the past many Native Indian children were required to attend residential schools where they were not allowed to speak their native language.

11. The Nisga'a Indians run their own school district and the curriculum includes a course on Nisga'a language and culture.

12. Afro-Americans usually have to learn a type of English different from Black English in order to go to college or to get certain jobs.

13. Starting in 1890 many Canadian provinces forced French speaking students to attend schools in English even where the French were the majority. Today, most Canadians of French origin outside Quebec do not speak French.

14. Many Jewish families who have been in this country for generations continue to practice Judaism and speak Hebrew.

15. Because Christmas is celebrated openly in stores, schools, and the media, many Jewish families chose to put up Christmas trees and even give presents on December 25, although Christmas is not a Jewish holiday.

16. The major school holidays are based on the Christian festivals of Christmas and Easter.

STUDENT HANDOUT

Find My Rule
(continued)

17. Many school boards have multi-cultural camps and clubs that try to promote respect for different cultural groups.

18. There are many restaurants and stores that specialize in food and other products from other countries.

19. Fast food companies like McDonald's are popular with young people. Even some children whose immigrant parents are vegetarian decide to eat hamburgers.

20. The influence of popular music on the radio has led many second generation immigrants to ignore the traditional music of their parents.

21. Latin American and Black music are popular both in their communities and among other cultures.

22. In the United States and Canada a man or a woman can legally have only one wife or husband. People from other countries who wish to live here and who have more than one spouse must abide by this law.

23. Festivals such as the Caribbean Carnival, Vietnamese and Chinese New Year's and St. Patrick's Day are popular celebrations in some North American cities.

24. In the 19th century the government banned the potlatch, the traditional native ceremony that formed a central part of their culture.

25. With the return of the right to hold potlatches they have again become popular in native communities.

Structure 6
FIND-SOMEONE-WHO... (aka People Hunt)

Steps at a Glance

❶ The teacher or students prepare questions that are put in a survey or worksheet form.

❷ The teacher distributes one of these to each student who then mills about the room trying to find someone who knows the answer or fits the characteristic.

❸ That person then answers the question and signs his or her name next to it.

Students circulate around the room getting other students to answer and sign a list of questions. This structure can be a class builder to help students become better acquainted or a review exercise.

Social Skills

- Summarizing

In these adaptations from the scavenger hunts of old, students search for someone who has a particular characteristic or knowledge. The items in the hunt can be in the form of "Find someone who has… a pet, visited another country, etc.," or in the form of a bingo card, acrostic, or worksheet.

The content can be mildly personal to help students get acquainted at the start of the year or it could include questions that review material, practice skills, or survey student opinions.

Structure 6 FIND-SOMEONE-WHO

STEPS

❶ **TEACHER OR STUDENTS PREPARE QUESTIONS THAT ARE PUT IN A SURVEY OR WORKSHEET FORM**
(See the examples that follow.)

❷ **TEACHER DISTRIBUTES ONE OF THESE TO EACH STUDENT WHO MUST MILL ABOUT THE ROOM TRYING TO FIND SOMEONE WHO KNOWS THE ANSWER OR FITS THE CHARACTERISTIC**

❸ **THAT PERSON THEN ANSWERS THE QUESTION AND SIGNS HIS OR HER NAME NEXT TO IT**

A student may sign only once. Students must find a different person for each question.

The goal is to complete the form or get as many answers as possible in the time limit.

In one version of Find-Someone-Who students fill out the form first. If the form has questions about characteristics, students would then go on to hunt for classmates with the same characteristic. If the items on the form are not about characteristics but are open ended questions like, "What would be the most effective means of reducing air pollution?" students would write down their answers first and then find people with the same answers.

Laurie Robertson, Kagan Cooperative Learning consultant, uses this structure with worksheets. Each student has a copy, then mills about the room until the teacher says, "Find someone who knows." Students find someone who knows the answer to one of the questions on the worksheet. After interviewing that person, they write the answer on the sheet in their own words. The answer-giver checks that it is accurate and signs it, before the two split apart and search for someone else who knows an answer to another questions.

This means that a weaker student who starts knowing no answers, after one or two interviews, will become Someone Who Knows and assume a higher status.

IDEAS FOR USING FIND-SOMEONE-WHO IN SOCIAL STUDIES

- **Get acquainted activity**
  At the start of the year when you want students to know each other's name and build trust you can use a People Hunt like the one here adapted from Laurie Robertson.

- **Introduction of a theme**
  To introduce a unit and attach a feeling of fun and excitement to the main theme a Find-Someone-Who form like the one reproduced here that Thomas Armstrong uses to introduce the idea of multiple intelligences and the examples from the narrative of Globingo and Lobingo.

- **A worksheet**
  After a lecture or video, students can review their knowledge using "Energy Hunt" or something similar.

Notes

STUDENT HANDOUT

People Hunt

Instructions: Fill in answers for yourself. Then circulate throughout the class and find another person and ask him or her a question for a match. If you get a yes, sign each other's People Hunt sheets. If you get a not, that person asks you a question looking for a match. Continue alternating questions until you find a match, then form new pairs. Try to get all your boxes filled.

	Self	Friend
1. Favorite color		
2. Favorite school subject		
3. Favorite dessert		
4. Favorite TV show		
5. Favorite musical group		
6. Favorite season of the year		
7. Favorite place to visit		
8. Favorite period in history		
9. Place where you learn world news		
10. Favorite animal		
11. Favorite sport		
12. Favorite hobby		
13. Miles you live from school		
14. Number of brothers and sisters		
15. Favorite topic in Social Studies		

(Adapted from Robertson, L. in Kagan, *Cooperative Learning*. 1992, p. 9:5.)

Structure 6 FIND-SOMEONE-WHO

STUDENT HANDOUT

Human Intelligence Hunt

(Adapted from Thomas Armstrong, *Multiple Intelligences in the Classroom*, 1994, p. 44)

Instructions: **1.** Find people who can do the following and have them *perform* the task listed. **2.** Once that person has performed the task to your satisfaction, he or she should initial the blank space next to the task on this sheet. **3.** A person may perform only one task. To complete this sheet you must have seven different sets of initials.

Find someone who can:

_____ whistle the national anthem.

_____ stand on one foot with her eyes closed for at least five seconds.

_____ recite at least four lines from any poem he has learned.

_____ draw a quick diagram explaining how an electric motor works.

_____ briefly share a dream that she has had in the past two weeks.

_____ complete this numerical sequence: 36, 30, 24, 18 and explain the logic behind it.

_____ honestly say he is relaxed and comfortable talking to other people during this exercise.

Energy Hunt Worksheet

Instructions: Find someone who knows the answer to one of these questions and have him or her explain it to you. Write it in your own words on this sheet. That person should check that your interpretation is correct and then sign the answer. Be prepared to answer that person's questions. Continue with another student until the worksheet is complete and all questions are signed.

1. What are the advantages and disadvantages of hydro-electricity?

2. What are the advantages and disadvantages of thermal electricity?

3. What are the advantages and disadvantages of nuclear power?

4. What are the advantages and disadvantages of geothermal electricity?

5. How does global warming work?

Cooperative Learning and Social Studies: Towards Excellence and Equity by Tom Morton
Kagan Publishing • 1(800) 933-2667 • www.KaganOnline.com

NARRATIVE OF LESSONS USING FIND-SOMEONE-WHO

Globingo and Lobingo

Themes
- Global connections
- Individual development and identity
- People, places, and the environment

Pete Clarke, the coordinator of a provincial program to encourage the teaching of global education, introduces the concepts of interdependence and identity to teachers and students through Find-Someone-Who activities. He uses the Globingo form (adapted from Pike and Selby, 1988, p. 114.) on the following page as a warm-up, but a warm-up with a point. After people have shouted their Globingos and returned to their seats, he ask for some of their answers: "Who found someone who speaks another language at home? Who were they? (To that person:) What languages do you speak? What countries would you like to visit? Who has someone who can sing a song from another country? (To that person:) What song can you sing? Would you sing it for us?"

He goes on to ask them to identify the common theme, global interdependence, and then to give him all the ways that we depend on the world and they depend on us. He continues this theme with further questions like "What if there was a plant disease that destroyed all the tomato crop in Mexico, how would that effect us? How might a civil war in China effect us?"

The conclusion that Pete Clarke draws from the discussion is that we are not citizens of any one country; we are world citizens. Later, he uses the second form, Lobingo. (The one reproduced here is specific to Vancouver where festivals like the dragon boat races are very popular. It would need to be revised for each locality.)

Again, after everyone has at least one Lobingo, he discusses some of their responses and then asks for the common theme, that they all concern being a Canadian and living in Vancouver. "You all got Lobingos, but what would have happened if I had done this in Hong Kong or Sydney, Australia?" The questions lead the audience to consider how we are citizens of our local area and of our country as well as world citizens. They know and feel certain things that other people do not. We are connected to the world, but we are also connected to our local roots. All of us have many group identities, national, local, and family as well as global.

Structure 6 FIND-SOMEONE-WHO

STUDENT HANDOUT

Globingo

Instructions: Find people who fit the descriptions in the squares below. Ask them a question and have them sign their name. This is an opportunity to meet someone new so a person can sign only once per sheet. When you have four signatures in a row, either horizontally, vertically, or diagonally, call out "Globingo." Try for as many Globingos as you can.

Find someone who...

has travelled to some foreign country.	has a pen pal in another country.	is learning a foreign language.	has a relative in another country.
Name:	Name:	Name:	Name:
Country:	Country:	Country:	Country:
has helped a visitor from another country.	enjoys a music group from another country.	has a family car that was made in another country.	enjoys eating foods from other countries.
Name:	Name:	Name:	Name:
Country:	Country:	Country:	Country:
can name a famous sports star from another country.	is wearing something that was made in another country.	has talked to someone who has lived in another country.	lives in a home where more than one language is spoken.
Name:	Name:	Name:	Name:
Country:	Country:	Country:	Country:
saw a story about another country in the newspaper recently.	learned something about another country on TV recently.	owns a TV or other appliance made in another country.	has a parent or other relative who was born in another country.
Name:	Name:	Name:	Name:
Country:	Country:	Country:	Country:

Student Handout

Lobingo

Instructions: Find people who fit the descriptions in the squares below. Ask them a question and have them sign their name. This is an opportunity to meet someone new so a person can sign only once per sheet. When you have four signatures in a row, either horizontally, vertically, or diagonally, call out "Lobingo." Try for as many Lobingos as you can.

Find someone who...

has eaten a Nanaimo bar. Name:	can say hello in English and French. Name:	has an electric kettle. Name:	knows what a maple tree looks like. Name:
has canoed or kayaked. Name:	has heard a Brian Adams song. Name:	knows what a dragon boat is. Name:	says "eh" when he or she speaks. Name:
knows who won the Stanley Cup. Name:	knows where skid row is. Name:	knows the date of Canada Day. Name:	lives in a dominion. Name:
knows who Anne of Green Gables is. Name:	has eaten a Macintosh apple. Name:	likes maple syrup. Name:	knows what all these questions have in common. Name:

Structure 7
FORMATIONS

Steps at a Glance

❶ The teacher directs the class to form a particular shape or tableau of a scene with their bodies.

❷ The class discusses the formation.

Students make a still life tableau of a historic or contemporary event. Formations can help make an abstract topic concrete, synthesize information, and develop class or team synergy.

This is one of several kinesthetic structures that can help make an abstract topic concrete. Students "feel" a situation, have a chance to synthesize information, and can develop class or team synergy.

In a Class Formation the teacher directs the students how to position themselves. The Team Formation, however, is more akin to a Team Project.

For the teacher who is stressing the uses of multiple intelligences, the Team Formation can be introduced with reference to the kinesthetic and intra-personal intelligences needed for the group to create a successful formation.

Structure 7 FORMATIONS

STEPS FOR A CLASS FORMATION

❶ **TEACHER DIRECTS THE CLASS HOW TO FORM A PARTICULAR SHAPE OR TABLEAU OF A SCENE WITH THEIR BODIES**

❷ **CLASS DISCUSSES THE FORMATION**
This can also be done as a whole class, for example, when a teacher reviews geography with a Class Formation of the outline of a country.

Students can also pair with a student next to them and use Think-Pair-Share to consider questions given by the teacher. For example, if the class recreates life in a trench in World War One, they could be asked to think about how the soldiers might have reacted.

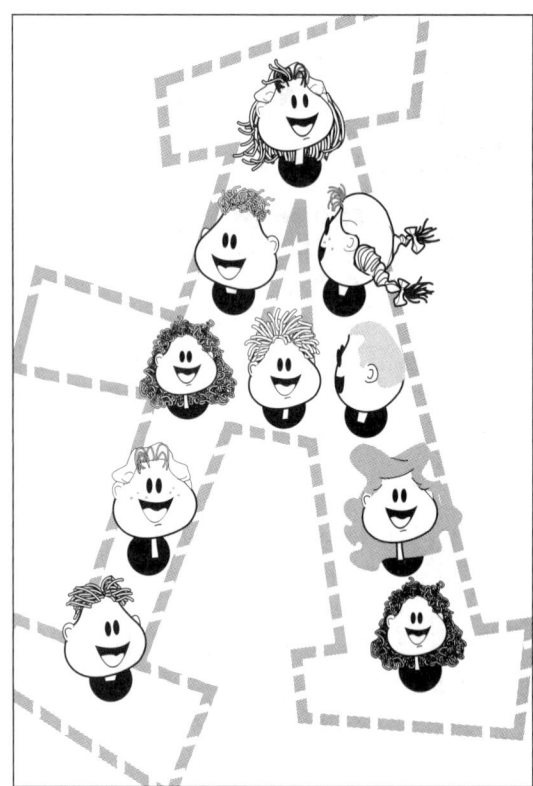

STEPS FOR A TEAM FORMATION

❶ **PRESENT STUDENTS WITH THE EVENT THAT IS TO BE INTERPRETED AS A FORMATION**
Explain that their group task is to make a still-life portrayal of this event. There should be actors and a narrator. If there are not enough human characters for the formation, some of the group may portray non-human characters, like a mountain or a horse.

Students should try to create the scene as realistically as possible so that the class will recognize what is going on. Ask them to step inside the characters and show their feelings with facial expressions and body postures.

They should also make the scene dynamic by facing the class and varying the positions of the actors. Some characters can sit, crouch, or squat. You might allow them to use a chair or props, but limit these or they may become the focus of their preparations.

They could make more than one Formation like different scenes in a play.

❷ **ALLOW TIME FOR PRACTICE**

❸ **GROUPS PRESENT**
(This could be done formally with a procedure from improvisational theatre as shown in Figure 1.) The narrator explains the team's interpretation and the team answers questions from the class.

❹ **REFLECT ON THE FORMATION**
This might be content oriented as in Class Formation or it could be a reflection on process, e.g., a Team Discussion of what helped the group or teacher observations of effective use of kinesthetic and intra-personal intelligences.

Notes

Cooperative Learning and Social Studies: Towards Excellence and Equity by Tom Morton
Kagan Publishing • 1(800) 933-2667 • www.KaganOnline.com

Ideas for Using Formations in Social Studies

With the Whole Class

- **Outline map**
  The class forms the shape of a country, continent, or river and the teacher asks questions about its geography. For example, with an outline of the United States the teacher walks across the classroom country asking questions like, "As I move west tell me what kind of terrain I am crossing?" and "I have to cross a river here, what might it be?"

- **Trench warfare**
  History Alive (1994) describes a lesson where students relive the conditions of World War One. Desks are aligned into two sets of two rows three feet apart on either side of the room. When the bell rings, students are assigned to one of two facing "trenches," German and French. Students crouch down crowded together while the teacher shows slides, reads from All Quiet on the Western Front, and plays a recording of the sounds of artillery and machine guns.

- **Riding the rods in the 1930s**
  Students climb on board their desks and then suspend themselves underneath as the hobos rode underneath the railcars. The teacher is the railway police.

- **A battle scene**
  One of our favourite formations is the Battle of Quebec. Two rows of students form the disciplined lines of the British redcoats, their rifles at their sides, another group to their left are the Canadien and Native snipers taking aim at the British, while the rest of the students are the French who take the position of soldiers running towards the British. The teacher acts as the generals.

- **Trial scenes**
  Like those Joan of Arc, Socrates, or the Nuremberg trials

- **A buffalo jump**

- **A civil rights lunch counter sit-in**

- **A slave ship from Africa to the Americas**

As Teams

- **Photographs, drawings, or political cartoons**
  For example, in the cartoon "Caught in the Middle" from the War of 1812, Thomas Jefferson holds up his hands threatened on one side by Britain with a club while on the other side a dandy looking Napoleon picks his pocket. Students discuss possible reactions of the three figures, take the form of the cartoon depiction, and then extend this into a mini-role play.

- **Current events**
  Teams who have been following news items interpret them for the rest of the class by portraying one or two scenes that reflect the event.

- **Interpretation of a narrative**
  For example, in a lesson from *Along the Silk Road* (1994), different groups of students are assigned different parts of a story about Zhang Qian and asked to recreate them as a tableau.

FIGURE 1

Team Presentation of a Formation

1. Prepare a realistic, still life portrayal of the event. Everyone should have a role. Make your scene interesting with the actors in dramatic positions.

2. The team lines up facing the audience.

3. To the count of 4, the team forms its scene. (Narrator may be part of the scene.)

4. The narrator stands aside to explain the background, the characters, and their viewpoints.

5. The narrator rejoins the formation.

6. To the count of 4, the team returns to line up.

7. The team answers questions from the audience.

NARRATIVE OF A LESSON USING FORMATIONS

Demonstrating Orographic Rainfall

Themes
- People, places and environment

Skills
- Reference and information-search
- Interpreting information
- Synthesizing information
- Classifying information
- Analyzing information

Mr. Glick's 10th grade class had started a geography unit on the forest. He started first with some inquiry lessons on where and why it rained. To review the students' knowledge of condensation and evaporation he used the fog on the classroom windows, what Mr. Glick called his "bargain basement science lab." Students also read maps of wind, precipitation, and elevation and constructed a cross-section of Washington state along the line of latitude that crosses Seattle and Spokane, before suggesting answers to the inquiry questions.

To help reinforce their understanding of orographic rainfall, he divided the class into two and asked them to line up in two lines according to their birthdays (just months and days, not by years) without talking. He then announced with some fanfare that through his magical powers he was going to transform one line into geographers and the other into Washington State. One line, in other words, was to be a human cross-section from the Pacific Ocean to the Olympic Peninsula, Puget Sound, Cascades, and Interior Plateau. The ocean and plateau students had to crouch and spread their arms flat while the mountain ranges stretched their arms high and leaned against each other.

Using a white balloon as a prop to represent a cloud, Mr. Glick then asked the students—the geographers—in the other line to explain the life of the cloud as it first formed over the ocean. Each student opposite was asked questions as the cloud made its way, cooling and warming, raining and drying up, across the state's terrain.

Mr. Glick then announced with tongue in cheek that he had made a mistake and mixed up the geographers with Washington. To fix his error he waved his magic wand again and asked that students to switch roles and review again orographic rainfall.

Later, the class did a Team Web to understand the connections between the rainfall and forests. Finally, as a challenge question they considered why Peru and Northern Chile with similar topography have deserts on their coasts.

Structure 8
INSIDE-OUTSIDE CIRCLE

Steps at a Glance

❶ The class forms two concentric circles with students facing each other.

❷ Students pair to complete the task.

❸ The circles "shift and share."

The class makes two concentric circles with students facing each other to form partners with whom they discuss various questions; they also rotate the circles to hear answers from different students. Students can have various sources of information for discussion and review or they can have various different audiences for a presentation.

Social Skills
- Taking turns
- Listening

Variations
- Team Inside-Outside Circle
- Role Play Inside-Outside Circle

The Inside-Outside Circle (IOC) is an active structure useful for a variety of purposes:
- interviews for classbuilding;
- role plays—each circle with a different role;
- practice of oral presentations;
- unit openers;
- review; or
- part of a constructive controversy.

Structure 8 INSIDE-OUTSIDE CIRCLE

STEPS

❶ CLASS FORMS TWO CONCENTRIC CIRCLES WITH STUDENTS FACING EACH OTHER

Divide the class in two with one half forming an inside circle facing out and the other half an outer circle facing inwards. Students should each be facing a partner.

Teacher Tips: If the pairing up looks a bit ragged, then ask them to touch right toes to be sure they are opposite someone.

If there is an odd number of students then have two students "twin." This means they answer and ask questions together and move as one when it is time to rotate.

❷ STUDENTS PAIR TO COMPLETE TASK

Students pair to complete the task assigned such as discussing a question, showing a flash card, or playing a role. Although the usual rule to stay with your group should usually apply, the teacher might also say something like, "I want both of you to be able to answer. If you can't, then ask the pair next to you." At any time the teacher can move to whole class discussion.

❸ CIRCLES "SHIFT AND SHARE"

Ask one of the circles to shift one or more places to the left or right so that students are in front of a new partner. The new pairs can repeat the same task if the goal is practice or to have multiple perspectives on a question, or they could share ideas on a new topic. Continue rotation, sometimes varying the number of spaces and direction.

VARIATIONS

TEAM INSIDE-OUTSIDE CIRCLE

In traditional group presentations, the students address the whole class one group at a time. In Team Inside-Outside Circle, half of your class can present at the same time. In much less time than a whole class presentation, students can practice their presentation repeatedly.

ROLE PLAY INSIDE-OUTSIDE CIRCLE

In a role play or as part of a constructive controversy, the different circles can be assigned different roles or arguments. After several rotations there will be a greater chance that students will have heard and understood a variety of points. The discussion can be done individually or in teams of two.

Ideas for Using Inside-Outside Circle in Social Studies

- A class builder at the start of the year. Students discuss mildly personal questions like "What is your favourite sport or school subject?" and open-ended questions about social studies like "What was you best memory of a social studies class (or other class if they have no good memories of social studies)?"

- A list of items to master, for example, vocabulary words and their definitions, countries and their exports, or land-form names and illustrations. Each student in the circle can have one of 15 or so different items. If students in a class of 30 with circles of 15 go around the whole way, they will have reviewed all the items.

- A series of teacher-made questions for a unit opener. For example, before studying geographic regions the teacher might ask the pairs in Inside-Outside Circle to consider the following:

   Besides political regions what kind of specific areas can you think of in this country?

   Describe one of the regions.

   How do you know where the boundaries of this area are?

   In what area of the country (state or province) do most people live? Why?

   For each question students Shift and Share to hear several responses.

- A series of student-made questions as review at the end of the unit.

- Practice of oral presentations as individuals or as teams.

- A review where different circles have different aspects of the same topic, eg, one could give the causes of an event, another the effects; one could define a concept and the other give an example; or one could suggest a learning activity for a unit and the other could think of how it should be evaluated.

- A role play with one circle playing one role while the other circle's role is different, eg, environmentalists and presidents of a nuclear power plant or union organizers and factory owners. One student teacher from Nova Scotia that we supervised assigned a junior high class research assignments on various figures in the Middle Ages—priest, knight, vassal, lord, trader, leper, peasant woman, and the like—two students per figure. They then formed Inside-Outside Circles with each partner in a different circle to meet and learn about a whole Medieval community.

NARRATIVE OF LESSONS USING INSIDE-OUTSIDE CIRCLE

Teaching About Revolutions

Themes
- Time, continuity, and change
- Power, authority, and governance

Recurring Issues
- Appropriate use of force to achieve social goals
- Individual needs vs. common good

Skills
- Synthesizing information

Sister Gagné was soon to begin her senior Humanities unit on revolutions. It was early in the school year. The students and she were new to each other and to cooperative group work, so she thought an activity like Inside-Outside Circle that combined getting acquainted with an academic discussion would be a good start. She had the class form the two facing circles and explained the purpose and procedure. She also added to her instructions that they should introduce themselves to each new partner whom they met.

Her questions reflected the general themes of revolutionary ideals, actions and reactions:

- If you could create an ideal school, a perfect place, what would it be like? (The circles rotated several times on this first question to help students talk to many different classmates. They also shared a few of their ideas with the whole class and Sister Gagné stressed the most radical ideas for the next few questions.)

- Suddenly, you are the leader and you have the power to change all the schools. What would you do to bring about your changes?

- What problems might you have?

- Would you force people to change and do things your way?

- Can we force people to be good?

The ideas from this introduction became an advanced organizer that Sister Gagné referred to for the next few lessons.

She also used the structure a few weeks later to give students an audience for a research assignment on the French Revolution. She had asked them to research in pairs and then write individually a description of the following people or groups and an explanation of their viewpoint towards the revolution: Louis XVI, Danton, Robespierre, Lafayette, the Sans-Culottes—her favorite name, Marie Antoinette and the women to whom she is supposed to have said, "Let them eat cake," the Poissardes who were the fish wives and market women, and others for a total of 14 topics for a class of 28.

When the students had finished their research, the class again used an Inside-Outside Circle with the pairs divided, each one in a different circle facing each other.

By starting with partners facing each other before shifting, no student ended up with someone who had the same topic. This time the circles made a complete "revolution"—Sister Gagné's joke—and as they introduced themselves in role, they gained a deeper understanding of many of the actors in this revolutionary drama.

To synthesize this information at the end of the Inside-Outside Circle, students formed into groups of four to create a Team Web of these historical actors and drew connections among them.

Structure 9
JIGSAW

Steps at a Glance

❶ The teacher prepares materials, questions and groups.

❷ Students start in their home groups.

❸ Students meet with an expert partner, that is, someone who has the same material to study.

❹ Partners master the material.

❺ Expert partners meet with two more students to form an expert group.

❻ If the material to be taught is complex or long, then partners can return to plan the teaching.

❼ Students return to their home groups to teach.

❽ The teacher recognizes team learning.

Students start in a "base group," then meet in an "expert group" to learn different parts of a larger topic and return to teach that material to the "base group." The Jigsaw gives a purpose and audience for student learning and can help a class cover material a bit more quickly than individual study. It can also be used to give multiple perspectives to a topic.

Social Skills

- Checking for understanding
- Summarizing
- Asking questions
- Teaching others

Variation

- Scavenger Hunt

The Jigsaw is a very popular way to help students learn social studies content. At its simplest, it means that each student in a team masters material and teaches it to the others. Like a jigsaw puzzle, the whole of the content is not complete until each team member has added his part.

Students start in a heterogeneous home team or base group. From there they break into expert groups, that is, groups who have the same materials, and then return to teach to the home team.

The need to teach gives a purpose and audience to the students' learning. In preparing and teaching the student synthesizes the material. If the other group members are active in their learning—questioning and elaborating—then the student will also sharpen his or her thinking. When the Jigsaw parts represent different points of view on an issue, like workers, owners, the public, and government on the General Strike, students can also practice perspective-taking, seeing several opinions and arguments at the same time.

Although the steps of this structure seem simple and powerful, the Jigsaw can demand a lot from both teachers and students in preparation and skills. This may be why so many people tinker with the format. In addition to describing Elliot Aronson's 1978 original version of Jigsaw, and Robert Slavin's Jigsaw II, Spencer Kagan (1992) describes nine other variations. The procedure below describes Partner Expert Group Jigsaw with references to Jigsaw II.

STEPS

❶ TEACHER PREPARES MATERIALS, QUESTIONS AND GROUPS

The materials may be pages from the text book or something more elaborate, but they must be at a suitable level for the students. The expert groups may be homogeneous in reading level which would permit some students to work on more difficult or longer material and some on simpler, shorter passages.

In Jigsaw II students start with a pre-test that they rewrite after the completion of the Jigsaw.

❷ STUDENTS START IN THEIR HOME TEAMS

They may make a team name connected to the theme of the unit.

❸ STUDENTS MEET WITH AN EXPERT PARTNER, THAT IS SOMEONE WHO HAS THE SAME MATERIAL TO STUDY

❹ PARTNERS MASTER THE MATERIAL
This can begin with Pairs Read.

❺ EXPERT PARTNERS MEET WITH TWO MORE STUDENTS TO FORM AN EXPERT GROUP WITH WHOM THEY CHECK THAT THEY HAVE DONE THE ASSIGNMENT THOROUGHLY AND CORRECTLY AND PLAN HOW THEY SHOULD TEACH IT TO THE OTHERS

The teacher needs to explain how they should go about teaching, for example, use of a visual aid.

❻ IF THE MATERIAL TO BE TAUGHT IS COMPLEX OR LONG, THEN THE PARTNERS CAN RETURN TO PLAN THE TEACHING

❼ STUDENTS RETURN TO THEIR HOME TEAMS TO TEACH

Students who are being "learners" should be active in asking questions, paraphrasing, and elaborating.

❽ THE TEACHER RECOGNIZES TEAM LEARNING

In the Jigsaw II variation students write an individual post-test. Students receive improvement points based on the extent of their gains from the pre-test. Depending on the total of the team's improvement scores, the team receives public recognition for its result.

Without the pre-test score, students may still receive public recognition based on every member of the group achieving a certain level on the test, for example, 60 percent.

Teacher Tips: Be prepared for absences and weak students. A weak student might be paired with a more reliable one in a home group of five and then move with that student to the expert group. If a student is absent, two groups can join for the teaching of the section that person is responsible for.

The students' communication skills need to be very good, if a Jigsaw is to reach its potential. For example, some students have a very limited understanding of how to teach assuming that they need only show their notes for the others to copy. Figure 1 gives a checklist of important group skills that the teacher or students may complete (Steinbrink and Stahl, 1994). Students should have these skills explained to them before teaching. The use of roles like task-master, encourager, materials manager, and checker can also be helpful.

VARIATION

SCAVENGER HUNT

In this structure teams receive a list of simple questions to answer or definitions to find. The students divide up the task, work individually on their parts and then share the results amongst themselves. It is a short and simple kind of Jigsaw that demands less of the students as students need only copy each other's answers if at all.

It can be given to students early in the year as a kind of experiential exercise: students complete the task without extensive directions from the teacher and then reflect on how well they worked together. Because it so clearly saves time, it also serves as a good demonstration of the value of cooperation. Moreover, it is a useful way to practice skim reading and finding the various parts of a textbook or newspaper.

The items on the scavenger hunt sheet may involve various levels of difficulty from vocabulary searches and conceptual understandings to making inferences and determining cause-effect relationships. One hunt can have 10–20 items and take fifteen to thirty minutes. Those who finish first should be encouraged to make up additional questions.

FIGURE 1
COOPERATIVE SKILLS CHECKLIST FOR A JIGSAW

Students in a team...	Always	Seldom	Never
shared materials			
encouraged all members to participate			
summarized materials out loud			
criticized ideas without criticizing people			
integrated different ideas into single positions			

Ideas for Using Jigsaw and Variations in Social Studies

Jigsaw

- Different pages from a chapter.

- Different parts of the environment, such as, the role of water, air, wind, land, animals and plants in an ecosystem.

- Different historical figures, like Roosevelt, Stalin, Churchill, and Hitler and their roles in World War II.

- Different countries and their positions on population, arms trade, or economic development.

- Different clues for a crossword puzzle. For a simple two part jigsaw using a crossword, give a copy of the puzzle to everyone, but split the clues up with one person receiving the Down clues and the other the Across clues. Make a rule that they have to share their clues orally. (This is more of a teambuilding exercise than an efficient way to master information.)

- Different perspectives on controversial topics, for example, *Jigsaw* and *Jigsaw Plus* (Coelho, 1991, and Coelho and Winer, 1991) have fictional case studies with worksheets of different viewpoints at varying reading levels on questions like Who Discovered America? and How to Save the Biramichi River (a polluted river)? The American version of these books is All Sides of the Issue (Coelho, Winn-Bell Olsen, and Winer, 1989).

- If you can obtain copies of textbooks or newspapers from different countries, these can be used as the parts of a Jigsaw. Like the different points of view of a controversy, the use of contrasting sources can form a Jigsaw to encourage perspective-taking. For example, the American *Patterns of Civilization*, vol. 2 (Beers, 1983) and the Canadian *Our Land* (Bowers and Garrod, 1987) give different accounts of the American Revolution.

- Students may also be given topics and assignments that are presented in different forms, for example, some expert groups may conduct interviews, another study statistical tables, another readings from journals and another video tapes. This may allow students of different abilities a better chance to contribute equally to the base of knowledge.

Scavenger Hunt

- A hunt of questions on a theme like government, economy, geography, environment, conflict, or cooperation using the newspaper;

- A hunt for definitions of vocabulary or explanations of events in a chapter of the textbook;

- A hunt that requires skill in using a resource, for example, questions that ask students to use the gazetteer (index in an atlas) and table of contents or to read maps of elevation and climate in an atlas;

- A hunt that requires the resources of the library; to avoid copying, questions can be personalized, for example, use the computer periodical catalogue and find the title of the cover of Time magazine the day of your birth and find the first name of a politician in the encyclopedia whose family name begins with the same first letter as yours.

AN EXAMPLE OF A SCAVENGER HUNT

Scavenger Hunt-Citizenship: Government and Law

As a team look through the newspaper and locate the following items. Circle them with a pen or pencil. Be sure to indicate below the page on which each item is found. When you are finished, fold the paper back into its original form so that the teacher knows you are finished.

1. A picture of a politician ___
2. An article about two or more countries co-operating ___
3. An article showing how someone has shown positive leadership ___
4. A story or letter related to a complaint by a consumer ___
5. An item from the sports section involving the breaking of rules ___
6. A comic strip showing two people or groups in conflict ___
7. An ad for a job with the government ___
8. A news item about a crime ___
9. An editorial talking about a political issue ___
10. A letter to the editor critical of the government ___
11. An item about a government outside of the North America ___
12. An article about events in a foreign country that could affect this country ___
13. An article dealing with an important local issue ___
14. A picture showing people trying to influence government ___
15. A picture showing how government affects the lives of its citizens ___
16. An ad for a movie that involves the law in some way ___
17. A map ___
18. A news item related to education ___
19. The word "court" ___
20. An item about immigrants or immigration ___

Finished quickly? What strategies did your team use? _____

_____

_____

Make up 5 more questions. _____

_____

_____

Structure 9 *JIGSAW*

NARRATIVE OF LESSONS USING JIGSAW

The Underground Railroad

Themes
- Time, continuity and change
- Individual development and identity
- Power, authority, and government

Values
- Freedom and equality

Skills
- Analyzing information
- Evaluating information

Recurring Issues
- Private property vs. freedom and equality
- Respect for the law vs. freedom

Jane Sitaya uses a jigsaw of primary and secondary source documents in her unit on the Underground Railway. The primary sources include the music and words of "Follow the Drinking Gourd," a historical cartoon, an excerpt from the memoirs of Alexander Ross, and newspaper articles on Harriet Tubman. The secondary sources are from the atlas, school library and the textbook. Together these form the following worksheets for expert groups.

Ms. Sitaya begins the unit by posing two general questions: first, Why would people run away? and secondly, What would someone need—what abilities and resources—to run away from the authorities? Students use a RoundTable brainstorming to answer the first question and share these with the class. Teams add new ideas from the other groups to their lists and then sort them into categories like "fear for life," "legal trouble," "to be united with family or love," "economic improvement" and "freedom." They repeat the exercise with the second question to come up with categories like "courage," "help from others" and "intelligence." This work forms an advanced organizer for the unit that Ms. Sitaya refers to at different points.

For the jigsaw, which lasts two periods, Ms. Sitaya asks students to play the roles of Taskmaster, Encourager, Checker, and Materials Manager.

After the teams have finished teaching each other the key ideas from their sources, they discuss informally which sources were the most helpful in trying to understand the Underground Railroad: the primary written sources, the primary visual sources, the primary musical source, or the secondary sources. They then form a Human Graph and discuss as a class their reasons for their choices.

To evaluate the jigsaw and the unit, Ms. Sitaya does not use a pre and posttest. In fact, she does not evaluate using a test at all. Instead she asks students (1) to write complete notes and be able to explain them and (2) work with their home team on a Team Project that uses the information that they have learned. They have the choice of creating and performing a sketch or writing and performing a song. Their project has to answer the focus questions: why would someone run away on the Underground Railroad, that is, it should show the conditions of slavery and the pros and cons of running away from it; and what would they need to run away, the abilities and resources of the passengers, conductors, and station masters.

The notes are marked by Ms. Sitaya, but the team project is graded with the help of peer and self evaluation using the forms reproduced here.

Structure 9 JIGSAW

 **Sheet 1**

Harriet Tubman

Harriet Tubman was called the Black Moses. She was born in Baltimore and fled to freedom in Philadelphia and later, St. Catherine's, Ontario. The interviews here are from the Commonwealth *of July 17, 1863, and the* Freeman's Record, *March, 1865, p. 34–38.*

Read and Discuss: Read the passage and then discuss the questions below with your expert group.
1. Make a list of the things that Harriet Tubman did to help the slaves escape.
2. What kind of abilities or intelligences did Harriet Tubman need to have to save so many of her people?
3. Find out who Moses was and what he did. Compare Tubman to the original Moses. Why would she be called the Black Moses?

• •

(With) her simple brave motto, "I can't die but once," she began her work which has made her Moses,—the deliverer of her people. Seven or eight times she has returned to the neighbourhood of her former home, always at the risk of death in the most horrible forms, and each time has brought away a company of fugitive slaves, and led them safely to the free States, or to Canada. Every time she went, the dangers increased. In 1857 she brought away her old parents, and, as they were too feeble to walk, she was obliged to hire a wagon, which added greatly to the perils of the journey…

She would never allow more to join her than she could properly care for, though she often gave others directions by which they succeed in escaping. She always came in the winter when the nights are long and dark, and people who have homes stay in them. She was never seen on the plantation herself; but appointed a rendezvous for her company eight or ten miles distant, so that if they were discovered at the first start she was not compromised. She started on Saturday night; the slaves at that time being allowed to go away from home to visit their friends—so that they would not be missed until Monday morning… If the escape was not discovered before Tuesday morning, she felt secure of keeping ahead of the (slave owners); but if it were, it required all her ingenuity to escape. She resorted to various devices, she had confidential friends all along the road. She would hire a man to follow along the one who put up the (wanted) notices, and take them down as soon as his back was turned. She crossed creeks on railroad bridges by night, she hid her company in the woods while she herself not being advertised (on the wanted posters) went into the towns in search of information. If met on the road, her face was always to the south, and she was always a respectable looking darkey, not a poor fugitive. She would get into the cars near her pursuers and manage to hear their plans.

• •

Check for Understanding: When your expert group has finished discussing the questions, check that each person understands the answers.

Write Answers: Write out your answers in complete sentences. Each person should have his or her own set of notes.

Choose Key Points to Teach: You will be teaching your home team about Harriet Tubman. Choose the three most important points that they should know about her.

Make Teaching Aids: Prepare a drawing, map or other aid that will help the members of your home team understand what you teach them.

Plan a Review: Decide how you will check to be sure that your home team understands and remembers what you have taught them.

Rehearse: Practice teaching your lesson with your expert group.

Alexander Milton Ross

Sheet 2

Dr. Alexander Milton Ross was a Canadian abolitionist (someone who wants to abolish slavery). This story is from his Recollections, *pages 32 to 55.*

Read and Discuss: Read the passage and then discuss the questions below with your expert group.
1. Why would the abolitionists refer to men and women as "packages of hardware" and "dry-goods"?
2. Describe what happens at a slave auction.
3. Why would Ross call slavery "unchristian?"
4. Given what happens at a slave auction and Ross' opinion that it was "unchristian," why would clergymen (Christian ministers) describe slavery as wise and a benefit to Blacks?

• •

My preparations being now completed, I engaged passage by steamer, to New Orleans, on a mission, the subject and details of which had occupied my mind exclusively for many weeks. I was accompanied to the steamer by two noble-hearted and steadfast friends. Whenever a slave succeeded in making his or her escape I was to send them the information, and they in turn notified our friends north of the Ohio river to be on the lookout for "packages of hardware" (men) or "dry-goods" (females), and their Ohio friends concealed the fugitives for a time, if necessary, until they could be safely sent to Canada…

During my stay in New Orleans I occasionally attended the slave auctions. The scenes I witnessed there will never be effaced from my memory. The cries and heart-rending agonies of the poor creatures as they were sold and separated from parents, children, husbands, or wives, will never cease to ring in my ears. Babes were torn from the arms of their mothers and sold, while parents were separated and sent to distant parts of the country. Tired and over-worked women were cruelly beaten, because they refused the outrageous demands of their wicked overseers. The horrid traffic in human beings, many of them whiter and more intelligent than the cruel men who bought and sold them, was, without exception, the most monstrous outrage upon the rights of human beings that could possibly be imagined…

My experience in New Orleans served to intensify my abhorrence and hatred of that vile and unchristian institution of slavery, and to nerve me for the work I was engaged in. On several occasions while in the Slave States I attended divine worship, and invariably remarked that whenever the subject of slavery was mentioned, it was referred to as a "wise and beneficent institution;" and one clergyman in particular declared that "the institution of slavery was devised by God for the especial benefit of the colored race…"

• •

Check for Understanding: When your expert group has finished discussing the questions, check that each person understands the answers.

Write Answers: Write out your answers in complete sentences. Each person should have his or own set of notes.

Choose Key Points to Teach: You will be teaching your home team about Alexander Milton Ross. Choose the three most important points that they should know about him.

Make Teaching Aids: Prepare a drawing, map or other aid that will help the members of your home team understand what you teach them.

Plan a Review: Decide how you will check to be sure that your home team understands and remembers what you have taught them.

Rehearse: Practice teaching your lesson with your expert group.

Structure 9   JIGSAW

 **Sheet 3**   # Follow the Drinking Gourd

"Follow the Drinking Gourd" was a song of the Afro-American slaves in the 19th century. Moses in the song refers to Harriet Tubman, a famous conductor on the Underground Railroad. In some versions, the words are "old man" instead of Moses.

Read and Discuss: Read the song lyrics and discuss the questions below with your expert group. If your teacher has a recording of the song, listen to it as well.
1. The words to "Follow the Drinking Gourd" have a religious meaning, but they also give secret instructions on how to escape on the Underground Railroad. (This was a system of secret hiding places and people to help escaped slaves on the way north to free American states and Canada.) Explain these instructions. Explain the religious meaning.
2. Why would the slaves give coded instructions like these in a song?
3. The drinking gourd in the lyrics refers to the Big Dipper constellation. What is so special about the Big Dipper that makes it important for the song? Draw a diagram of it and Polaris.
4. Besides an idea of where to travel, what else would the slaves need to be able to run away on the Underground Railroad?

• •

When the sun comes back and the first quail calls,
Follow the drinking gourd,
Moses is awaitin'
For to carry you to freedom
Follow the drinking gourd.

CHORUS: Follow the drinking gourd,
For Moses is awaitin'
For to carry you to freedom,
Follow the drinking gourd.

Now the river bank'll make a mighty good road
The dead trees will show you the way.

Left foot, peg foot, travellin' on,
Follow the drinking gourd.

CHORUS

Now the river ends between two hills,
Follow the drinking gourd.
There's another river on the other side.
Follow the drinking gourd.

CHORUS

• •

Check for Understanding: When your expert group has finished discussing the questions, check that each person understands the answers.

Write Answers: Write out your answers in complete sentences. Each person should have his or own set of notes.

Choose Key Points to Teach: You will be teaching your home team about the Underground Railroad. Choose the three most important points that they should know about what it was and how it worked.

Make Teaching Aids: In addition to your drawing of the Big Dipper, think of any other aids that will help the members of your home team understand what you teach them.

Plan a Review: Decide how you will check to be sure that your home team understands and remembers what you have taught them.

Rehearse: Practice teaching your lesson with your expert group.

The Escape Routes of the Underground Railroad

The Underground Railroad was not really underground, nor was it a railroad. It was underground in the sense that it was a secret organization that helped slaves excape from American slave states north to freedom. It was a railroad in the sense that it was a system of travel for the runaway slaves. It also used the language of the railroad as code words. Another expert group will teach you about Alexander Ross, a Canadian doctor who visited Vicksbury, Mississippi, to help free slaves and Harriet Tubman, who was a conductor on the Underground Railroad who helped hundreds of slaves escape to St. Catherine's, Ontario.

Discuss: Use your atlas and work with your expert group to answer the following:

1. Trace a map of eastern North America from Ontario to the Gulf of Mexico. Locate Vicksburg, Mississippi and St. Catherine's, Ontario and place these on the map.
2. Draw one or more likely routes for travellers on the Underground Railroad from Vicksburg to St. Catherine's. Remember that the escaping slaves must travel in secret. Indicate on your map any physical obstacles that they might encounter as they followed your route. Explain why you think the slaves would follow your routes.
3. Finally, use the map scale to calculate how far it is from Vicksbury to St. Catherine's. Estimate how many days it might take someone in the 19th century to walk that distance and write this on your map.

Check for Understanding: When your expert group has finished your work with the atlas, check that each person has a clear map and can explain why the slaves would follow the routes you chose.

Choose Key Points to Teach: You will be teaching your home team about the escape routes of the Underground Railroad. Choose the three most important points that they should know about these routes.

Plan How to Use Your Map: Your map will be a good visual aid to help your home team understand your key points. Plan how you will use it when you teach, for example, using a pointer or asking questions.

Plan a Review: Decide how you will check to be sure that your home team understands and remembers what you have taught them.

Rehearse: Practice teaching your lesson with your expert group.

Structure 9   JIGSAW

Sheet 5

Henry "Box" Brown

This drawing illustrates the escape of Henry Brown, a slave from Richmond, Virginia, a state where slavery was legal, to his friend in Philadelphia, Pennsylvania, a free state before the Fugitive Slave Act of 1850. Brown travelled in a packing crate sent by express. He lived in the box for 26 hours.

Brown later moved to Boston to become a conductor on the Underground Railroad helping other fugitive slaves escape. However, Samuel Smith, the white carpenter who put Brown in his crate, was later caught and imprisoned for eight years.

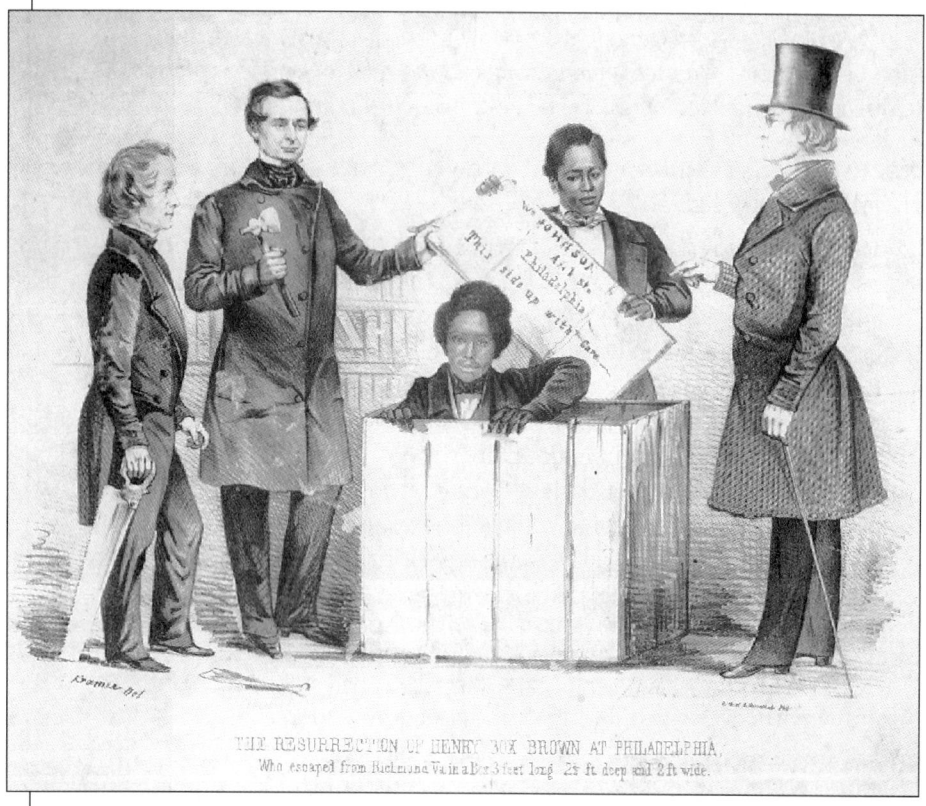

THE RESURRECTION OF HENRY BOX BROWN AT PHILADELPHIA.
Who escaped from Richmond Va in a Box 3 feet long 2½ ft deep and 2 ft wide.

Discuss: Look at the drawing and then discuss the questions below with your expert group.

1. What would have been some of the special problems and risks that Brown would have had during his time in the box?
2. What would he have needed to do to solve these problems?
3. Why would someone risk jail to help other people?
4. Make a list of other ways that you think the slaves might have avoided capture.
5. Research the Fugitive Slave Act and find out what it said and what influence it had on the Underground Railroad.

Check for Understanding: When your expert group has finished discussing the questions, check that each person understands the answers.

Write Answers: Write out your answers in complete sentences. Each person should have his or own set of notes.

Choose Key Points to Teach: You will be teaching your home team about Henry "Box" Brown and the Fugitive Slave Act. Choose the three most important points that they should know about these topics.

Make Teaching Aids: The drawing of Brown's escape will help your home team members understand how he escaped. Prepare another aid such as a map or diagram that might help them understand other key points.

Plan a Review: Decide how you will check to be sure that your home team understands and remembers what you have taught them.

Rehearse: Practice teaching your lesson with your expert group.

Structure 10
MIX-N-MATCH

Steps at a Glance

❶ Students or the teacher prepare items for review, such as a question and its answer or a word and its definition.

❷ Mix up the cards and distribute them to the class.

❸ Ask students to stand up and find the person with the card that matches their own.

❹ Tell students to freeze and then remix the cards to repeat.

Half the class has cards which are one part of a pair (like a vocabulary word), the other half has matching cards (like the definition), and they mill around to find their match. The purpose is twofold: to review academic content and to have fun.

Kittens practice hunting when they play with a ball. Students master course content as they play Mix-N-Match. The structure has high positive interdependence, individual accountability, simultaneity and participation plus playfulness.

Structure 10 MIX-N-MATCH

STEPS

❶ **STUDENTS OR TEACHER PREPARE ITEMS FOR REVIEW, SUCH AS A QUESTION AND ITS ANSWER OR A WORD AND ITS DEFINITION**
The match should be unambiguous. Questions, for example, should have only one clear answer. Place these on separate cards or sheets of paper. You will need as many cards as you have students, e.g., for 30 students you would need 15 vocabulary cards and 15 matching definition cards.

❷ **MIX UP THE CARDS AND DISTRIBUTE THEM TO THE CLASS**
If there are an odd number of students, then have two students join together to share one card between them.

❸ **ASK STUDENTS TO STAND UP AND FIND THE PERSON WITH THE CARD THAT MATCHES THEIR OWN**
You might also instruct them to discuss some questions on the item once they have found the match. For example, if they were to match a river with a country, they might also share other features of that country.

❹ **TELL STUDENTS TO FREEZE AND THEN REMIX THE CARDS TO REPEAT**
You can do this by taking up their cards to redistribute yourself, which is a bit time consuming, or by asking the students to pass the cards around a few times. Restart the game with each student having a new item to match. Continue through several rounds.

IDEAS FOR USING MIX-N-MATCH IN SOCIAL STUDIES

- Countries and capitals (or major river or export), event and date, word and definition, politician and his or her political position.

- Outline map of a country (or state, province, or river) and the country's name

- Drawing or contour elevation of a geographic term like delta, fjord, or isthmus and the name of the term

- Picture of a place or person and the name. (PCGlobe or MacGlobe can make the outine maps feasible.)

- Questions about a topic and their answers.

NARRATIVE OF LESSONS USING MIX-N-MATCH

Rhythms of Resistance in Southern Africa

Themes
- Culture
- Power, authority, and governance
- Global connections
- People, places, and the environment

Values
- Freedom to participate in the political process

Janet Bibb was planning a lesson on political change and culture in Southern Africa that she hoped would integrate social studies with music and literature. She wanted students to understand the role of popular music in expressing political and social themes as well as to learn the recent history and geography of Southern Africa. She would use Mix-N-Match often during the unit.

The class began by completing maps of the political boundaries of African countries, the major rivers and mountain ranges, and climatic zones. They reviewed these using a Mix-N-Match game with outline maps of 15 of the countries on one side that Ms. Bibb had prepared using MacGlobe and the matching names on another 15 cards. When pairs matched, they also tried to share other information that they knew about the country.

Two weeks later, after studying the music and politics of Southern Africa using especially the videos *Graceland* (1987) and *Rhythm of Resistance* (1979), Bibb used Mix-N-Match again. This time on one set of cards were photos or illustrations of instruments like the mbira or thumb piano, of the Zimbabwe ruins, of a gumboot (for the gumboot dance of the townships), and of people like Nelson Mandela and Miriam Makeba, as well as key vocabulary words like bantustan and the song title N'Kosi Sikeleli. The matching cards had explanations of the pictures and the words.

Students moved on to make their own thumb pianos and songs that expressed a political-social message. Student teams also made up questions and answers for review that they wrote on filing cards, one question on one card and the answer on another. This formed a Mix-N-Match practice test.

Structure 10 MIX-N-MATCH

STUDENT HANDOUT

Mix-N-Match Materials

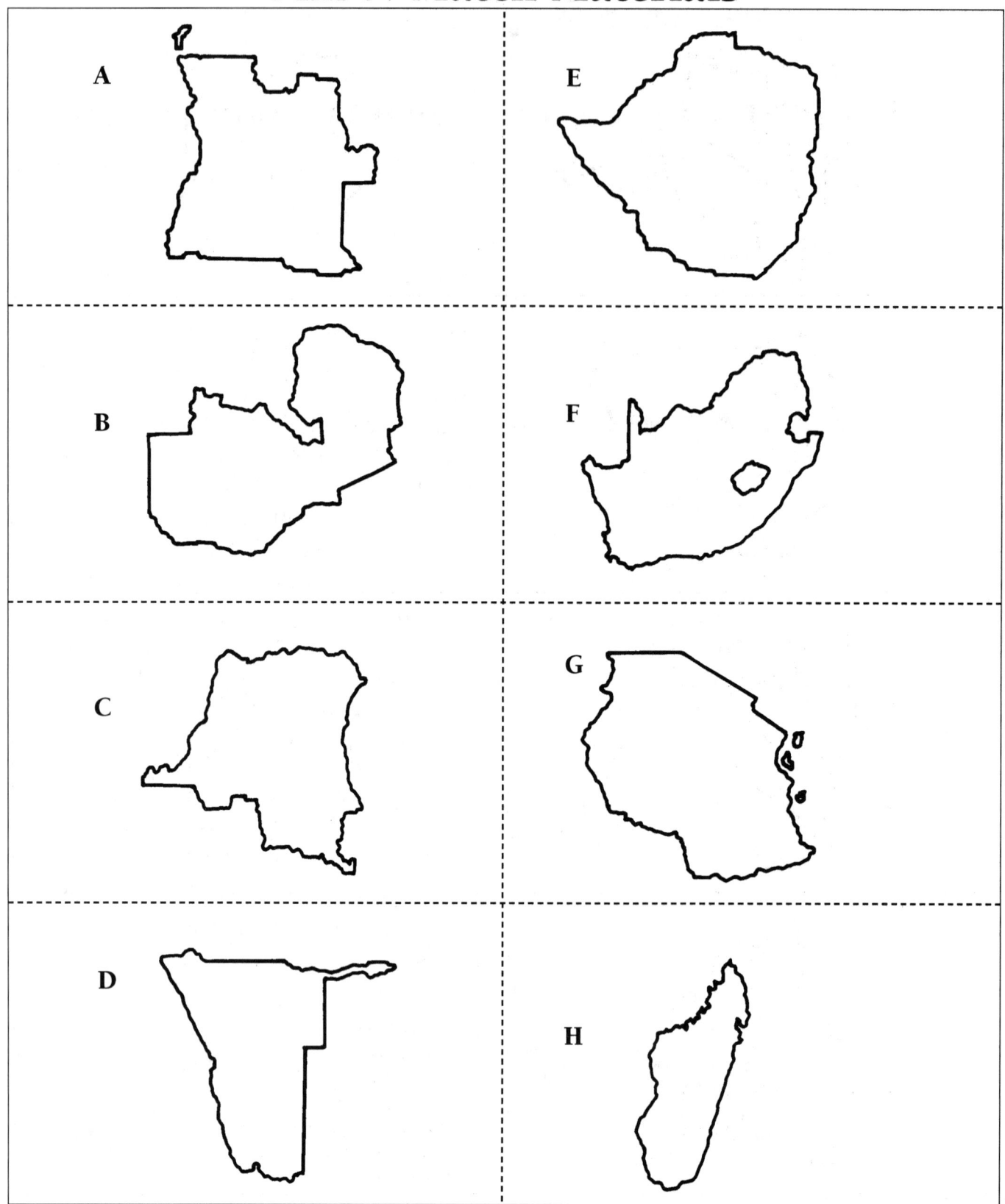

112 Cooperative Learning and Social Studies: Towards Excellence and Equity by Tom Morton
Kagan Publishing • 1(800) 933-2667 • www.KaganOnline.com

STUDENT HANDOUT

Mix-N-Match Materials (continued)

Structure 10 MIX-N-MATCH

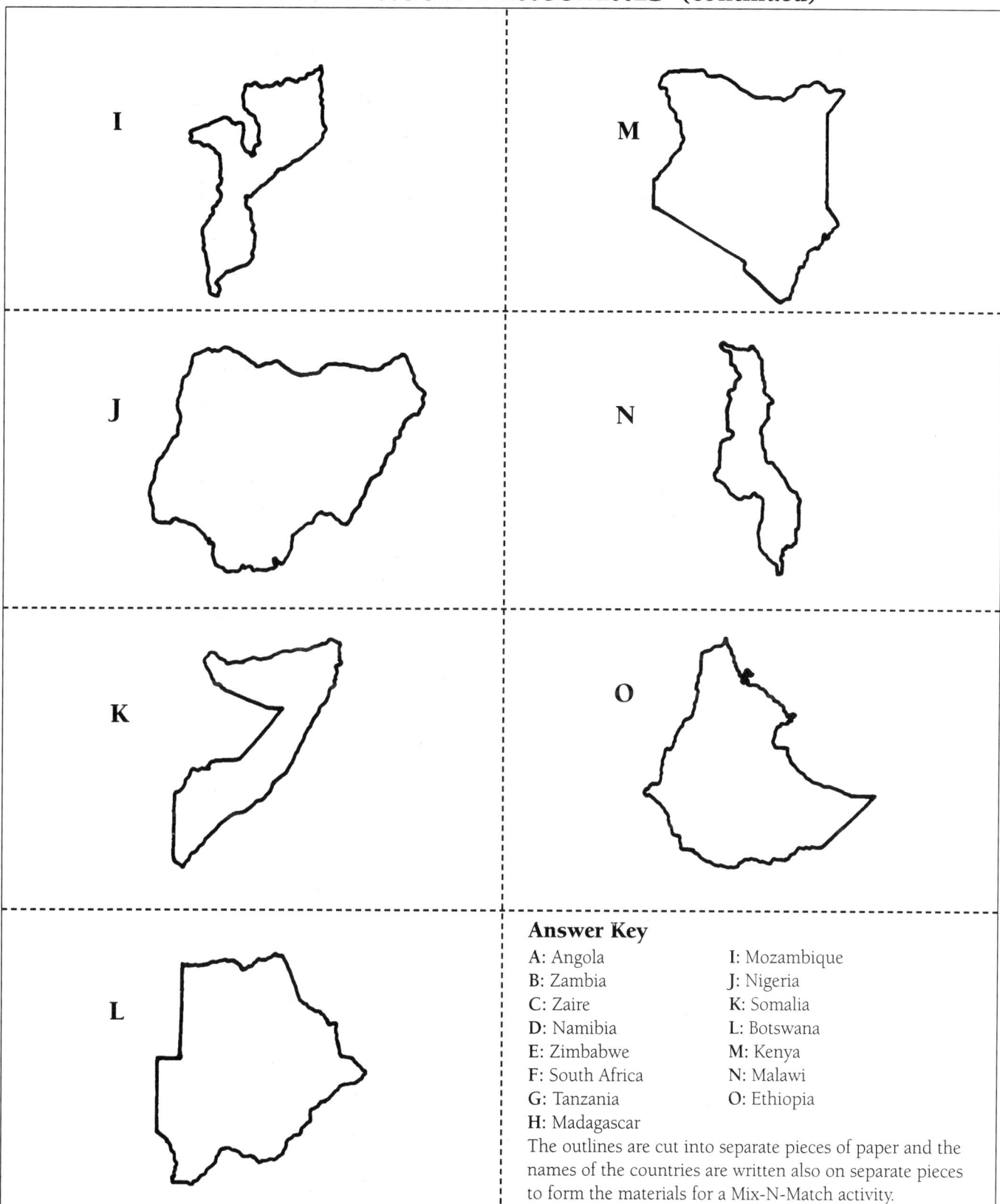

Answer Key

A: Angola
B: Zambia
C: Zaire
D: Namibia
E: Zimbabwe
F: South Africa
G: Tanzania
H: Madagascar
I: Mozambique
J: Nigeria
K: Somalia
L: Botswana
M: Kenya
N: Malawi
O: Ethiopia

The outlines are cut into separate pieces of paper and the names of the countries are written also on separate pieces to form the materials for a Mix-N-Match activity.

Cooperative Learning and Social Studies: Towards Excellence and Equity by Tom Morton
Kagan Publishing • 1(800) 933-2667 • www.KaganOnline.com

Structure 11
MYSTERY GAME

Steps at a Glance

1. Prepare an introduction and sets of clues, one set per group.
2. Introduce the mystery, procedure and social skills required.
3. The teams distribute the clues equally among group members.
4. Team members share their clues orally in order to solve the mystery.
5. Teams share their answers with Numbered Heads Together or Simultaneous Sharing.
6. Teams reflect on their group process.

Students share clues orally to try to solve a mystery. This structure is useful to teach communication and thinking skills as well as to create curiosity about a topic.

Social Skills
- Organizing
- Listening
- Summarizing
- Asking for justification
- Checking for agreement
- Checking for understanding

Puzzles, riddles, and mysteries are good hooks. A good mystery can fuel a desire to go to the roots of a subject, what is called epistemic motivation.

A Mystery Game combines cooperative learning with inquiry. It gives students a setting to practice hypothesizing, assessing evidence, attending to details and looking for contradictions, that is, the methods of the historian or social scientist. The rules encourage wide participation and oral communication so this structure is a good vehicle for teaching social skills like summarizing or paraphrasing.

The first time with this structure the teacher may wish to use a mystery like "Hootchy Kootchy" which is unrelated to social studies especially if the goal is to practice social skills. In the initial game the teacher might also want to share out loud his or her own thought processes in solving the mystery. A "think aloud" strategy gives students a model for thinking in clear and concrete terms.

Preparing original mysteries and clues will take some careful judgement of the level of your students. The first few games should probably have a puzzle that has a single right answer and straight forward clues. Later games can have greater complexity with misleading clues and nuanced answers.

The structure comes from Gene and Barbara Stafford in *Developing Effective Classroom Groups* (1977, 1990).

STEPS

❶ **PREPARE AN INTRODUCTION AND SETS OF CLUES, ONE SET PER GROUP**

❷ **INTRODUCE THE MYSTERY, PROCEDURE AND SOCIAL SKILLS REQUIRED**
The skills may include active listening, summarizing, or checking for understanding. Give one set of clues to each team.

❸ **TEAMS DISTRIBUTE THE CLUES EQUALLY AMONG GROUP MEMBERS**

❹ **TEAM MEMBERS SHARE THEIR CLUES ORALLY IN ORDER TO SOLVE THE MYSTERY**
They may not show or give their clues to another group member. This ensures that a low-status student does not give his or her clues away and then tune out. It may also restrain a domineering student who might otherwise take all the information and work alone. They may, however, take notes as others report their clues.

❺ **TEAMS SHARE THEIR ANSWERS WITH NUMBERED HEADS TOGETHER OR SIMULTANEOUS SHARING**
The teacher asks them to explain their reasoning.

❻ **TEAMS REFLECT ON THEIR GROUP PROCESS**
Ask them to discuss questions like the following:

- Did you feel you were listened to?
- Did you listen to others?
- What helped you solve the mystery?
- What hindered you?

IDEAS FOR USING MYSTERY GAME

The clues given below need to be cut into separate pieces. The rules for each game are the same:

1. Distribute clues equally amongst group members;
2. Share the information orally, but do not show the clues to other group members.

Who Killed Ned Nasty? (Example of a mystery unrelated to social studies that can be used as a model.)

A crime has been committed. As a group find out what the crime was, who committed it, why it was done, and how.

Ned Nasty was found dead in his Toronto home on Boxing Day, December 26.

The body had been dead 24 hours when it was found.

George Xenon was a top executive in Aardvark Resources, a forestry company.

Ned Nasty, although 80 years old, was a very active owner of a professional sports team and several resource companies. He had purchased Aardvark Resources in early December and announced the dismissal of all of Aardvark's upper level management.

Zoé Spot and her friend, Wendy Mark, left for a two week holiday on December 17 in Trinidad in the Caribbean Sea.

Yolanda Snarly, girlfriend of Ned, had learned that she was going to be left out of Ned's will.

There were traces of poison found in Ned's blood from the Hootchy Kootchy fish.

The day before Christmas, Ned Nasty's company had announced its intention to clearcut log an area of land which is the only known habitat of the hooting loon.

George was in Los Angeles on Christmas day playing Santa Claus at a Christmas party.

On Christmas Eve, Ned Nasty went carolling with neighbors and invited them in for a rum punch afterwards.

Wendy and Zoé had a huge argument while on holiday. Wendy stayed, but Zoé left and came home a week early.

The Hootchy Kootchy fish is found only in the Caribbean. Its poison slowly paralyzes its victim and kills in about 12 to 24 hours.

Yolanda broke both her legs in a skiing accident the week before Christmas and was in bed the whole holidays.

Zoé was a militant environmentalist who was opposed to clearcut logging.

Wendy and Zoé live next door to Ned Nasty.

Answer: Zoé Spot killed Ned Nasty with poison from the Hootchy Kootchy fish because he had ordered clearcut logging that would hurt the habitat of the hooting loon.

What Killed the Soldiers?

What was the leading cause of death in World War One? Why was it so devastating?

1. Battles and bullets killed some 14,000,000 soldiers, sailors and civilians in World War One.
2. High temperatures, low pulse, pains in the eyes, head or back were among symptoms of the disease that swept the world in 1918–1919.
3. Schools, hotels and even provincial legislatures in Canada were turned into hospitals during the 1918–1919 epidemic.
4. Chlorine gas was a new horror weapon first used by the Germans in 1915 at Ypres. Over 6,000 died from the gas or were left with lung disease after that one battle.
5. The world wide epidemic was called Spanish flu because the king of Spain was among its early victims.
6. Streets in some European cities were lined with bodies and there were traffic jams outside cemeteries during the epidemic.
7. The deterioration of health services caused by warfare made the outbreak of disease and its spread more likely.
8. Some military doctors saw death rates of ⅓ of their patients in French hospitals near the front during 1918–1919.
9. The virus that caused the epidemic may have begun in rat-infested trenches in France, but not identified as a distinctive disease until later.
10. In 1916 German airships dropped bombs on London.
11. The worldwide epidemic causes social disruption. Children were left without parents, or families without a wage earner.

Structure 11   **MYSTERY GAME**

12. In 1918 and 1919 an unidentified disease killed 27,000,000 people world wide.
13. It wasn't until 1933 that the virus that caused the 1918–19 epidemic was identified. The disease enters the body through the respiratory tract. There is no known cure although some vaccines are available for certain strains of this virus.
14. Doctors recommended wearing masks with cotton gauze over the nose and mouth to prevent the spread of the epidemic, but his did not work.
15. Strong doses of whiskey and towels packed with vinegar were recommended to prevent the spread of the disease, but this did not work.
16. Returning soldiers helped spread the disease to the United States and Canada where it made its way to the most remote communities. Some entire villages were exterminated.
17. Most deaths from the epidemic were related to complications like pneumonia.
18. The first outbreaks of the world wide disease in France occurred where American troops were stationed.

Answer: An influenza epidemic called the Spanish Flu was the leading cause killing some 27 million during and after the war. It was devestating because of the poor state of health care, the lack of knowledge of the disease's causes, the lack of antibiotics to treat complications, and the return of infected troops to their communities.

The Case of the Missing Days

Why do many people celebrate Christmas on January 7th, 13 days after December 25th? Why did Canadians and Americans go to sleep on the evening of September 2, 1752, and wake up on September 14?

1. Throughout the world people have used the moon as a measure of time. Twenty-eight days makes a lunar month. It is an easy way to reckon dates. However, for most people the important dates, such as when to plant crops, are those that involve the seasons.
2. For following the seasons a lunar year is of no use. The seasons are determined by the rotation of the earth around the sun and have no relation to the cycle of the moon. A lunar year of 13 months of 28 days makes only 364 days while a solar year, the time it takes the earth to circle completely the sun, is about 365¼ days.
3. The first people to develop a calendar based on the sun were the Egyptians who developed a year that had 365 days. There were 12 months of 30 days with five days added at the end of the year to celebrate the Egyptian gods. There were also leap years to make up for the extra ¼ days.
4. A solar year is not exactly 365 days or 365¼ days; it is 365 days, 5 hours, 48 minutes, and 46 seconds. Thus the months of the Egyptian calendar would gradually occur in a different season. The error was very small. It took 1460 years for a month to completely "wander" through all the seasons.
5. The Egyptian calendar was the most accurate calendar of the time of Julius Caesar so he adopted it to make his Julian Calendar.
6. Along with Christmas the most important Christian festival is Easter, which celebrates the resurrection of Christ from the grave. In 325 A.D. the Church decided Easter should be the first Sunday after the full moon next after March 21, the equinox or time of equal day and night. This was done in the Julian calendar.
7. The Julian calendar, like the Egyptian calendar, was not exactly the same as the solar year. The 365¼ day year was actually 11 minutes and 14 sec-

Notes

onds more that the time for the earth to orbit the sun. Over the centuries, these minutes and seconds added up and dates slowly lost their relation to the sun and the seasons. Easter was occuring earlier and earlier. By the 16th century, the date from which Easter was calculated, the equinox, was no longer on March 21. It was occurring on March 11.

8. In 1582 Pope Gregory XIII reformed the calendar. He announced that October 4 was to be followed by October 15. This meant that the equinox would again occur on March 21 as it did in 325 A.D.

9. The Gregorian Calendar also changed the system of leap years so that there would be no more wandering dates.

10. After Pope Gregory took 10 days out of the calendar there were demonstrations demanding the return of lost days. Servants demanded their usual full monthly pay for the shortened month but employers refused.

11. The Gregorian Calendar came from the Pope in Rome and was adopted by all Catholic countries. However, by that time in history there were many other Christian churches who did not recognize the Pope as their head. The Eastern Orthodox Churches in what is now Greece, Russia, and the Ukraine continued to calculate their holidays according to the old Julian Calendar as they do today.

12. The Protestant churches in Britain and British North America did not adopt the Gregorian Calendar until 1752. By that date the Julian calendar year had wandered 11 days off the solar year.

13. In 1752, when Britain adopted the Gregorian calendar, New Year's Day was to be January 1 and not March 25 as had been the case for centuries and the day after September 2, 1752, was to be called September 14, 1752. This law applied as well to the British colonies in North America, what are now the United States and Canada.

14. Slowly, Western influence spread the calendar of Pope Gregory throughout the world, often as part of a campaign to modernize. For example, Japan started to use it in 1873 and China in 1949.

15. Many religions follow a wide variety of calendars for setting festival dates. Moslems use a completely lunar calendar so their New Year's day or Ras Al-Sana can be in any season. The Jewish, Hindu, Chinese, and Vietnamese calendars are a mixture of both the lunar and solar years. This is why the Chinese and Vietnamese New Year's wanders but not too much. It is between January 21 and February 20, the first day of the second moon after the Winter Solstice.

Answer: Christians of the Eastern Orthodox church celebrate Christmas on January 7 because they follow the Julian calendar for religious days. When countries in Europe and North America left the Julian calendar for the Gregorian one that most people use today, the governments of the time had to subtract some days to get the calendar in line with the solar year. This created confusion and hostility.

Structure 11 *MYSTERY GAME*

NARRATIVE OF LESSONS USING MYSTERY GAME

Images of the World

Themes
- Time, continuity, and change

Skills
- Interpreting information
- Evaluating information
- Reference and information-search

John McBride began his 10th grade unit on world geography with a Mystery Game he calls "Guess the Country." Each cooperative team received envelope A with clues that describe a country. (The clues of both A and B are given on the next page.) McBride explained the rules of the Mystery Game and then gave the following instructions:

The clues in the envelope describe a well-known country. Share these clues orally to find the country in part A then put them back in the envelope and follow the same rules to guess the country in envelope B. When you have finished, list the reasons and sources for the information that led you to your guesses, e.g., newpapers, personal knowledge, social studies class, and the like.

The answers for both Part A and Part B are the same: India. However, the teams all had guessed industrialized countries for Part A and were very suprised to learn the modern side of India. Mr. McBride asked students to share their lists of the sources of information that led them to arrive at their answers and to consider why no one chose India for country A. Students suggested a variety of answers including the media coverage of third world countries or how school text books treat third world countries.

As a follow-up, Mr. McBride asked the class to collect newspaper articles and a journal record of stories on foreign countries over the following days. When they brought them to class, he asked student teams to sort them according to common subject matter. They fit them into categories like disasters, wars, and elections and noted that almost all were negative.

Mr. McBride wanted students to practice library research and generally broaden their knowledge of the world, so he assigned teams to research a country and to keep its name secret from the other teams. The task was to use almanacs, yearbooks, CD Rom disks and other references to create a list of at least twelve clues that describe the country and run their own Mystery Game.

Because some of the assigned countries were not well known to the students, when they played the game the teams who were guessing were allowed to look in a standard school atlas.

The goal of fooling their classmates led teams to find some curious facts that went beyond a simple profile. Some were a bit too obscure and Mr. McBride ruled these inadmissible.

An unintended and pleasant side effect was that groups used very, very quiet voices. One group tried to lead another astray by staging a conversation on a country different from their assigned one.

(The clues for this game are based on "Use the Clues", David Pardoe, *Tommorow's World*, Canadian Red Cross, 1982, p. 142. All rights reserved.)

Structure 11 *MYSTERY GAME*

Guess the Country   Part A

1. This country is an exporter of manufactured goods.

2. It has a written constitution. It is a democracy with an assembly of elected representatives.

3. This country is an atomic power.

4. This country has launched its own satellites, and has made major scientific contributions to the world including algebra.

5. This country is second in the world for the number of daily newspapers published.

6. This country is fourth in the world in number of universities.

7. This country is rich in the arts—painting, sculpture, singing, and dance—and is the world's leader in the production of feature films.

8. It produces over a million radios and 300,000 television sets a year.

Guess the Country Part B

1. This country has one of the oldest cultures in the world. It is the birthplace of two of the world's major religions. It has 16 official languages.

2. This country contains 18% of the world's population.

3. This country has a major sacred river to which millions travel each year.

4. This country's population doubles every 35 years.

5. This country receives large amounts of foreign aid.

6. The elections in this country are associated with great turmoil and massive public demonstrations.

7. Flooding, droughts, and epidemics occur frequently in this country.

8. The average life span is 58 years. Infant mortality is high.

Structure 12
NUMBERED HEADS TOGETHER

Steps at a Glance

❶ Students number off one to four in their teams.

❷ The teacher poses a question requiring multiple answers.

❸ Team members put heads together to answer question.

❹ Teacher calls number and students with that number raise hands to respond.

Students number off in teams. The teacher poses a question for team members to discuss and then calls a number. Students with that number respond to the question. Numbered Heads Together gives an opportunity for purposeful talk with high individual accountability.

Social Skills

- Checking for agreement
- Checking for understanding

Variations

- Stand and Deliver
- Simultaneous Numbered Heads Together
- Stir-The-Class

"Watch carefully, ladies and gentlemen. Spinning wheel got to go round. Where it stops nobody knows."

Numbered Heads Together is a versatile academic structure and with a little ham acting and a prop it makes a fun schtick.

It has usually been used for mastery of material that is moderately complex where the teacher poses a question which has multiple answers, but answers that are factual. However, many teachers with whom we've worked have also used it successfully with more open-ended questions much like Team Discussion, but with greater individual accountability.

Cooperative Learning and Social Studies: Towards Excellence and Equity by Tom Morton
Kagan Publishing • 1(800) 933-2667 • www.KaganOnline.com

Structure 12 NUMBERED HEADS TOGETHER

Steps

❶ Students number off one to four in their teams

If you have a group of three, then student number three answers when either three or four are called. In a group of five, team members four and five can answer together. (A spinner from Kagan Cooperative Learning solves this problem as well.)

❷ Teacher poses a question requiring multiple answers

❸ Team members put their heads together to answer the question, making sure each member can respond

Students can give a visual sign like thumbs up when they are ready to answer.

❹ Teacher calls a number and students with that number raise their hands ready to respond

The teacher can choose the number by the role of a dice, the choice of a card, or the spin of a spinner. Props like these add to the game show atmosphere of Numbered Heads Together.

The groups can also be assigned a number. In this case a second number is called to indicate the team to respond first. If a question has multiple parts, different teams could be asked to answer only part of the question. Another way to involve more students after the first answer is to ask the corresponding numbers of the others teams to respond to it.

Numbered Heads Together can also be used group by group. The teacher visits one group at a time and randomly calls the number of a person to respond to a question. This is a simple and effective way to ensure individual accountability.

Teacher Tips: Sometimes only a few teams respond when the teacher calls a number. In this case, ask them to put their heads together again.

Remember to give credit to the whole team for a good response and, likewise, responsibility to the whole team if the answer is inadequate.

Variations

Stand and Deliver

Having students stand up when their number is called is a popular twist on Numbered Heads, although some teachers dislike the pressure it may put on the student. Vanston Shaw (1993) in *Community Building in the Classroom*, however, suggests even more pressure: the first student to stand answers first and receives team points for the answer on the overhead projector.

Simultaneous Numbered Heads Together

For greater participation, students can give their answers simultaneously either by a choral response on the count of three, with a visual signal like thumbs up or thumbs down, or by writing at the blackboard. Simultaneous blackboard sharing also allows the class to reflect on the variety of responses.

Stir The Class

This structure literally came to Spencer Kagan in a dream. Groups line up together in one large class circle facing towards the center and each group numbers off amongst its members. The teacher poses a question and groups huddle together to answer it. When discussion is finished, the groups return to line up in the circle. The teacher gives a number and each student with that number rotates to share answers with the next group. The student stays with that new group for the next question.

IDEAS FOR USING NUMBERED HEADS TOGETHER IN SOCIAL STUDIES

Below are several ways to introduce this structure:

- "Make sure that everyone in your group can answer these 'who, what, when, where, why' questions that we made up. In a few minutes we'll roll the dice to hear your ideas."

- "As a group, list all the political positions in the federal government that we've studied and their responsibilities. The key social skill here will be checking, because any one of you may have your number come up on the spinner to represent your team."

- "Number off in your group.... Now take a few minutes and be sure everyone in your group can name and describe at least three landform regions in North America. Try it without looking at your notes first, but refer to them if you need to. I'll call a number in a few minutes."

- "Use your atlas to find the locations of all the countries in OPEC and be sure everyone is ready to come up and point to them on the wall map at the front. When you are sure everyone is ready, double check to be sure."

- Different groups can be given different perspectives to consider. For example, when considering a particular current event, the teacher might say something like the following, "I want these two groups to consider how geography might be a factor in this event. These groups should consider history. Your groups, government. And your groups, economics."

- Groups can also be assigned to consider an event from the point of view of different countries or historical figures, for example, one group could give an opinion on the Crusades from the perspective of a peasant; another from that of a knight; another, a priest; and so on.

- Towards the end of a Team Discussion the teacher can say, "I want you to summarize what you've decided on so far and take the next few minutes to be sure that all members of the team are ready to stand up and deliver an explanation of your team's ideas."

NARRATIVE OF LESSONS USING NUMBERED HEADS TOGETHER

Neighborhood Field Study

Themes
- People, places and environment
- Civic ideals and practices

Skills
- Acquiring, organizing and using information

Follow-Up
- Social and political participation

Recurring Issues
- How should we use land?

The social studies class of Guadalupe Bohorquez has a large number of recent immigrants. To ensure they have a base knowledge of geography skills, to help them become familiar with their neighborhood, and to consider some conceptual questions about urban land use, Ms. Bohorquez has them work in pairs to map the neighborhood. She then moves to a Sort structure and Numbered Heads Together to have them interpret their maps. As well as being a unit based on concepts and consideration of values conflicts, this field study is also a multi-ability unit using spatial, kinesthetic, and social abilities.

Before mapping the neighborhood, students practice using their pace length to determine distance. With the desks pushed to the side they find out how many steps it takes them to walk 8 meters, then calculate how long their average pace is. After testing their measuring ability on the hallway and cafeteria of the school, they are almost ready. They still need to be sure how to check on each other, because the task is a cooperative one and accuracy is very important.

Each pair of students takes a different block. Each block has one street that is mainly commercial. Their task is to walk around the block measuring the width of each lot and recording how the land is used, eg, the type of business or residence. Each member of the pair has a role, pacer and recorder, that they switch half way through. Both partners check.

When the class returns to the room for the next class, Ms. Bohorquez moves the pairs into fours and uses a Sort to consider how they might categorize their types of land use. She approves of the

Structure 12 NUMBERED HEADS TOGETHER

student labels like "where people live" and "stores," but adds to them what she calls "fancy talk vocabulary:" residential, commercial, institutional, and recreational.

The next step of the lesson is her first, quick use of Numbered Heads. Groups list the main features of a map (scale, compass direction, border, legend, title) then a number is called and those students report. Then Ms. Bohorquez gives them paper and crayons and assigns a common scale and common colors for the map legend.

Once all the pairs have finished their maps she posts them together on the wall. Because her two different classes do a different part of the neighborhood, the final result is almost a 30 block map of the school community giving considerable data to think about how land is used.

In their groups of four, students now number off and huddle together to answer the following questions interspersed with spins of the spinner and reports to the whole class:

- What could we say about how the land is used around our school? Why this particular type of land use?

- How is the area similar to and different from other neighborhoods? Why those similarities? Why those differences?

- Suggest some ideas about how the neighborhood has changed in the last ten years, hundred years? How could we find out?

- What do you like about the area? What would you suggest is missing here?

When the teams report, Ms. Bohorquez uses Stand and Deliver. To involve more students and vary the pace, she sometimes goes all around the room seeking responses from everyone and another time she takes only one response and asks everyone to think about it, calls another number, and has that student rise to react to the first response.

Ms. Bohorquez processes at several stages—after the field study, part way through the Sort, and at the end of Numbered Heads Together. The first time she gives students a Participation Pie like the one on p. 28 and asks them to divide it up according to the amount of participation each person did. Since they had quite specific roles, the circles are mostly all divided in half, which is what Ms. Bohorquez wants. It gives her a good chance to give some positive feedback and publicly talk about some of the contributions she saw made by her lower status students.

Later, groups refer to their Participation Pie and write about how well they followed their ideas for improvement.

Often, Ms. Bohorquez extends the exercise to have students write letters to the community weekly paper, *The Echo,* about what they like in their neighborhood and how it could be improved. Later in the year, they do a study of local history documents about the community which they compare to their neighborhood today.

Structure 13
PAIRS CHECK

Steps at a Glance

1. Teams of four break into two and each pair works on a single worksheet.
2. The coach checks to be sure the answer is correct.
3. Students switch roles and repeat the first two steps.
4. Pairs check.
5. If the team is in agreement, they celebrate with a group handshake.

Students in pairs take turns completing problems on a worksheet intermittently checking their answers with another pair. The structure is intended for students to help each other master skills.

Social Skills
- Taking turns
- Asking for justification
- Helping
- Praising

A group worksheet is a common teaching strategy. However, if the teacher merely gives a group a common worksheet to complete, there may be uneven cooperation. In Pairs Check, where students take turns to complete a problem, help, praise and check, they are much more likely to work together to complete the task.

Pairs Check is most powerful when students are able to help one another skillfully. If they only tell each other the answer without explanation and prompting, the learning may not be much beyond that of individual work.

Pairs Check is most commonly used in social studies for the practice of geography skills, although it has wider application in teaching reading strategies, text analysis, and even concept attainment.

Structure 13   PAIRS CHECK

STEPS

❶ TEAMS OF FOUR BREAK INTO TWO AND EACH PAIR WORKS ON A SINGLE WORKSHEET
One student works on the question while the other takes the role of coach, helping if needed.

❷ COACH CHECKS TO BE SURE THE ANSWER IS CORRECT
If not, the two try to reach agreement as to a good answer. If they can't, they may ask the other pair for their opinion. However, if the coach does agree, then he or she gives some exaggerated praise. For example, "You deserve the Nobel Prize for social studies!" or "You are so brilliant, I need to wear sun glasses!" (For more fun, share with the class any good examples of super praise that you hear during the lesson.)

❸ STUDENTS SWITCH ROLES AND REPEAT THE FIRST TWO STEPS
The coach answers the question, while the worker now becomes the coach.

❹ PAIRS CHECK
The original team of four reunites and compares answers. If they disagree and are unable to figure out why, they raise all four hands.

❺ IF TEAM IS IN AGREEMENT, THEY CELEBRATE WITH A GROUP HANDSHAKE

Teacher Tips: The worksheet can ask pairs to check with each other after each line of problems or after two or three lines. Because groups finish at different rates, it is a good idea to have a sponge at the end, that is, an involving question that extends the learning.

IDEAS FOR USING PAIRS CHECK IN SOCIAL STUDIES

- **Geography Skills**
  - latitude and longitude
  - reading elevation on a topographic map
  - reading bar graphs, pie graphs, line graphs, and tables
  - compass directions and bearings
  - determining distance using scale
- **Reading Strategies**
  - writing a summary
  - finding the main idea
  - generating questions
- **Text Analysis**
  - identifying loaded language; euphemism; passive voice; logical fallacies; or fact, opinion, and argument
- **Variation in the Final Stage of Find My Rule**
  - given a Pairs Check form with examples and non-examples of a concept, the pairs take turns to identify if the item is an example of the rule or not.

NARRATIVE OF A LESSON USING PAIRS CHECK

Reading Strategies

Skills

- Reading comprehension
- Summarizing information
- Metacognitive skills

All of Robert Doyle's social studies department were surprised at the results of recent standardized reading tests. Every class, including the gifted, was reading well below national norms.

This was the impetus for the department to make improving reading instruction as its professional goal for the next three years. One of the main approaches has been teaching students cognitive strategies like generating questions, using context, and finding the main idea. For example, to find the main idea students were given these steps and rules:

Step 1: Find the topic sentence.

Step 2: If there is no topic sentence, identify the topic and find the most important information about that topic. You can usually find it by looking for words that are repeated and their synonyms.

Rule 1: Leave out unimportant or repeated information.

Rule 2: Put the main idea in your own words.

Rule 3: Give steps or lists a title.

The teachers have used whole class instruction, sharing their thinking out loud as they looked for the main idea of a paragraph, and individual seatwork, giving frequent prompts to students to follow the steps and rules.

However, Doyle has also encouraged other teachers to try Pairs Read and Pairs Check. Below is one of his Pairs Check worksheets using a passage from a grade 11 geography textbook.

The more confident senior students especially like to play with the exaggerated praise. Doyle monitors looking for good examples that he writes up on the blackboard and uses over the next few days to the great appreciation of the students.

Structure 13 *PAIRS CHECK*

The Pairs Check worksheet includes a "Sponge" for groups who finish early that asks them to represent the main ideas visually. Graphic organizers are another of the department's approaches intended to improve both reading and writing. (At the time of writing, the social studies department is waiting for the results of testing to see if there have been any reading gains.)

Notes

Structure 13   *PAIRS CHECK*

Names: _____

PAIRS CHECK WORKSHEET

Finding the Main Idea

Instructions: You are to work in pairs in your team. Both of you should read paragraph 1. One of you should then play the role of the Thinker and write down the main idea and two supporting details. Try to say what you are thinking out loud. The second member of your pair acts as Coach. Coaches, if you agree that person one has done the task correctly, give him or her some exaggerated praise. If you do not agree, try to help that person use a reading strategy to find a better answer. When you have finished, switch roles and move to the second paragraph.

When you have each finished a paragraph, share your answers with the other pair. If you don't agree, figure out why. When all of you agree your answers are good, give a team handshake.

	Main Idea	Supporting Details
The demand for a resource may be altered by changes in technology. This can happen as a result of either technical improvements in production, or the development of more economical substitutes. Take the example of copper.		
In the second millennium BC, early copper mines in the Middle East extracted ores containing from 3 to 15 percent copper. Anything less was not considered worth mining. Yet many copper mines today... exploit ores which contain only 0.5 percent copper. This change in demand results from improved mining technology. Large-scale equipment operating in open-pit mines makes possible the mining of low-grade copper ores…		✓ Checked your answers?
The demand for copper is affected in another way by the new technology of fibre optics. These fine filaments or fibres of glass which transmit light waves can carry hundreds of times more information than copper wires can. Fibre optic cables are also less liable to corrosion. For these reasons and many more, fibre optics are taking the place of copper in telecommunications. The drop in demand for copper causes a drop in its price. This may make some mines uneconomical to operate—despite the improved mining technology.		
On the other hand, an increased demand for a metal will cause a rise in its price and possibly lead to the reopening of mines previously considered uneconomic. For example, the sharp increase in the demand for gold in the late 1970's caused the price to rise to over $800 (U.S.) an ounce in January, 1980. Many gold mines were reopened, but some closed down again when gold prices fell in the mid-1980's.		✓ Checked your answers?

From *Towards Tomorrow: Canada in a Changing World.* Copyright © 1988 Harcourt Brace & Company Canada, Ltd. Reprinted with permission of the publisher.

Sponge: Finished? Construct a diagram that represents the main ideas.

Pairs Check Worksheet

page 2

Finding the Main Idea

Passage	Main Idea	Supporting Details
In theory, international trade ought to benefit all countries which engage in it. Trade enables countries to specialize in those forms of production to which they are best suited. Nevertheless, international trade has usually operated to the benefit of western countries, which have been able to buy their raw materials cheaply from Third World suppliers. The benefits felt by these suppliers are relatively low. This is because the cost of the resources used in making an article such as a computer or bicycle is very much less than the final cost of manufacturing. Most manufactured articles require several stages in manufacturing before final consumption. Then there are the costs of marketing the finished product. Thus, only a few dollars of the price of a typical $200 article would go to the cost of the raw materials. If these materials came from a Third World country, they might well have been bought by a company which paid only a royalty to the government, and probably low wages to its workers there.		
Third World countries often sell their resources at such low cost because they are in competition with each other. Except during the oil crisis period (1973–1980), world prices in recent years have been low both for minerals and agricultural commodities. For instance, how much of the price you pay for a banana actually goes to the Third World producer? (Just 10 cents per $1.) Thus, the benefits from the use of these resources have been felt more in western industrialized nations than in the less developed countries of the world. The problem is worse for those nations that depend on a single product for much of their exports. For example, copper accounts for over 90 percent of Zambia's exports. If the price of this commodity falls, the whole nation is adversely affected.		✓ Checked your answers?

Sponge: Finished? Construct a diagram that represents the main ideas.

Structure 13 **PAIRS CHECK**

Names: _____

PAIRS CHECK WORKSHEET

Finding the Main Idea

Instructions: You are to work in pairs in your team. Both of you should read paragraph 1. One of you should then play the role of the Thinker and write down the main idea and two supporting details. Try to say what you are thinking out loud. The second member of your pair acts as Coach. Coaches, if you agree that person one has done the task correctly, give him or her some exaggerated praise. If you do not agree, try to help that person use a reading strategy to find a better answer. When you have finished, switch roles and move to the second paragraph.

When you have each finished a paragraph, share your answers with the other pair. If you don't agree, figure out why. When all of you agree your answers are good, give a team handshake.

	Main Idea	Supporting Details
		✓ Checked your answers?
		✓ Checked your answers?

Sponge:

Cooperative Learning and Social Studies: Towards Excellence and Equity by Tom Morton
Kagan Publishing • 1(800) 933-2667 • www.KaganOnline.com

Structure 14
PAIRS COMPARE

Steps at a Glance

1. A group of four divides into two pairs.
2. Both pairs should now join together to take turns sharing their answers.
3. The pairs switch tasks.
4. Team Discussion to come up with as many answers as they can that neither pair alone could think of.

Students work in pairs to create a list of answers to a question, compare their list with another pair, and then work as a team to find still another answer. Pairs Compare lets students explore in depth questions to which there are multiple answers.

Social Skills
- Taking turns
- Listening
- Checking for agreement
- Checking for understanding

This structure is a blend of RallyTable, RoundRobin, and Team Discussion. It is used to consider questions that have multiple answers. This can be at the beginning of a unit when the teacher wants to establish the prior knowledge of students or at any other point for review. The Team Discussion pushes students to go deeper with their answers.

The steps of Pairs Compare also help the teacher reinforce the social skills of taking turns, listening and checking.

Structure 14 PAIRS COMPARE

Steps

❶ A GROUP OF FOUR DIVIDES INTO TWO PAIRS

One person should be an "A" and the other, a "B." The pairs consider a question that has multiple answers using RallyTable, that is, each member of the pair takes a turn writing an answer.

❷ BOTH PAIRS SHOULD NOW JOIN TOGETHER TO TAKE TURNS SHARING THEIR ANSWERS AS FOLLOWS

The "A" of one pair gives one of her pair's answers while the second "A" from the other pair looks to see if it is on his list. If it is, he checks it off; if not, he adds it to his list. The first "B" then gives her answer, while the other "B" looks at his list to check it off or add it.

❸ PAIRS SWITCH TASKS: THE SECOND "A" GIVES AN ANSWER WHILE THE FIRST "A" LOOKS IF IT IS ON HER LIST

Then "B" shares an answer, and the other "B" checks the list. The group

continues alternating roles. They have finished when both lists are the same.

This crisscrossing RoundRobin, while complicated at first, ensures maximum participation and complete notes.

❹ LAST STEP IS A TEAM DISCUSSION TO COME UP WITH AS MANY ANSWERS AS THEY CAN THAT NEITHER PAIR ALONE COULD THINK OF

Although this is a Team Discussion, participation is the most equal if the pairs take turns recording answers like a RoundTable.

Ideas for Using Pairs Compare in Social Studies

- Before a field trip ask each group to come up questions to which they might find answers during the trip. These could be shared with Stand-N-Share to try to have every student ready with a different question to explore.

- As a review, list all the important facts about a field trip, an event, a place, or a person.

- List all the causes or effects, for example, causes and effects of war and peace, of unemployment, and of economic development; influences on weather; or sources and solutions of pollution.

- List examples that fit categories, for example, examples of developed countries and developing countries, major exports and imports of Japan, or skills needed for a good learning team.

- List all the pros and cons of some controversial decision. For example, Spencer Kagan told us of when he visited a Canadian classroom where the teacher was discussing the expulsion of the Acadians in 1755, which Longfellow portrayed in his poem "Evangeline." Invited by the teacher to lead the class in a discussion of history that was unfamiliar to him, he relied on the students to develop reasons why the British should or should not expel the Acadians using Pairs Compare.

- Complete almost any graphic organizer, for example, a Venn diagram comparing countries, a web of student knowledge of the Cold War, or a fishbone of causes of the American Revolution.

- Predict the outcomes of a trend as an alternative to brainstorming or a Future Wheel. For example, students could be asked to predict all the possible consequences of deforestation or of global warming or of some government action that may have just been reported.

Structure 14 *PAIRS COMPARE*

NARRATIVE OF LESSONS USING PAIRS COMPARE

Land and Logging

Themes
- People, places, and environment
- Production, distribution, and consumption

Skills
- Classifying information
- Analyzing information
- Evaluating information
- Decision-making

Jim Kelly teaches a unit on the ecology and economy of forests to his middle school social studies class. Early in the unit students use Pairs Compare to list from their own knowledge all the products that come from trees. They share the information using the Stand-N-Share structure described in Structure 19.

Kelly also adds a twist to make Stand-N-Share almost an extra step in Pairs Compare. In Stand-N-Share, the teams give each member one idea to report to the class and then everyone stands up. One student in the class is asked to share an idea and then sits down. Anyone else in the class with the same idea then sits down as well. This continues until all students are sitting. Kelly asks the class, however, to check their list during the sharing to see if the items mentioned by other groups are on their own list and to add them if they are not.

Another lesson has students play Woolly Thinking to create a class model of a forest ecosystem. Students play the roles of a mature Douglas fir tree, a snag, a beetle, a bear, a salmon, and other plants and animals that they interconnect with each other using colored yarn. (The roles and an explanation of the procedure are given in Structure 21.)

To help students remember all the interdependent connections Kelly follows this with Pairs Compare with a web at the end of which each student has a diagram of the forest ecology as best the group can recall.

The class next studies a fictional, but very realistic, account of a dispute over logging described in Elizabeth Coelho and Lise Winer's *Jigsaw Plus* (1991). Their jigsaw has four different viewpoints on whether a forest should be logged or left as is. Once the students have finished teaching their sections of the jigsaw, the group summarizes the controversy using Pairs Compare and the Decision Making Sheet on the next page.

Notes

As a class the students first establish the problem and the goals. The island has a rich rain forest eco-system that is also part of the traditional culture and economy of the native people and logging may destroy this. However, logging provides employment and supplies tax revenue. The goal is both to preserve the forest and reap economic benefits.

The class continues to suggest several alternative solutions such as no logging, the development of tourism, selective logging, and clearcut logging with close supervision before using Pairs Compare to develop the arguments for and against.

Structure 14 *PAIRS COMPARE*

Decision-Making Model

Problem:	Goal(s):

Alternatives:	Pros & Cons:

Decision(s):	Reason(s):

Structure 15
PAIRS READ AND PAIRS VIEW

Steps at a Glance — PAIRS READ

1. Students work in pairs.
2. Both students silently read.
3. Pairs decide if there is anything that can help answer questions.
4. Both write down main points of discussion.
5. Pairs decide on the 5 points they think are most important.

Steps at a Glance — PAIRS VIEW

1. In pairs students designate an A and a B.
2. Teacher starts video and stops it every ten minutes.
3. A summarizes for B the ideas and information presented so far.
4. After 3 minutes, the teacher starts video again.
5. After another 10 minutes, video is stopped again and B takes lead while A listens.
6. Continue pauses and alternating roles.
7. Discuss video with whole class.

In Pairs Read students read a section of a longer passage, then one member of the pair completes a task like giving the main idea. For the next section, the other partner takes a turn giving an answer and they continue like this to the end of the passage. Pairs View is similar except that the pairs discuss a section of a video when the teacher stops the tape at five to ten minute intervals. This structure gives students an opportunity to check their comprehension as well as giving them practice in a particular learning strategy.

Social Skills

- Taking turns
- Listening
- Summarizing
- Checking for agreement
- Checking for understanding

Structure 15 PAIRS READ AND PAIRS VIEW

Reading the textbook and watching videos are the two most common ways of gaining information in social studies classrooms. Here are two structures that can improve comprehension and skills: Pairs Read and its equivalent for viewing film or videos, Pairs View.

Pairs Read has many different forms and authors. Our description here is adapted from that of David and Roger Johnson (1994).

STEPS FOR PAIRS READ

❶ **STUDENTS WORK IN PAIRS, ONE OF WHOM SHOULD BE A GOOD READER, TO TAKE THE MAJOR HEADINGS OF THE TEXT AND TURN THEM INTO QUESTIONS**
The teacher may want pairs to share these and then designate some common questions for the whole class or let students work on their own questions.

❷ **BOTH STUDENTS SILENTLY READ A PARAGRAPH OR ABOUT 10 LINES OF TEXT**

❸ **AT THE END OF READING, PAIRS DECIDE IF THERE IS ANYTHING THAT CAN HELP ANSWER THE QUESTIONS**
They should be prompted to summarize the paragraph, clarify any words that are unfamiliar, and elaborate.

❹ **BOTH WRITE DOWN THE MAIN POINTS OF THEIR DISCUSSION AND CONTINUE TO THE NEXT PARAGRAPH AND SO ON UNTIL THEY HAVE FINISHED THE WHOLE PASSAGE**

❺ **AT THE END OF READING THE PAIRS DECIDE ON THE 5 POINTS THAT THEY THINK ARE THE MOST IMPORTANT AND SHARE THESE WITH THE CLASS OR ANOTHER PAIR**
A variation of this is to ask the students not to pose questions, but to find the main ideas of each of the paragraphs. Teammates both read a paragraph silently. Then one student takes the role of summarizer, giving the main idea in his or her own words and one or two key details. The second student becomes the accuracy checker, listening carefully, correcting any misstatements and adding anything left out.

The students then switch roles and move on to the next paragraph. At the end of the passage the pair prepare a written summary and process how well they worked together.

STEPS FOR PAIRS VIEW

This is basically the same as Pairs Read but is used with video or film. It is intended only for those that are lengthy and documentary, not with a short video when it would be unnecessary or with those videos that tell a story where frequent pauses might hurt enjoyment of the narrative.

Structure 15 *PAIRS READ AND PAIRS VIEW*

❶ **IN PAIRS STUDENTS DESIGNATE ONE PERSON TO BE AN "A" AND THE OTHER, A "B"**
Tell them that their common goal is that they both can explain the contents of the video and give the procedure that they should follow.

❷ **THE TEACHER STARTS THE VIDEO AND STOPS IT ABOUT EVERY TEN MINUTES (FIVE WITH YOUNGER STUDENTS)**

❸ **WHEN THE VIDEO IS STOPPED THE FIRST TIME, "A" SUMMARIZES FOR "B" THE IDEAS AND INFORMATION PRESENTED SO FAR**
"A" tells "B" what he or she finds the most interesting about what they have so far seen, and identifies anything that is confusing and tries to clarify it. "B" listens, gives feedback on the summary and helps clarify any confusing points. The teacher may also ask students to take notes or fill out a worksheet as desired.

❹ **AFTER THREE MINUTES OR SO, START THE VIDEO AGAIN**

❺ **AFTER ANOTHER 10 OR SO MINUTES, THE VIDEO IS STOPPED AGAIN AND "B" TAKES THE LEAD WHILE "A" LISTENS AND HELPS**

❻ **CONTINUE THE PAUSES AND ALTERNATING ROLES.**

❼ **DISCUSS THE VIDEO WITH THE WHOLE CLASS RANDOMLY CALLING ON "AS" OR "BS" TO RESPOND SIMILAR TO NUMBERED HEADS**

IDEAS FOR USING PAIRS READ AND PAIRS VIEW IN SOCIAL STUDIES

Almost any text passage or lengthy audio-visual presentation can be used with Pairs Read and View. There are several different approaches, however, that might be used before, during and after gathering the information.

- **Prereading or Viewing Strategies**
  The teacher
  - discusses with the class what they already know about the topic
  - provides a worksheet or a graphic organizer like a web on which students take notes
  - presents an Advanced Organizer, that is, a conceptual framework around which students may build the information that they gather, such as the idea of supply and demand before reading a passage on economics
  - relates the text or video to the central questions or goals for the unit and suggests how the information may help answer them

- **Tasks for Reading or Viewing**
  The students
  - compare the material with another topic already studied
  - formulate an implicit question answered in each paragraph
  - identify the opinion and supporting evidence in paragraphs
  - identify bias in paragraphs
  - time length of interviews and commentaries in news or documentary programs

- identify the sources of evidence in news or documentary programs, eg. who is interviewed and who is not
- record types of images and later classify them.
- predict what will happen next

● **Postreading or Viewing Strategies**
- Pairs create a dialogue or sketch, for example, after a video on Brazilian agriculture, they could create a dialogue between a North American consumer and a farm labourer
- Pairs rank ideas in order of most to least important
- Each student prepares exam-type questions, then the pair chooses the top 5 and passes these to another pair to answer or to the teacher to give to the whole class
- Pairs prepare a diagram or poster of the information they've read or viewed
- Pairs create a metaphor to express their understanding of the topic
- Pairs share results of their work with the class or another group
- Pairs prepare a Team Statement or Team Web about the topic

Notes

NARRATIVE OF LESSONS USING PAIRS READ

The Return of Martin Guerre

Themes
- Individual development and identity
- Individuals, groups, and institutions
- Time, continuity, and change

Skills
- Comprehension

In teaching the Middle Ages and Renaissance, Janet Thompson wanted to emphasize the social history. The story of Martin Guerre and the movie of the same name with Gérard Depardieu gave her fascinating resources to consider how French families lived some 450 years ago and to discuss, as well, the similar processes for deciding on the reliability of evidence in courts and in history.

Janet Thompson used some of her usual methods to help her students develop their reading, an anticipation guide and Pairs Read. Both were intended to develop the students abilities to find the main ideas in a passage and predict (anticipate) what is to come. The students started in pairs.

She began with the anticipation guide and Think-Pair-Share. The guide is intended as an anticipatory set and an opportunity to clarify vocabulary like curse, adultery, rely on, reliability, court proceedings, and testimony. Some of the questions such as number 2 that says, "Most married couples…," are designed to have students look closely at the text and make careful judgements.

The students filled out the form individually predicting if the statements would turn out to be true or false. They shared their predictions and reasons for them with their partner, then with the class. After the reading, the class would return to their anticipation guide to write down what the the reading said.

Next, Ms. Thompson distributed the Martin Guerre story and asked the class to use Pairs Read. In this case, she did not ask them to take notes while they were reading, only to write down the main points and predictions at the end.

She continued by asking for some of the predictions from the class and a vote as to the man's guilt or innocence before reading the following out loud:

Just as Jean de Coras was about to recommend that the prisoner was indeed Martin Guerre, a man with a wooden leg appeared at the doors of the Parliament of Toulouse and said that his name was Martin Guerre. In the next few days, things became clearer. Pierre, Bettrande and others recognized the one-legged man as Martin, even when the judges arranged a test in which he had to be picked out of a line-up. It seems that the soldier who had passed through Artigat told the truth. Martin had served as a courtier for a nobleman and had lost a leg in combat in Flanders. How he found out about the trial at Toulouse or how he was able to arrive just in time is not known.

The prisoner eventually confessed that he was indeed, Arnaud du Tilh. He claimed that he had tricked Bettrande and that she was blameless for all that had happened. In September of 1560 Arnaud made a public confession in front of the church at Artigat. He apologized to all and to Bettrande for tricking her as he climbed the ladder to the gibbet. Just before he was hanged, he asked for mercy from God through his son, Jesus Christ.

After this we hear no more of Martin, Bettrande, Pierre or any of the other characters in this story who were to become so famous.

Ms. Thompson then returned to Think-Pair-Share to consider these questions:

- How did the judge try to determine the reliability of a witness?

- What other evidence was there for or against the man claiming to be Martin Guerre?

- How do we know the history of Martin Guerre?

She then asked the class to return to their anticipation guides and complete the column "What does the reading say?" Finally, students wrote a summary of what they learned about life in 16th century France and about how judges and historians find the truth.

STUDENT HANDOUT   NAME: _____

Anticipation Guide for "The Return of Martin Guerre"

	What do you think? (True or False)	What does the reading say?
1. People in France in the 1500's believed in witches and spells.		
2. In 16th century France most married couples stayed together all their lives.		
3. In France of this time it was a serious offense to commit adultery.		
4. There were no photographs in the 16th century.		
5. There were no written records of court proceedings in 16th century France.		
6. In France at this time judges relied on the testimony of witnesses to determine the truth.		

The Return of Martin Guerre

Instructions: Read section A silently and then one of you should give the main points of the section and predict what will happen next. The other partner listens, paraphrases, and then gives his or her answers. Reach agreement on the main points. Do the same with each section but switch roles each time. At the end, decide on the five most important points of the passage and one prediction, write these down and share them with the class.

A. In 1527, the peasant Sanxi Daguerre and his family, including his young son, Martin, his wife and younger brother Pierre left the French Basque country to live in the village of Artigat, a three-week walk away. They acquired land on which they grew millet and grapes for wine making and kept sheep. They also set up a tile business.

During their early years here, they adapted to the customs of the community. This included learning the local French dialect and changing their family name to Guerre.

One indication of the success they enjoyed was the marriage of their son, Martin, to Bettrande de Rols, daughter of one of the most prosperous families in the area. This happened in 1538 after eleven years in Artigat. Both were in their early teens, perhaps thirteen or fourteen. Marriage at this age was unusual at the time.

B. The early years of the marriage were uneventful. There were no children for more than eight years. This was unusual for married couples in those days since there was no such thing as family planning or birth control. It was suggested that Martin was impotent or "bewitched."

After almost ten childless years, the couple saw a "wise woman" who lifted the spell. Soon a son, named after his grandfather, was born.

It appears that Martin was not happy with life in Artigat. It must have been difficult with Martin, his wife and their young son, his parents and his sisters, all living in the same household. In 1548, he quarreled with his father Sanxi over some grain he had "stolen." That summer he left his family, his infant son and his wife.

C. Bettrande received no news from or about her husband for many years. She was left to raise her son as best she could. In those days women had few rights, for example, unless there was absolute proof of Martin's death, Bettrande could not remarry. There was no such thing as divorce. During this time Martin's father forgave him for his theft, but both parents died without hearing any news of their son. Martin's uncle Pierre took over the family businesses and looked after Bettrande and her son. Then, in the summer of 1556, a man showed up at Bettrande's door saying he was Martin, her husband. She warmly received him and took him back.

D. It had been eight years since anyone had seen Martin. In those days, there were no photographs or other clues such as painted portraits to remind people what long lost relatives and friends really looked like. They had only their memories to go by. Martin looked shorter and not as slim and athletic as he had been in his youth. Of course, some people gain weight as they get older. Then there was the fact that Martin did not look like his son, but, then again, he looked like his sisters. While his uncle did not recognize him immediately, his wife, after showing some surprise at first, recognized him as her long-lost husband, especially after he had reminded her of events on their wedding day.

Martin was quite sick, but after Bettrande nursed him back to health he made his appearance in the village as the heir to the Guerre property. He recognized people by name and reminded them of the times when he lived in town before. So most people accepted him as Martin Guerre. During the next few years Martin established himself as a merchant, in addition to managing his other properties inherited from his father.

E. Pierre had been looking after the Guerre properties, including his own, in Martin's absence. He had, for a peasant, control of a lot of territory. At first he welcomed his nephew back into the family, but gradually his attitude changed. First, there was Martin's new appearance, but most people, including his wife, recognized him. Second, Martin seemed to have forgotten much of his native Basque language. Third, Martin sold part of his inherited property. This was common in this area, but in the Basque country where the Guerres came from, it was almost never done.

Martin had some complaints of Pierre as well. He suspected that his uncle had withheld some of his inheritance. When he could not get some straight answers from his uncle, Martin decided to sue him late in 1558 or early in 1559.

F. The doubts Pierre had about Martin now came into the open. For the next year he talked openly about the "imposter". The town was split. The family was split as well with Bettrande insisting that the man she lived with, who had since his return fathered several daughters, was indeed Martin. After all, wouldn't she know?

Pierre wanted to take Martin to court as an imposter, but for months there was no case other than his suspicions. Then a couple of events changed everything. First, a soldier passing through Artignat declared that this man was an imposter. He had seen the real Martin in Flanders in Belgium far to the north. There he had lost a leg in battle and now had a wooden one. But before anyone could check on this story the soldier had gone on his way. Shortly afterward Martin was put in jail for arson. While there was no proof of Martin's guilt, his imprisonment in Toulouse gave Pierre time to check out the soldier's story. He came across an innkeeper in a village some distance away who was told a secret by an acquaintance, Arnaud du Tilh. Arnaud was reported to have said, "Martin Guerre is dead; he has given me his goods."

Pierre now decided to charge Martin. When Martin was released from prison he was rearrested and reimprisoned. Pierre and his family, including Bettrande's mother, put great pressure on her to join them. Bettrande was in a real bind, for if she was not careful, she would be accused of adultery. Adultery would, at the very least, have disgraced her and her daughters forever. Nevertheless, while sending money and goods to Martin in prison, Bettrande swore a complaint against the man saying he had tricked her into believing he was her long lost husband. Such impersonation was punishable by death.

G. The trial at Rieux could have gone either way. There were 150 witnesses. Thirty to forty of them, including Martin's four sisters and his brothers-in-law who testified that the person who came into their midst just a few years before was indeed the long lost Martin. More than forty-five witnesses testified that the prisoner was Arnaud du Tilh, or at least not Martin Guerre. These included Arnaud's uncle, Pierre Guerre, and Bettrande.

The prisoner testified in his defense and impressed all, including the judge, with his detailed knowledge of the life of Martin Guerre. It seemed that only the real Martin could know so much. His accounts matched those of his wife, despite attempts to catch him up on details. As to why his wife should be testifying against him, he stated that it was due to the coercion of his uncle and her relatives. On the basis of all this, the judge rendered a verdict.

H. On the strength of the numbers of witnesses, given that their reliability seemed to be about equal and without photographs, pictures or handwriting samples the prisoner was declared to be an imposter and sentenced to death. The prisoner appealed to a higher court, the Parliament of Toulouse, the largest city in southern France. Jean de Coras, one of the judges in the Parliament, was to record the proceedings and make a report including recommendations for judgement.

About thirty witnesses were called. Pierre Guerre and Bettrande de Rols testified in front of and were questioned by the defendant. She spoke with some nervousness and gave every indication that she was under pressure from those around her. The prisoner professed his love for her and said that this was all staged by his uncle.

At this point both Bettrande and Pierre were imprisoned and they, along with the prisoner, were questioned separately. The prisoner's story matched Bettrande's almost perfectly. The additional witnesses added little. While the numbers from the two trials were slightly against the defendant, those witnesses for the defendant seemed more credible, especially Martin's four sisters. The testimony of Pierre Guerre was suspect and the prisoner seemed to be genuine. Bettrande seemed, to Jean de Coras, to be a virtuous woman caught in a soap opera. At neither trial would she swear that the prisoner was not Martin Guerre. At the end of the summer Jean de Coras was ready to make his report.

Write down the five most important points of the story up till now and your prediction as to what will happen next.

Finished early? Complete the second column of your Anticipation Guide.

Structure 16
ROUNDROBIN AND ROUNDTABLE

Steps at a Glance

❶ The teacher poses a question that has multiple answers.

❷ In RoundRobin students take turns giving an answer or idea orally. In RoundTable students write down or construct answers in turn on a single sheet of paper.

Students take turns giving answers orally or in writing to a question that has multiple answers. These structures are useful for sharing information either for team building or for short academic tasks.

These sister structures are useful for sharing information either for teambuilding or for short academic tasks to punctuate a lesson. They also encourage taking turns and listening.

The difference between the two is that RoundRobin answers are spoken and RoundTable answers are written or constructed.

Social Skills

- Taking turns
- Listening (for RoundRobin)

Variations

- Sequential RoundTable
- Simultaneous RoundTable
- RoundTable Brainstorm
- Reaction Wheel
- RallyRobin and RallyTable
- Team Boggle

Structure 16 ROUNDROBIN AND ROUNDTABLE

STEPS

❶ **TEACHER POSES A QUESTION THAT HAS MULTIPLE ANSWERS**
The answers required should be factual, not conceptual or controversial. The questions should also be easy enough so that all students can contribute at least some answers. If the teacher sketches a scenario or gives guided imagery, students can often generate more responses.

❷ **IN ROUNDROBIN STUDENTS TAKE TURNS GIVING AN ANSWER OR IDEA ORALLY. IN ROUNDTABLE STUDENTS WRITE DOWN OR CONSTRUCT ANSWERS IN TURN ON A SINGLE SHEET OF PAPER**
A student may ask for help if he or she has no answer, but should still write down the answer for his or her turn.

The written RoundTable makes it easier for the teacher to monitor responses, but it can take longer than RoundRobin.

ROUNDROBIN

ROUNDTABLE

VARIATIONS

SEQUENTIAL ROUNDTABLE
This is done with one paper circulating.

SIMULTANEOUS ROUNDTABLE
Instead of one paper, students have two, three, or four papers circulating.

ROUNDTABLE BRAINSTORM
This is the same as a Sequential Roundtable but with the rules of brainstorming in force. Spencer Kagan does this with roles in a version called 4S Brainstorming. The roles are Speed Captain (who might say, "Let's get some more ideas."), Super Supporter ("Another great idea."), Chief of Silly (Let's have a crazy idea), and Synergy Guru (Let's combine these two ideas.").

Students may also write their ideas down first on separate slips of paper and then present them in a Roundtable manner. This encourages students to build on the ideas of others and later makes it easier for the team to categorize them.

REACTION WHEEL
This structure is a version of Simultaneous Roundtable but it uses only one piece of paper, large poster paper on which there is a circle divided into segments, at least as many as there are students in the group. Students are then given a question to consider and in their segment they write their answers simultaneously, preferable in felt pen. The teacher then instructs the groups to rotate the circle to read their teammates' writing and to react according to directions from the teacher. The teacher can continue with other instructions that further extend or synthesize the information. The advan-

tage of the Reaction Wheel over Simultaneous RoundTable is that it is large enough so that groups may easily read it if the teacher wishes to use Simultaneous Sharing. It is especially useful as review or a pre-writing exercise.

RallyRobin and RallyTable

These follow the same steps as RoundRobin and RoundTable, but are done in pairs. They can be combined with Think-Pair-Share and Pairs Compare. RallyRobin can also be used with Passport Paraphrase in Corners.

Team Boggle

Boggle is the Parker Brothers trademark for a hidden word game. Team Boggle is a teambuilding game based on the RoundRobin structure. Each team member in turn contributes a word. The letters of the word must connect to the previous letter by the side or corner. For example, in the example on this page "nod" counts, but "ran" does not. As in the regular RoundTable, students may pass.

Each word is worth the square of the number of letters it contains. A two letter word is worth 4 points (2x2) but current is worth 49 points (7x7).

The goal of Team Boggle is to make as many points as possible in a brief time period, four or five minutes. You may want to give clues such as "Find a 49 point word that means movement of water or air." The example given here has a particular theme, climate, but any word with any meaning is acceptable.

TEAM BOGGLE

C	O	N	R	A
U	E	D	O	T
R	N	S	P	E
R	E	A	C	O
C	A	N	T	N

Structure 16   ROUNDROBIN AND ROUNDTABLE

Ideas for Using Roundtable/Roundrobin in Social Studies

Sequential
- List all the facts about a field trip, an event, a place, or a person. For example: "Take turns listing all the countries in Africa," "Come up with all the different forms of communication that you can think of with one person at a time giving an idea," or "Each person in turn add to the web outline on the Civil War."

- List all the different questions you might ask about a topic, for example, before going on a field trip, starting a chapter, or listening to a guest speaker.

Simultaneous
- List all the examples that fit under different categories. For example, at the start of an economics unit or as review have groups write "Production," "Distribution," and "Consumption" on the top of three different pieces of paper. On each page a student writes one example of an economic activity that accomplishes each of these three economic stages and then passes the page clockwise to another team member to write another example.

  Similar instructions could be used with different categories such as the attributes of natural regions like the Arctic ice cap, tundra, taiga (coniferous forest), and deciduous forest; examples of criminal and civil crimes; responsibilities of municipal, provincial/state, and federal governments; or all the similarities between Canada and the United States and all the differences.

Reaction Wheel
- Most of the topiocs used for a Simultaneous RoundTable could be done with a Reaction Wheel, but it is most suitable for occasions where you want all students to have "fat answers," that is, when you want them to have detailed notes before drafting an essay or writing an exam. Because it is in poster form and in felt pen, it is easily readable by other students if they make a Gallery Tour, Teams Tour or other Simultaneous Sharing.

- The reaction side of the structure might be used with a scenario like the following:

"Think back beyond the time of the dinosaurs, to a billion years ago to Pre-Cambrian time and imagine what the earth was like… Now think about what the world looks like now. How has the earth changed? What have been the forces that have caused those changes? In your segment of the wheel I want you to list all the different forces that work to change the earth."

(Allow a few minutes and then ask groups to rotate the wheel.)

"Put a check beside the answers that you agree with and write a question mark beside the answers about which you have a question."

(Repeat this first reaction stage until all segments have been read and received a reaction and the original section is back to the student who first wrote it. With a RoundRobin each student can now answer any questions.)

Following are some other reactions that a teacher might ask students to write:

"Rotate the paper again and underline all those forces for change which are natural and circle those that are of human origin."

or

"Rotate the paper again to look at another segment and put a E beside those processes that erode or wear down the surface and a P beside those that push up new material."

NARRATIVE OF LESSONS USING ROUNDTABLE AND ROUNDROBIN

Current Events Study

Themes
- Civic ideals and practices

Skills
- Using community resources
- Interpreting information
- Analyzing information
- Summarizing information

Ms. O'Brian had assigned her base groups to follow a particular news event during the previous week. Each student was to cut out three newspaper or magazine articles on the assigned topic and write a summary of each one. She then decided to use a Reaction Wheel to begin a Know/Want to Know/Learned (KWL) sequence.

When the students met in their base groups, she gave each group a large sheet of poster paper and asked them to divide it into six sections. Next to each section they wrote one of the question stems below, a different one for each section. (In brackets is her elaboration on these questions.)

- Who? (For example, who were involved in this event and what do you know about these people)?
- What? (For example, what were the events that were described in your articles?)
- When? (List recent events and their dates and as much of the history as you know.)
- Where? (Give the places that these events occurred and any information about them.)
- Why? (List causes of the event.)
- So what? (Why is this event important? Suggest any effects that these events might have on us and others.)

Following the steps of the Reaction Wheel, students wrote their answers to one of the questions in a blank section first, then rotated the wheel to read and add to the previous student's writing in another section. At the end they decided as a team one important answer for each team member and then shared with the class using Stand Up and Share.

Ms. O'Brian next asked the teams to turn over the paper and make a similar circle with six sections and the same six question stems. Only now students were to create their own questions that would help focus their learning as they followed the topic during the next few weeks. Using the same sentence stems for each section, students wrote questions in each of the sections, then rotated the wheel once more putting a check beside the question that they felt was the most important to answer in that section.

Each student made a record of the questions in each section that received the most checks. The first one finished made an extra copy for Ms. O'Brian to help her evaluate their learning in the next few weeks.

During this current events study, Ms. O'Brian also used other Rounds and Rallies: a RallyRobin to review causes and effects and an idea from Jeanne Stone (1994) for a Simultaneous RoundTable. Students write on four papers each one considering the current event from the perspective of a different social science: how geography influenced the event, how history was a factor, what the impact of governments was, and how economics might have been an influence.

Structure 17
SEQUENCING

Steps at a Glance — ONE-DIMENSIONAL

1. Teacher makes a set of cards for each team.
2. The group places the cards face down in front of them and each person in turn takes a card until they are all distributed.
3. Each group member describes or reads what is on one of his or her cards and suggests where it might go in the sequence.

Steps at a Glance — COMPLEX

1. As before, prepare the necessary cards, one set per team, and have the teams distribute them equally among team members.
2. Ask students to put them in sequence in which they occurred.

Students are given items out of order and asked to put them in order based on cause and effect or chronology. Because students have to organize numerous events or causes and effects, Sequencing can help them master the material and see the connections among things.

Social Skills
- Encouraging
- Checking for agreement
- Checking for understsanding

If history is, as Winston Churchill once said, "one damn thing after another," the least we can expect our students to do is to get the right order of damnation. And there are lots of other social sciences with plenty of curricular chaos where some logical or chronological order could help students.

Sequencing is simply putting something in order. When you do it with someone else with some positive interdependence and individual accountability, it becomes a cooperative structure.

Structure 17 SEQUENCING

It is mostly used to organize content—to get one thing after another—either as a preview or review. However, Sequencing can also be used to teach inductively. For example, in analyzing the jumbled paragraphs of a document students must look for meaning, causal links, and the transitional devices of writing to decide on the order.

Sequences can be of two general types:
- One-dimensional, most commonly a timeline, and
- Multi-dimensional such as a web chart of a system with arrows indicating relationships.

STEPS FOR ONE-DIMENSIONAL SEQUENCING

❶ **WITH LINEAR SEQUENCES LIKE A TIMELINE OR EVEN WITH A SIMPLE WEB CHART, THE TEACHER CAN ENSURE MAXIMUM INDIVIDUAL ACCOUNTABILITY BY USING BLIND HAND**

The teacher makes a set of cards for each team. To do this, the teacher divides up the sequence into its component parts, puts each one on a separate card, and jumbles up the order.

❷ **GROUP PLACES CARDS FACE DOWN IN FRONT OF THEM AND EACH PERSON IN TURN TAKES A CARD UNTIL THEY ARE ALL DISTRIBUTED, MAYBE TWO OR THREE EACH**

❸ **EACH GROUP MEMBER DESCRIBES OR READS WHAT IS ON ONE OF HIS OR HER CARDS AND SUGGESTS WHERE IT MIGHT GO IN THE SEQUENCE**

He or she does not show it to the other students. Once all team members have decided where the card should go, the student places it down on the table or diagram, and another student continues with another card, and so on.

STEPS FOR COMPLEX SEQUENCING

❶ **FOR MORE COMPLICATED CONSTRUCTION THERE NEEDS TO BE A GREATER FLOW OF INFORMATION AND MATERIALS**

As before prepare the necessary cards, one set per team, and have the teams distribute them equally amongst team members.

❷ **ASK STUDENTS TO PUT THEM IN SEQUENCE IN WHICH THEY OCCURRED**

To ensure individual accountability students could work in pairs then share with another pair or work as a larger team with roles like that of Encourager, Gatekeeper, or Checker.

IDEAS FOR USING SEQUENCING IN SOCIAL STUDIES

- **One-dimensional**
  • simple timeline, that is, putting events on a line that represents chronology
  • annotated timeline, that is, students write explanatory notes of events on a timeline. This can be done as a review without any text or it can be done as an advanced organizer with the textbook open: given a series of events students have to read the book to understand the event and learn when it happened.
  • ordering paragraphs or sentences

- **Multi-dimensional**
  • ecological systems, for example, the food chain, or ecological problems, for example, the construction of a dam on a salmon spawning stream and its consequences
  • weather systems, for example, the life cycle of a thunderstorm
  • economic systems, such as the relationship of consumer spending, business investment, and wages
  • social systems, such as the various factors in population growth and stabilization
  • systems in government, for example, the steps in how a law is made
  • physical models, like a castle

Structure 17   *SEQUENCING*

NARRATIVE OF A LESSON USING SEQUENCING

Forest Ecology

Themes
- People, places and environment
- Global connections

Skills
- Summarizing information
- Synthesizing information

The grade 6 class of Catherine Malarchuk was studying a unit on the ecology of temperate rain forests. She wanted them to understand the interrelationship of rain, soil, rivers, and trees and chose a Sequencing exercise to do this. Because the number of cards was small, she chose the Blind Hand procedure described above.

(For this activity she also appointed one group member to play the role of recorder to record ideas or information.)

She gave each group the following instructions and diagram with the steps listed below cut out in cards.

After discussing the diagrams as a class, Malarchuk then asked the teams to make a similar diagram but without the forest, imagining that it had been cut, and predicting the consequences. Which stages of the sequence would still be there? Which would be different?

The groups shared their answers using Neighbor Show and Tell and then returned to reflect on their group process with feedback from the observer.

Malarchuk also wanted the students to write two paragraphs, first, about the forest system and, secondly, about their predictions. She reviewed the vocabulary of transition words that would be needed for writing about a sequence of events. For example, the first paragraph would need phrases like "so that" and "as a result," and the second would be introduced by "However, if..." and use the subjunctive "were."

Structure 17 **SEQUENCING**

The Forest System   NAMES: _____

1. Distribute the cards equally amongst group members. Do not show them to the others; instead, one group member should read out the information on the card to the group. Decide as a group where it should go on the diagram below.
2. When you have decided, write the number of that card on the diagram.
3. Move to the next person and follow the same steps. Continue until the diagram is complete.
4. As a group consider what would happen to the rainfall, soil, and river if there were no trees. On the other side of the page draw a similar diagram but without the trees and predict the results.

Cards to be cut out by the teacher:

1. Evaporation from leaves.	4. Tree roots keep the soil loose so rain soaks in easily.
2. Water seeps slowly into the river all the time, so that the river never runs dry.	5. Rainwater drips slowly onto the ground.
3. Trees catch rain.	6. Underground water level remains high.

Cooperative Learning and Social Studies: Towards Excellence and Equity by Tom Morton
Kagan Publishing • 1(800) 933-2667 • www.KaganOnline.com

Structure 18
SIMULTANEOUS SHARING:
(TEN VARIATIONS)

This is a list of ten ways that students can share the results of their work as a team with other teams at the same time. Teams can share their ideas and listen to new ones from other teams while avoiding a series of time-consuming and often repetitive reports to the whole class.

Social Skills
- Listening

When student teams share their ideas with other teams, they can learn new ideas from them and sharpen their own thinking. Moreover, having an audience beyond the teacher gives their work importance and context. Lastly, when students know that each team member needs to be ready to report, there is a strong sense of positive interdependence.

However, if each student or team reports to the class, it can be time-consuming and repetitive without any simultaneous interaction. Here are ten ways for sharing that can avoid these problems.

VARIATIONS

BLACKBOARD SHARING
Each team selects a representative or the teacher chooses one. The representatives go to the blackboard and write or post their teams' best answers simultaneously. The teams can continue working while this is going on.

CAROUSEL SHARING
One person from each team stays at the team's workplace to become the spokesperson. The others rotate from team to team learning as much as they can to incorporate later into revisions of their work. The spokesperson stays behind to explain the team's work to the other teams as they rotate through.

CHORAL SPEAKING
This type of response works best when the probable response or series of responses are brief and clearly defined. After discussion in their teams, on a given signal, all students answer out loud simultaneously.

GALLERY TOUR
(adapted from Jeanne Stone, 1992) Completed team products are displayed around the room. Near each product should be a sheet of paper where other groups can write questions or comments about the products. To start each team stands in front of their own product in the classroom. At the teacher's signal, they pass from one product to the next until they have viewed all the products in the classroom. Students are encouraged to write questions or comments about each product they see next to that product. Using their own paper, students should also make a record of any ideas that they see on each product which are different from their own. Remind students that they don't need to list a new idea twice. Students return to their team and discuss what they recorded from the other products that could improve their own. They can also discuss any questions and comments the other students made on the paper next to their product.

NEIGHBOR SHOW AND TELL
Each team turns to one of its neighbors and shows and tells about what they have done.

SHOWING
If the product of the team's work is something that can be expressed in a few words or a number, then the teams can write these in a large, clearly visible form on a sheet of paper. On a cue from the teacher, the teams can show these simultaneously. The kind of questions and responses that are suitable for Corners could be used in this manner.

STAND-N-SHARE
This works best following a Team Discussion on a topic that will likely produce several ideas. The team then gives everyone at least one idea to report to the class. Next, the teacher has all students stand up. One student is asked to share an idea and then sits down. If anyone in the room has the same or similar idea then that student should sit down as well. Continue until all students are sitting.

TEAM INSIDE-OUTSIDE CIRCLE
This is described in the section on Inside/Outside Circle. The class follows the same steps of that structure but do so as a team to present their information.

TEAMS TOUR
(adapted from Stone, 1992)
In each of the four rounds of this structure, one of the team members travels to another team to share his or her team's products with that team.

> **Round 1:** Student #1 travels with the team's product one team to the right (or left). The students who stay, #2, #3, and #4, listen to the presentation from the visiting #1. All members return to their original teams.

Round 2: Student #2 travels with the team's product two teams to the right (or left). Students #1, #3, #4 stay and listen to the presentation from the visiting #2. All members return to their original teams.

Rounds 3 and 4: Continue following the same steps with #3 and #4 touring three and four teams to the right (or left).

VOTING

After discussing a values question or one that requires some evaluation, on a given signal students can show their opinion by voting. The simplest method is thumbs up, thumbs down, or thumbs waving in between. A more dramatic method is as follows. Given a controversial statement,

- If students strongly agree, they wave their arms in the air;
- If they only agree, they just raise their arms;
- If they are unsure, they fold their arms;
- If they disagree, they make the gesture of thumbs down with their hand;
- If they strongly disagree, they motion up or down with their hand.

Structure 19
SORT

Steps at a Glance

1. The teacher gives teams data or students generate their own.
2. Next, students group their data based on similarities.
3. Teams give labels to their categories.
4. Teams share their categories.
5. The teacher records the categories and leads a class discussion on their importance.

Students group data into categories and define the characteristics of their category. A Sort helps students make sense of and master large amounts of information.

Social Skills

- No specific skills, but asking for justification and encouraging would be useful

Variations

- Structured Sort
- People Sort
- Sort and Predict

A Sort is often thought of as a way to teach thinking skills; however, there is also considerable research evidence (Joyce and Weil, 1986) that strategies like these can also improve the mastery of information. It seems that when students form their own categories of data as they do in a Sort, they can hold information better than when the categories are given to them. It is the kind of information processing that historians and social scientists do.

The variation Sort and Predict has become a staple pre-reading strategy for many teachers. It gives an anticipatory set for the concepts in the reading and introduces key vocabulary.

Steps

❶ Teacher gives teams data or students generate their own

Teams can generate their own by RoundTable, Jigsaw, Pairs Compare or Team Discussion.

Teacher Tip: Monitor to check if the student responses reflect a realistic diversity of possible answers. If the responses are too one dimensional, you may want to prompt them to consider other possibilities.

❷ Next, students group their data based on similarities

This can be done relatively informally by saying, "I want you as a team to group your occupations (countries, government responsibilities, et cetera) into two (or more) categories."

For greater individual accountability, ask the students to write their items on separate sheets of paper first and then have them use Roundtable to place an item in one of the categories while explaining the reason for their choice. In this case no item should be placed unless all agree. A student may suggest a change in any category during the sorting, but again the team needs to agree before anything is changed.

❸ Teams give labels to their categories

❹ Teams share their categories

This can be done by Numbered Heads Together or any one of the numerous ways of Simultaneous Sharing. This stimulates students to see their information from different perspectives. At this stage, the teacher can also use Find-My-Rule to open even more perspectives. If the data is extensive, you could also ask teams to build more concepts by subdividing their categories.

❺ Teacher records categories and leads a class discussion on their importance

You may also ask the teams to repeat the same steps to create new categories.

Variations

Structured Sort

Spencer Kagan (1992) refers to what we have called simply a Sort as an Unstructured Sort. He distinguishes it from a Structured Sort where students are given a category system into which they place certain data. For example, they might be asked to draw a Venn Diagram and then be given a list of items that they should place inside the Venn.

The category system that students draw could be a matrix, an agree-disagree line, the steps of a staircase, or any other graphic organizer that is appropriate to the content.

People Sort

Each student is given an item. The teacher designates sides or corners of the room to represent different concepts to which the item might belong. The student decides where his or her item fits and moves to the appropriate place.

This could also be done with students organizing themselves into a huge Venn Diagram or any other graphic.

A People Sort is both classbuilding and review. It also gives clear feedback to the teacher and students as to how well the class understands the concepts being studied.

SORT AND PREDICT

Faye Brownlie and Susan Close (1992) have extended the Sort to create a very effective pre-reading strategy. First, the teacher selects twenty to thirty key concept words from the text. In groups, students sort these words into four or five categories plus one unique category. (It's the unique category that pushes the students to extend their thinking.) After groups share and explain their group answers, students choose five or six words on which they need more information. The selection becomes a focus for their reading. Finally, students predict the contents of the text.

IDEAS FOR USING SORT IN SOCIAL STUDIES

SOURCES OF DATA

- **Students Prior Knowledge**
  Students can list and sort products that they consume or the clothes that they are wearing in a unit on trade. For media studies they could list the TV programs that they watch. In geography they can pool together all the countries or types of industries that they know or brainstorm all the factors that make up a complex concept like a developed country to form a web. To begin looking at social skills they could brainstorm and sort all the different attributes of a good cooperative learning group.

- **Textbooks**
  Generally, the teacher selects the key concept words for Sort and Predict. However, students can skim read the headings and titles looking for key words to categorize and predict. Students can also search in their textbooks for other information, such as all the different actions of a historical figure to categorize his or her politics or all the different references to a particular country or group to analyze the point of view of the textbook authors.

- **Atlases**
  From an atlas students can find data on rainfall and temperature in order to categorize climatic regions or demographic and economic data on their own and other countries.

- **Library References**
  Students can research paintings or music from different eras, countries or styles. Statistical data on demography and economics can found in almanacs and yearbooks and then sorted. Teams could also summarize and sort articles from newspapers or magazines.

- **Surveys and Interviews**
  Students can prepare a common set of questions about work, habits of consumption, or the like for a survey of parents and neighbours that could be grouped and presented as graphs. They could prepare questions on the environment or patterns of consumption and survey their classmates.

- **Field Studies**
  A field trip can gather data on neighborhood businesses, land use, cemetery tombstones, cars, or forest vegetation.

- **Teacher Prepared Material**
  The teacher could reproduce posters some that illustrate propaganda and others that do not. The teacher could prepare a list of factual statements and opinions or a list of statements that reflect various political ideologies. (If students do not arrive at the concept of propaganda or fact and opinion, the teacher could move to Find-My-Rule.)

NARRATIVE OF LESSONS USING A SORT

Economics Field Study of the Parking Lot

Themes
- Production, distribution, and consumption
- Civic ideals and practices
- Power, authority and government
- Culture

Skills
- Acquiring information from community resources
- Classifying information
- Interpreting information
- Analyzing information
- Synthesizing information

Values
- Individual consumer choice and collective welfare

Ms. Hill's sixth grade class is studying a unit on economics. To help to illustrate the relationships between consumption and production and to practice research skills she decides to have the class do a brief field study in the school parking lot.

First, she explains to the class the importance of the auto industry for the country: one in six workers is employed directly or indirectly in the auto industry. She then asks the class what they might look for in the cars in the lot. Different classes suggest everything from color to cleanliness, but she makes sure that they include the make so she can later consider the country of origin.

The parking lot is a large one so she has groups of four divide into pairs with each pair responsible for gathering data on half the lot. The pairs take turns recording and making the observations. She double checks to be sure that no pair overlaps on the other pairs' territory and counts cars twice.

Back in the classroom, the pairs pool their data, categorize it, and give labels to the categories, that is, they are asked to do a Sort. Ms. Hill provides the countries of origins of the car companies. Team representatives share their responses at the blackboard.

For the next step, Ms. Hill asks the students to play the role of economists. Using Numbered Heads Together, sometimes Think-Pair-Share and even Brainstorming, she leads them to consider these questions:

What did you notice?

Do you think we would find the same results in a different parking lot?

What does this tell us about society or about the economy?

Sometimes the students focus on the age of the car and speculate that people are not replacing them because times are tough. Other times they compare the teacher cars to student cars and hypothesize about the tastes of teachers vs. students. However, Ms. Hill also wants to focus on the demand for foreign cars and how this influences domestic production so she guides the discussion with these questions for the teams to consider:

What would happen if the number of sales of Japanese cars were to increase? decrease?

(To probe more deeply here she sometimes has to specify how this might influence different groups like factory workers, owners, the government, the consumers, and the like. In the early 1980's under pressure from the American companies and government, Japanese manufacturers agreed to a voluntary restriction. This led to prices for the Japanese cars going up, American car sales stabilizing, American car manufacturers being under less pressure to equal the quality of Japanese cars, and Japanese companies starting to manufacture in North America to avoid restrictions. In recent years, however, the sales of Japanese cars have declined.)

How could we find out if your considered guesses are correct?

Later, Ms. Hill will use a Team Web to consolidate student understanding of how the consumption and production are connected and a Values Line to consider the issue of "Buy American" versus buy the best and cheapest product whatever the origin.

Structure 20
TEAM DISCUSSION

Steps at a Glance

❶ The teacher poses a reflective question, one that can generate a variety of responses.

❷ Teams discuss the question and the teacher monitors.

❸ Students share their ideas with the class or with a Simultaneous Sharing.

Students work as a team to decide on a common answer or create a single product. This is a flexible structure that can be used for almost any academic task or for team building.

This is an informal structure that is appropriate for almost any topic. It is the equivalent of the "Heads Together" in "Numbered Heads Together" or the "Square" in "Think-Pair-Square." It has, however, a low level of positive interdependence and individual accountability and no guarantee of equal participation, so you may want to consider some of the variations that follow.

Social Skills

- Encouraging participation
- Checking for agreement
- Checking for understanding
- Listening

Variations

- Teammates Consult
- Team Statement
- Team Thesis
- Team Project

Structure 20 TEAM DISCUSSION

STEPS

❶ TEACHER POSES A REFLECTIVE QUESTION THAT CAN GENERATE A VARIETY OF RESPONSES

To encourage high quality discussion you may wish to specify that students should practice specific behaviours like asking for justification or paraphrasing. To raise positive interdependence you may want to ask for a consensus answer.

❷ TEAMS DISCUSS QUESTION AND TEACHER MONITORS

When a team displays some quality discussion, you could ask the team to repeat what they said as a model for the class.

❸ STUDENTS SHARE THEIR IDEAS WITH CLASS OR WITH A SIMULTANEOUS SHARING

VARIATIONS

TEAMMATES CONSULT

For lengthy or involved work using Team Discussion, for example, completing a worksheet, there are some risks with using a straight Team Discussion. The high status student might dictate answers to the rest of the group or students might not even discuss answers at all, a situation that Roger Johnson calls "individual work with talking."

One way to encourage greater co-operation is to build roles into the structure and follow the steps of Teammates Consult:

Step 1. Pens Down. All teammates put their pens down in the center.

Step 2. Team Discussion. One student is the Reader who reads the first question of the assignment and all students seek the answer from the textbook or their own knowledge.

Step 3. Check for Agreement. The student on the left of the Reader is the Checker who ensures to see that everyone understands and agrees with the answer.

Step 4. Individuals Write. When there is agreement, then all students pick up their own pens and write their answers in their own words.

Step 5. Roles. Students progress to question two and rotate roles of the Reader and Checker.

TEAM STATEMENTS

This variation is a great way to move students towards a deeper understanding of a topic or to look afresh at what you may already have studied. It can become a slogan for a poster or a leitmotif for a unit.

Students first write individually their statement on a topic. You might give them some stems to complete like the following:

Democracy is...
The railroad resulted in...
The Cold War was...
Development means...

Next, each person reads his or her statement and the team tries to find the common thread. The team goal is to reach consensus on the statement and then share it with the class.

Students need to be clear that the statement should reflect the essence of the topic. It is not a list. It is not an invitation to a run-on sentence.

For example, in a unit on immigration some teams decided on statements like these for the topic of assimilation: "Assimilation is fitting in," and "Assimilation means you can't talk to your grandmother."

TEAM THESIS

A thesis might be defined as a limited topic plus a point of view on that topic, for example, "Assimilation for the Japanese in California has meant acceptance into the mainstream of American society." A team thesis is not as creative as a Team Statement because it is more rigid. It is also difficult for many students. However, it serves as an excellent starting point for an essay.

TEAM PROJECT

This is essentially the same as a Team Discussion but it refers to group work where the content is something concrete like a poster or a handshake. The single product adds positive interdependence, but individual accountability may still be low unless specified.

IDEAS FOR USING TEAM DISCUSSION IN SOCIAL STUDIES

- **Academic Projects**
  Ask teams to create a propaganda poster, a press conference on the eve of the Civil War, a model of a fur trading fort or medieval castle, a cardboard model of the landscape from the contour elevations of a topographic map, or a diagram of the ecosystem of an old growth forest.

- **Teambuilding Projects**
  After a team has had a chance to learn each other's names and talk about their likes and dislikes, they can become better acquainted and build an identity by creating one of the following: a team name based on the theme of the unit of study or their common likes; a team handshake; a team motto; a cheer; a rap song; an advertisement of the group's qualities; a poem that expresses their goals, expectations, and fears; or a TV commercial promoting the group's merits.

- **Inquiries**
  In a short discussion students might consider questions like the following: Given this information, where on the topographic map would people likely settle? Where would be a good place to locate the pulp mill? Where should the railroad be located?

  or

  In a longer lesson with learning centers, the Team Discussion would be on-going. For example, teams may go to different centers around the room and try to solve the mystery of the buffalo jump: how did bands of Peigan Indians convince these huge, dangerous buffalo to run to a small spot on the Prairies to kill themselves?

- **Complex Answers to Values Questions or Controversies**
  For example: "Given what we have learned, take some time now to decide what the level of immigration should be and why."

- **A Short Break in a Lecture for Students to Synthesize or Summarize (similar to Pairs View)**
  This can be done very informally with the following: "Now turn to your partner and come up with two main ideas from the lecture to this point."

- **Checking for Understanding at the End of a Lesson**
  The filmstrip is finished and there are five minutes left. Now is a good time for

the teacher to say something like, "Talk with your classmates across the aisle on what you learned today about our country's trade with the Pacific Rim and be ready to report in two minutes."

- **Review at the Beginning of a Lesson**
  While taking attendance or filling out that last minute form for the office, you can have students work productively if you ask them, "Talk with your teammates and be ready to report on what you learned yesterday about our country's trade with the Pacific Rim."

- **Completion of a Worksheet**
- **Pre-writing Activities**
- **Group Processing**
- **One of the Steps in Find My Rule**

NARRATIVE OF A LESSON USING TEAM DISCUSSION

Analyzing Arguments on Women's Role

Themes
- Time, continuity, and change

Skills
- Reading comprehension
- Interpreting information
- Analyzing information
- Evaluating information

Values
- Equality
- Political rights and freedoms

Critical thinking is an important outcome for Sam Assad's school. In his senior history class his main approach towards this elusive goal is to analyze primary source arguments with an organizer called Marker that he discovered at a cooperative learning workshop.

To illustrate the steps in Marker, Mr. Assad likes to use examples like the following journal entry on "wishes" from his daughter who is in grade two at Ecole Anne Hébert. (Translated from French.)

> "I want candies for me. For elephants, some water. Rabbits, carrots... For the giraffes to be happy. I want the sea to be not polluted with garbage. The other countries of the world I want to have a bit of money for their families because some of them are poor."

Using Marker, Assad suggests an analysis like the following:

M: the main idea would be that animals and people should have what they need or want and that the sea should not be polluted;

A: some assumptions that his daughter makes are (1) that the sea is polluted and (2) that if countries have more money that it would go to poor families;

R: the the form of reasoning might be (1) examples of needs and desires of animals and people; and (2) application of a moral principle - we should give money to other countries because this would help the poor, what might be called a principle of "doing unto others as we would have them do unto us."

K: key questions might be how can we make the giraffes happy or how could we best be sure that poor people in other countries receive help and what kind of help would be the best;

E: there is no evidence given;

R: there is considerable information that supports the author's claims, for example, we know that rabbits eat carrots, that there is pollution in our seas and that people are poor.

When Mr. Assad turns student teams loose with Marker and material closer to their course content, he likes to use Team Discussion so that there is a free exchange of ideas. Depending on the class, however, Sam adds a few more ingredients to his lesson mix to encourage participation and listening.

First, he insists on the roles that are described on the Marker worksheet. Second, he asks that each student take notes with common answers that all agree to and can explain. Third, he stresses, monitors and compliments good listening. Fourth, about five minutes before the time to report to the whole class, he asks students to switch to Numbered Heads Together:

"Even if you are not finished, we have limited time left so I want you to use Numbered Heads Together and check that everyone is ready to report to the class."

In processing he has students as individuals answer the questions below. Sam feels that the individual answers give him more honest feedback about how well the groups are working than group answers. He can then take steps to adjust his lessons or grouping based on the feedback.

1. On a scale of 1 (low)–10 (high) how well did your team members listen to you in your group discussion?
2. On a scale of 1 (low)–10 (high) how well did you listen to others?
3. How do you feel about the work that you just finished?
4. How might you improve next time?

An example of the kind of arguments that students analyze in Assad's class are two opposing viewpoints on suffrage for women on the following pages.

EXAMPLE

MARKER

(Adapted from O'Reilly, K. and Splaine, J. (1987) *Critical Viewing.* Pacific Grove: California in Rhoades, J. and McCabe, P. (1992). *Outcome Based Learning: A Teacher's Guide to Restructuring the Classroom.* Sacramento: ITA Publications.)

Directions: Divide the following roles among team members, then read the passage and complete the questions on this page.

1. **Reader/Checker:** Begin by reading the passage to your team, then as you work, check that all team members agree with what is written and can explain it.
2. **Recorder:** Write down the team's answers then read what you have recorded to your team to check for accuracy.
3. **Encourager:** Ask students who are reluctant to speak if they have any ideas. Try to motivate the team if it gets bogged down.
4. **Gatekeeper:** If one student is talking too much, ask him or her politely to give someone else a turn.

All team members should listen to each other and be ready to report the team answers.

M = What is the main point? Look for key words to identify the different parts of an argument.

A = What assumptions does the author make? What values and value judgements are apparent?

R = What type of reasoning does the author use? comparison? sampling? cause and effect?

K = What are some key questions about this topic? How well does the author answer them?

E = What evidence does the author offer to support the argument(s)? Does the author use factual evidence without identifying the source? If the author has evidence, evaluate it (e.g. is it primary evidence or secondary; is the source of the evidence reliable or possibly biased?)

R = What is Relevant information about this topic that you already know? Does that information agree with what the author claims? Do the author's claims seem to make sense based on your own experience?

EXAMPLE

The Woman's Sphere

In the economy of nature or rather in the design of God, woman is the complement of man. In defining her sphere and describing her influence, this fact is fundamental. Unless this fact be admitted as an axiom in every way self-evident, no reasoning on this subject is sound...

Woman is the equal of man, alike in the matter of intellect, emotion, and activity, and... she has shewn her capabilities in these respects... It would never do, however, from these premises, to draw the conclusion that woman behoves and is bound to exert her powers in the same direction and for the same ends as man. This were to usurp the place of man—this were to forget her position as the complement of man, and assume a place she is incompetent to fill, or rather was not designed to fill. This were to leap out of her sphere and attempt to move in another, in which, to move rightly, the whole moral relations of society would behove to be changed, and suited anew to each other, but which, because they are unchangeable, every attempt is fraught with damage, it may be with ruin, and woman becomes a wandering star, which, having left its due place, and violated its prescribed relations, dashes itself into shivers against some other planet... and goes out in the blackness of darkness for ever.

(Reverend Robert Sedgewick, 1856)

The Suffragist Position

Now politics simply mean public affairs—yours and mine and everybody's—and to say that politics are too corrupt for women is a weak and foolish statement for any man to make. Any man who is actively engaged in politics, and declares that politics are too corrupt for women, admits one of two things, either that he is party to this corruption or that he is unable to prevent it—and in either case something should be done...

There is another hardy perennial that constantly lifts its head above the earth... and that is that if women were ever given a chance to participate in outside affairs, family quarrels would result... If husband and wife are going to quarrel they will find a cause for dispute easy enough, and will not be compelled to wait for election day...

In spite of the testimony of many reputable women that they have been able to vote and get the dinner on one and the same day, there still exists a strong belief that the whole household machinery gets out of order when a woman goes to vote. No person denies a woman the right to go to church, and yet the church service takes a great deal more time than voting...

If one woman wants to vote, she should have that opportunity just as if one woman desires a college eduction, she should not be held back because of the indifferent careless ones who do not desire it. Why should the mentally inert, careless, uninterested woman, who cares nothing for humanity but is contented to patter along her own little narrow way, set the pace for the others of us? Voting will not be compulsory; the shrinking violets will not be torn form their shady fence-corner... We will not force the vote upon them, but why should they force their votelessness upon us?

(Nellie McClung, 1915)

Structure 21
TEAM WEB

Steps at a Glance

1. Give each team a large sheet of paper and give each student a different colored pen.
2. If this is to be a preview, the teacher can provide the sub-topics; otherwise, ask teams to use a RoundTable to add them.
3. Ask students to complete the details with each team member recording his or her contributions with a different colored pen.
4. Teams share their webs.
5. If web is used for pre-writing, supply students or elicit from them some of the language necessary for writing description or analysis.

Students create a large web diagram of a topic with each student having a different colored pen for writing items. Like graphic organizers in general, a web can help students see their thinking. Making a web as a team allows for sharing and helping while assigning different coloured pens ensures individual accountability.

Social Skills
- No specific skills, but asking for justification and encouraging would be useful.

Variations
- Team Visuals
- Future Wheel
- Woolly Thinking

The last few years have seen an immense interest in graphic organizers like the web because they can help students see their thinking, the visual equivalent of talking through ideas. A teacher can use a web to establish the students' prior knowledge, to help them explore a topic, or to review it. When lines or arrows are added, a web can also help students to see the connections among things.

The Procedure describes a few simple but effective steps to make this strategy a cooperative structure, the Team Web.

These steps can also turn other graphic organizers like a Venn Diagram, Grid, Flow Chart or Fishbone into cooperative structures. Another variation, the Future Wheel, helps students to consider the consequences of events. Woolly Thinking works as a class builder and a way to explore the relationships among topics.

Structure 21   TEAM WEB

STEPS

❶ **GIVE EACH TEAM A LARGE SHEET OF PAPER AND GIVE EACH STUDENT A DIFFERENT COLORED PEN**
If necessary, explain how the web works: the center circle is the main topic, the surrounding circles are sub-topics, and around the sub-topics one writes explanations. Students also draw lines among different parts to indicate logical connections.

❷ **IF A PREVIEW, PROVIDE SUB-TOPICS; OTHERWISE, ASK TEAMS TO USE A ROUNDTABLE TO ADD THEM**

❸ **ASK STUDENTS TO COMPLETE THE WEB WITH EACH TEAM MEMBER RECORDING HIS OR HER CONTRIBUTIONS WITH A DIFFERENT COLORED PEN**
The different colors allow the teacher to monitor individual accountability easily.

❹ **TEAMS SHARE THEIR WEBS WITH SIMULTANEOUS SHARING.**
The teacher may also wish students to make individual notes.

❺ **IF WEB IS USED FOR PRE-WRITING, SUPPLY STUDENTS OR ELICIT FROM THEM SOME OF THE LANGUAGE NECESSARY FOR WRITING DESCRIPTION OR ANALYSIS**
This might include transition words like first, second, another, also, in addition, moreover among many others.

Notes

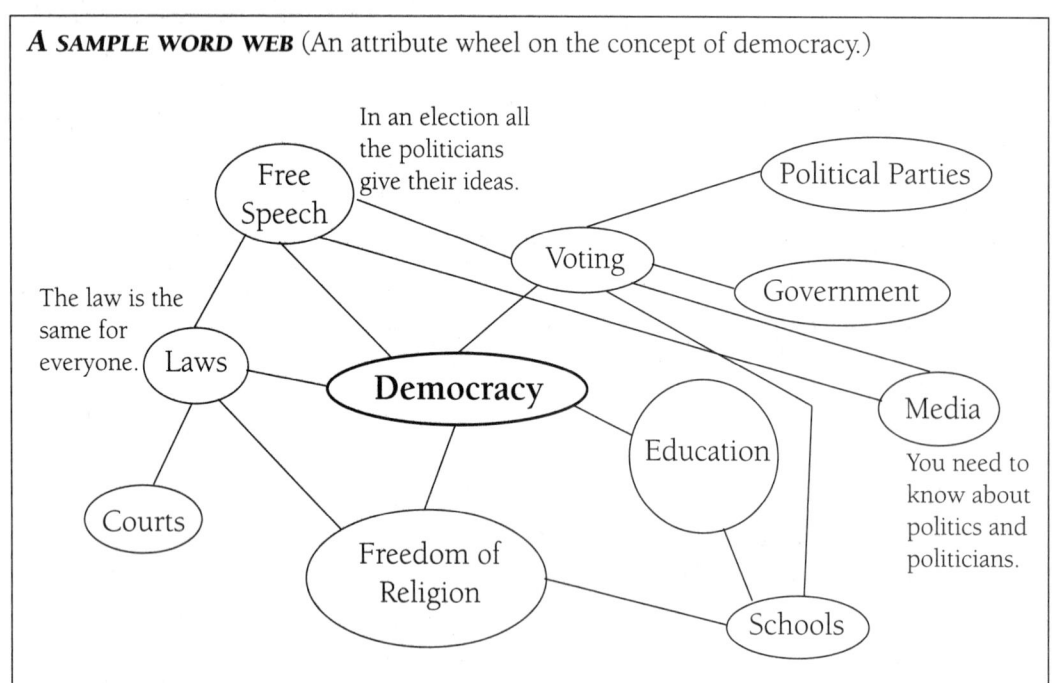

A SAMPLE WORD WEB (An attribute wheel on the concept of democracy.)

186   Cooperative Learning and Social Studies: Towards Excellence and Equity by Tom Morton
Kagan Publishing • 1(800) 933-2667 • www.KaganOnline.com

VARIATIONS

TEAM VISUALS
The same steps—a single product and each student writing with a different colored pen—can be applied to other graphic organizers. A Team Venn Diagram is especially useful in social studies when students are assigned different opinions on controversial issues. They can identify areas of agreement and in the overlap, areas of agreement. A Team Time Line is an excellent way to summarize a historical period.

FUTURE WHEEL
This structure is usually done with a large sheet of paper and a single felt pen for recording. Students draw an event, idea, or trend in the middle circle. Teams are then asked to consider what might be the consequences of the event, idea, or trend. Single lines are drawn out from the central circle and the consequences are also circled. Teams continue to consider further consequences stemming from their first order of consequences and draw double lines connecting the first order to the second order consequences. This is continued with third, fourth and even more orders of consequences (see page 191).

WOOLLY THINKING
(based on *Global Teacher, Global Learner* by Graham Pike and David Selby): This web variation for the whole class offers a powerful visual symbol of interdependence.

The teacher needs 10 sets of labels, 3 per set, each of a different color, plus 10 balls of wool of colors to match the labels. The exercise also requires a large open space in the classroom.

The teacher or class chooses 10 topics related to a major theme. For example, on the theme of development there could be health, shelter, food, environment, technology, industry, resources, education, urbanization, and government.

Student teams of three or two choose one of the topics and write the name down on their labels that they wear. Teams start with a brief 5 to 10 minute team discussion of everything they know about their topic and how it relates to the other topics. They should write this down on a single team paper.

Next, they select one student as a "static" negotiator and two as "mobile" negotiators. The static negotiators take up fixed positions in a large circle and tie one of the ends of their ball of wool around their wastes. They stay in the one position but negotiate with any of the mobile negotiators of the 9 other groups. These mobile negotiators go out and discuss with the stationary members of other teams what connections, links, or relationships they might have between their topics. Each time that they agree on a connection they write it down and pass the ball of wool across the circle and around the waste of the "static" negotiators of the 2 groups concerned. The wool should be kept taut and each time the ball is brought back to the static negotiator from whom it started. As the woolly web develops, it can become so closely woven that mobile negotiators may have to crawl underneath to continue their task.

In the end, the class discusses the negotiations and connections. The absence of connections can also be important to consider (see page 189).

Ideas for Using Team Web and Variations in Social Studies

Team Web
- Web a system of causes and effects.
- Web the qualities of a leader or hero through an analysis of behavior patterns displayed during various events, sometimes called a Character Map.
- Web the characteristics that define a concept, like democracy (see Sample Word Web on page 186), sometimes called an Attribute Wheel.
- Brainstorm prior knowledge of an event, place, or time, then categorize the ideas and write them as a web.
- Web the pattern of interdependence of people in the community, for example, student pairs place themselves in the center circle then web all the people that they have depended on since waking up that morning.
- Web the world in a lunch (newspaper, school, classroom), for example, groups can take a chocolate bar, a map of the world to draw on, and atlases and almanacs as resources. They locate their town and then draw lines on the map between that center and all the places on the world from where the chocolate bar's ingredients came. This can also be done with topics in the newspaper or the origins of students in the group, class, or school. The latter is sometimes called Routes and Roots.

Future Wheel
Students create a web of possible consequences

if

- fewer people voted
- the voting age were lowered to 13
- the oceans were polluted
- logging of trees were banned
- there were no more nuclear power plants
- there were fewer wild animals
- students do (or don't do) their homework
- students help and encourage each other

Woolly Thinking
- **Qualities for success in school**
  Effort, helpfulness towards others, willingness to ask for help, curiosity, willingness to fail, knowledge of a topic, listening to others, willingness to give ideas, planning, sense of humour

- **Topical issues**
  Hunger, human rights abuses, war, pollution, unemployment, overpopulation, arms production, dictatorships, "Third World" poverty, disease

- **An economic system**
  Taxes, business investment, government investment, consumer spending, wages, interest rates, exports, imports, currency value, employment rate.

- **The food chain**
  The sun; producers: pines, firs, deciduous trees, grasses, shrubs; *primary consumers:* insects, plant eaters like deer and hares, rodents like mice and squirrels, foraging birds like grouse or quail; *secondary consumers:* snakes, spiders, owls, insect eating birds like woodpeckers and sparrows; higher order consumers: cougars, coyotes, hawks, eagles, humans; *decomposers and scavengers:* decomposing earthworms and bacteria; scavengers like crows and vultures.

- **Temperate rain forest eco-system** (see the following role desriptions.)

Notes

AN EXAMPLE OF ROLE DESCRIPTIONS FOR WOOLLY THINKING

The following role descriptions represent the plants and animals of a temperate rain forest. They are divided into layers: the Canopy, the Understory, and the Forest Floor. Students should be in pairs sharing the same plant or animal role, but with one student as the static negotiator, the other as the mobile negotiator. There are nineteen roles to choose from. Your selection should include a rough balance of roles from the different layers.

The static negotiators with Canopy roles should stand on chairs; those with Understory roles should stand on the floor, and those with Forest Floor roles should sit on the floor. The mobile negotiators could use different colored wool depending on the layer of their role: blue for the Canopy, green for the Understory, and brown for the Forest Floor.

CANOPY

- You are a mature **Douglas Fir** tree between 200 and a 1000 years old and 70–80 meters high. Your branches and trunk provide shelter for many plants and animals while your needles, cones and sap give them food. Your roots keep the soil in place, preventing erosion. You also help keep the forest cool and moist.
- You are a **snag**, a tree that is still standing after it is dead. You may stay this way for a 125 years. Birds like eagles and owls perch on you while hunting. Other birds and mammals may use you for nests or dens and a place to store food. Lichen and moss grow on you.
- You are a large, hanging lichen called **old man's beard (or witch's hair)** that grows on the branches of conifer trees. Small mammals eat you as do deer when you fall to the forest floor in the winter. Other mammals and birds use you to make their nests. You add nutrients to the forest floor when you die and decay.
- You are a **spotted owl**. You nest in in the cavities or branches of large, live trees. The forest canopy protects you from predators. It also gives you warmth in winter. You prey on small mammals like the vole. Because some of these animals eat fungi, you help spread the fungi spores.
- You are an **eagle**. You perch on the branches of conifers looking for fish or small mammals to catch. You make your nest as well in the upper branches.

UNDERSTORY

- You are a **red tree vole** and you can spend your whole life in a single Douglas fir. You eat only its needles, line your nest with other needles, and drink rain and dew that is caught by the needles. Birds like owls and mammals like raccoons eat you.
- You are a **red huckleberry bush** that is growing on a decaying "nurse" log. You may reach a height of 4 meters. Your berries are delicious for deer, bears, and raccoons as well as human beings.
- You are **litterfall**. You are everything from microscopic fungal spores and spider threads to needles, lichen and branches. Much of you falls in the branches of the understory to make food for insects and mosses. Some falls in streams to be food for insects which are in turn eaten by fish. Most falls on the forest floor to decay and give nutrients to the forest plants and provide insulation for the tree's roots.
- You are a **mosquito**. Your larvae grow in puddles and the still pools of streams. Fish eat you. You feed on the blood of animals like the deer and bear.
- You are a **marbled murrlet**, a sea bird that spends most of its life over water. For years it was a mystery where you nested until in the 1970's it was established that you form your nests from lichen and moss in the branches of Old Growth forest. The canopy protects you and your young.

Cooperative Learning and Social Studies: Towards Excellence and Equity by Tom Morton

An Example of Role Descriptions for Wooly Thinking
(continued)

Forest Floor

- You are a **nurse log**, a dead tree that has fallen to the forest floor where you will slowly decay over several centuries. You keep moisture in the ground, especially important during the dry summer. Many animals find shelter in you. In addition, you provide food for insects and fungi. You have this name because you also "nurse" young seedling trees and bushes that feed on your nutrients.
- You are a **fallen log** in a stream. You decay more quickly than a log on land and will probably last only a 100 years. You slow the speed of the water and provide pools where fish and insects can live. As the current slows it also leaves deposits of gravel where salmon can spawn. Insects and fungi feed on you.
- You are a **Chanterelle mushroom**, the "fruit" of a chanterelle fungus which lives under the forest floor and forms a mychorriza with the roots of the Douglas Fir. This mychorriza is a special kind of root with very thin threads that gather water and minerals, to feed the tree. The tree in turn makes sugar from sunlight to feed you. You also cover the tree's root and protect it from infection. Small rodents and insects eat the mushroom. Humans too find the mushroom delicious.
- You are a **salmon** that lives best in the cold water, 5–15° Celsius (40–60° F.), that is found in the rivers and streams shaded by Old Growth forest. You eat insects and larvae and, in turn, can be eaten by bears and eagles. You spawn in gravel but cannot lay eggs in silt or mud.
- You are an **ambrosia beetle**. You are a fungus eating, tunnelling beetle who is one of the first to begin the process of decay in a log. When you settle in the log, so does fungus and this gives you your food source. Other insects like termites and ants follow your tunnels into the log.
- You are a **black bear.** You eat salmon, small mammals, insect grubs, birds and berries.
- You are a **Columbian black-tailed deer**. In the winter when the snow covers the ground in open areas, the forest gives you protection from predators and warmth. Here too, you can find food especially in the winter when storms leave lichen like Old Man's Beard on the forest floor.
- You are a **Pacific giant salamander** who eats insects, worms and frogs. You spend most of your time in the cool moisture under a log, but will wander about the forest floor and even into bushes and small trees.
- You are a **Pacific dampwood termite**. You help decompose dead trees turning them into nutrients for other trees and bushes. You are food for animals like the salamander, raccoon and bear.

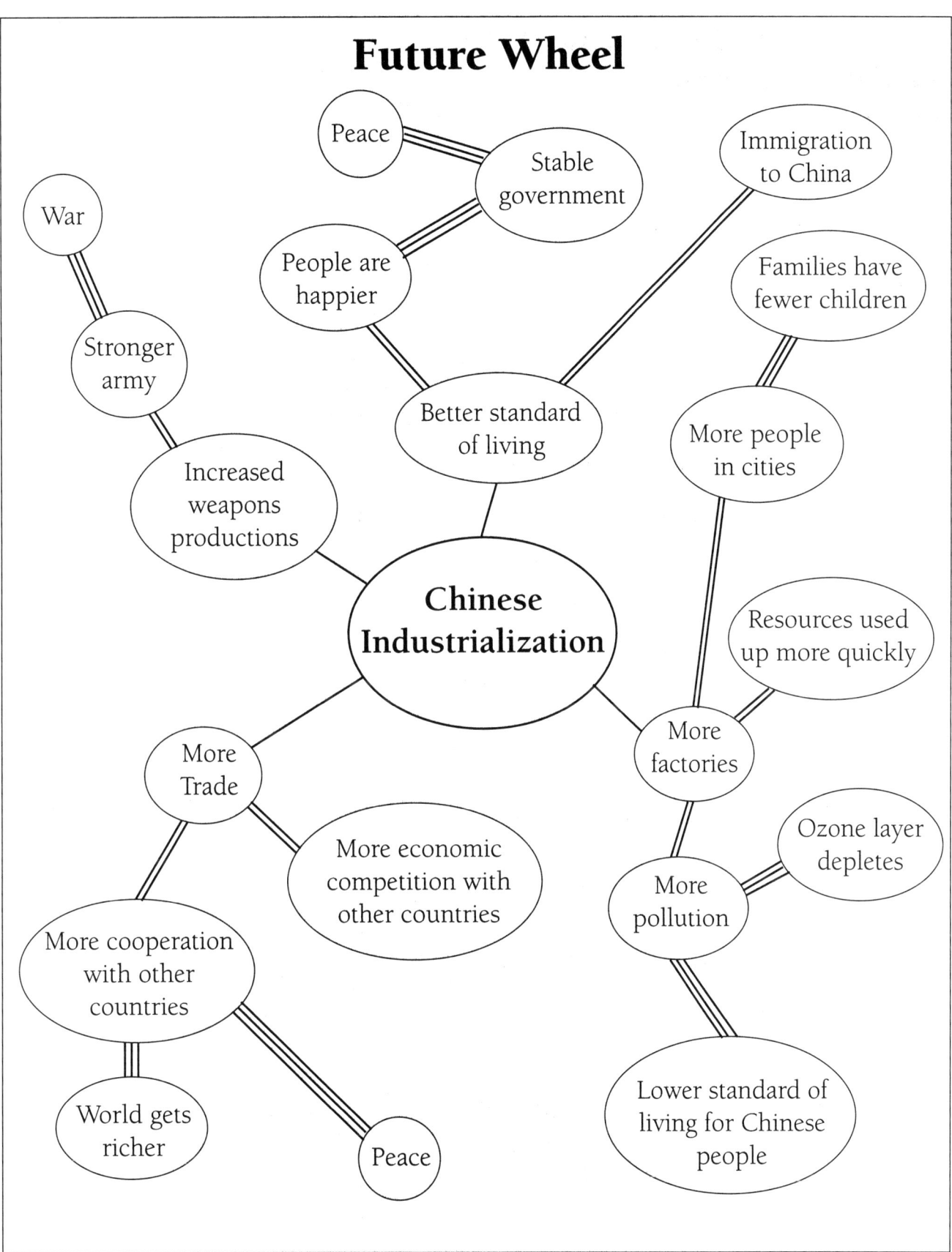

Narrative of Lessons Using a Team Web and Future Wheel

On China

Themes
- People, places and environment
- Culture
- Time, continuity, and change
- Global connections
- Science and technology

Skills
- Organizing information
- Using information

Before starting a unit on contemporary China with her middle school class Mrs. Webber wanted to access their prior knowledge. Using a Roundtable student teams of four each compiled a list of all the things that they knew about the world's most populous country. Webber then asked students to Sort their lists, give each category a name, and then construct a Team Web on poster paper. The teams posted these on the wall and held a Carousel Share.

Towards the end of the unit, Mrs. Webber used a Team Web for review. To be sure her class was going to be comprehensive in their review and that they could compare their work with other teams she provided them with the topics: recent history, economy, geography, government, culture, relations with other countries, and living standard. She monitored contributions by looking at the different colored writing of different students. Teams then showed their webs to their neighboring team and make individual copies of the review webs.

The class also reviewed the kind of language needed to analyze a system like "is connected to" and "helps" or "hinders" and wrote paragraphs on the links among these topics.

Next, Webber asked her class to consider what might happen if China were to continue its economic growth to become as industrialized as countries like Canada and the United States. Teams began a Future Wheel with Chinese Economic Growth written in the middle. Because the class had not discussed this topic before, the teams were a little slow to start, but once Mrs. Webber stopped the class to have some of the more successful groups share their possible future consequences, all of the groups began to generate elaborate Future Wheels.

Structure 22
THINK-PAIR SHARE

Steps at a Glance

❶ The teacher poses a "fat question" and students "Think" about it for at least 3 seconds, what is often called wait time.

❷ Students now "Pair" to complete a particular task.

❸ In the final "Share" stage students give their thoughts to the whole class.

The teacher assigns a question. Students think about an answer and then share their ideas with a partner and the class. This is a short and versatile structure that combines think time with purposeful talk.

Social Skills
- Taking turns
- Listening

Variations
- Think-Pair-Square
- Sketch-Pair-Write-Pair-Share

Think-Pair-Share sounds pretty literal and pedestrian, but it has lots of wiggles and waggles that make it very versatile. It is used when you want students to reflect on what Bellanca and Fogarty (1990) call "fat questions," those that require discussion and explanation, as opposed to "skinny questions" that require short and simple answers.

Think-Pair-Share is easy to implement and quick, so it works well in informal groups, perhaps as a change of pace during teacher-controlled direct instruction.

Structure 22 THINK-PAIR-SHARE

STEPS

❶ STUDENTS SHOULD BE IN PAIRS EITHER ON THEIR OWN OR AS PART OF A GROUP OF FOUR DIVIDED IN HALF

The teacher poses a "fat question" and students "Think" about it for at least 3 seconds, what is often called wait time. The research on wait time suggests that answers are more likely to be longer and more developed if students think about a question for three to ten seconds.

This "Think" stage can also take the form of guided imagery, writing or making a graphic organizer like a web.

❷ STUDENTS NOW "PAIR" TO COMPLETE A PARTICULAR TASK

This could mean coming to agreement on an answer, listening so as to explain their partner's idea to someone else, interviewing each other, creating a web, or writing a common answer.

❸ IN THE FINAL "SHARE" STAGE STUDENTS GIVE THEIR THOUGHTS TO THE WHOLE CLASS

Each answer is often followed by a second wait time of at least 3 seconds before the next comment. The sharing can also be done using one of the variations of Simultaneous Sharing.

VARIATIONS

THINK-PAIR-SQUARE

Instead of sharing with the class after the pairs share stage, pairs in a group of four can share their answer with the other pair, that is, a team discussion. This variation can increase participation.

SKETCH-PAIR-WRITE-PAIR-SHARE

This variation comes from a local study group on multiple intelligences. The teacher reads aloud a passage as students sketch any ideas that come to mind. After a minute of two pause for students to complete their drawing, they explain it to a partner. Next, they write underneath it a particular reading strategy like the main idea or predictions, pair again and share with the class.

IDEAS FOR USING THINK-PAIR-SHARE IN SOCIAL STUDIES

- **Review**
  There are many variations on how this can be done. For example, students can write as much as they know about the topic of study then pair up to draw a web that is passed to the next pair to read.

- **Analysis of a table of statistics, document, photo, or drawing**
  For example, the teacher provides students with a table comparing the results of surveys of Canadian and American attitudes towards questions having to do with freedom and authority such as opinions on gun control and bans on court room reporting. The teacher then uses Write-Pair-Share and Think-Pair-Share to consider the two questions "What do you notice about the results of these surveys?" and "What does this tell us about the attitudes of these two people?"

- **Inquiry-type questions or most any that begin with why or how**
  For example, students might be asked to speculate specifically on why General Hull was willing to surrender Detroit to Isaac Brock in the War of 1812 or, more generally, why does any one side in a battle win or lose?

- **Prediction**
  This could be real speculation about the future. For example, what do you think will happen to this current event? What will happen to this trend? How will we find out if we are right?

  It could also be prediction about something that has happened, but about which the students do not yet know the results. For example, what are all the possible things that can happen if you build a dam on a river like the Nile...? Let's read to see if your predictions are correct.

- **Dialogue on Controversies**
  One strategy designed to emphasize commonalities in arguments begins by asking students to write their opinion on a controversy and all their reasons why they hold that opinion. In the share stage, pairs construct a Venn Diagram. All the points of disagreement should go inside just their own circles while all the points of agreement should go in the overlap.

  A second approach intended to encourage perspective taking combines Think-Pair-Share with Peter Elbow's (1983) technique for teaching writing, called methodological belief. One of the goals in discussing controversies as well as studying the thoughts of a different time or place is for students to be able to enter the perspective of others. So prior to criticism of any position, the teacher asks the students to suspend judgement and use think-pair-share about how advocates of each position feel about the topic. They use the same structure again to try to identify the truth in each position with which everyone can agree.

Structure 22   *THINK-PAIR-SHARE*

Narrative of a Lesson Using Think-Pair-Share

Cartoon Analysis

Skills
- Information search skills with visual materials
- Analyzing information
- Synthesizing information

Ms. Rivas wanted to teach her students to identify the techniques of political cartoons as a step towards interpretation. She chose the following (based on Clark, 1991):

Light and dark: dark design creates a feeling of fear, disaster, or mystery; light design, in contrast, conveys hope, goodwill, or light-heartedness.

Lines: light, smooth lines can show humour or whimsey; crooked lines can indicate tension; dark lines seriousness.

Size: oversized figures can indicate power or threat; small ones can be powerless or threatened.

Caricature: this technique emphasizes physical defects so that well-known people look ridiculous, while still instantly recognizable.

Symbols: for example, an eagle or Uncle Sam for the United States and a beaver or maple leaf for Canada.

Exaggeration: an object, person, situation or idea is overstated.

Stereotyping: groups of people may be represented in an oversimplified and inaccurate way that makes them, nonetheless, easily recognizable. For example, a working class male might be drawn wearing a baseball cap and a t-shirt with a protruding stomach and a housewife might be drawn wearing a bathrobe and slippers with hair in curlers.

To illustrate her explanation of these techniques she showed a number of cartoons, mostly on themes relating to reform movements, on overhead transparencies. To help students in independent practice of identification of the techniques and interpretation, she used various forms of Think-Pair-Share.

For example, after showing the two cartoons drawn during the Suffrage campaign for the vote for women (see figure) she asked,

Structure 22   THINK-PAIR-SHARE

- Which cartoon seems to portray the Suffrage Campaigners in the most negative way? (Think, pair, and then vote.)
- What techniques did the cartoonist use to communicate his opinion? (Think-Pair-Share. Possible answers would be the use of lines and exaggerated facial features.)

Ms. Rivas also wanted her students to explore some of the issues that can arise about cartoons. For example, on symbolism she used Think-Pair-Share and Draw-Pair-Share to expand their knowledge of various symbols and also to discuss stereotyping:

- Look for any examples of symbolism in the cartoon? (then pair and share)
- Take some time to draw any symbols that you can think of for different countries like the United States, Mexico, Canada, India, or China. (then pair and show to the class)
- Why does a cartoonist use symbols? Why use stereotypes? (pair, share)
- What are some drawbacks in using stereotypes, like the Mexican sleeping in a huge sombrero? (pair, share)

Later, students brought in cartoons to share in a RoundRobin manner and drew their own political cartoons.

Cartoon courtesy of Charles Hou. Illustrated by Lou Skuce, *Toronto World*, March 3, 1912.

Cartoon courtesy of Charles Hou. Illustrator unknown, *Montreal Herald*, circa 1912.

Cooperative Learning and Social Studies: Towards Excellence and Equity by Tom Morton
Kagan Publishing • 1(800) 933-2667 • www.KaganOnline.com

Structure 23
THREE-STEP INTERVIEW

Steps at a Glance

❶ Foursomes divide into pairs with one of the pair starting as the interviewer and the other as the interviewee.

❷ The teacher sets the topic for the interview and time limits and students begin the interview.

❸ Pairs reverse roles and begin a second interview.

❹ Students take turns sharing with the team what they learned from their partner.

In a group of four, students divide into pairs and take turns interviewing a partner. Next, they summarize what their partner has said for the other group members. This can be used for team building, creating an anticipatory set, role playing or reviewing. Active listening is integral to Three-Step Interview.

Social Skills

- Listening (especially paraphrasing)

There is clearly a versatile structure with high individual accountability and simultaneous interaction. There is a drawback, however, in that it depends on the students' willingness to talk and so may not work as well with those who are reluctant. If this is the case with many of your students, you may need to spend more time with the skills of a good interviewer especially asking open-ended questions and paraphrasing and try to ensure that the assigned topic of discussion will elicit responses.

The topic for an interview could be a non-threatening question like what are your favorite foods and hobbies or what was the funniest thing to happen at school last year or a review question on material that the students know well.

Structure 23 THREE-STEP INTERVIEW

STEPS FOR GROUPS OF FOUR

❶ FOURSOMES DIVIDE INTO TWO PAIRS WITH ONE OF PAIR STARTING AS INTERVIEWER AND THE OTHER AS INTERVIEWEE

❷ TEACHER SETS TOPIC FOR INTERVIEW AND TIME LIMITS. STUDENTS BEGIN INTERVIEW

❸ PAIRS REVERSE ROLES AND BEGIN A SECOND INTERVIEW

❹ STUDENTS TAKE TURNS SHARING WITH TEAM WHAT THEY LEARNED FROM THEIR PARTNER

STEPS FOR GROUPS OTHER THAN FOUR

❶ FOR GROUPS OF THREE STUDENTS DO A ROUNDROBIN WITH TWO TEAM MEMBERS INTERVIEWING THE THIRD

❷ FOR A GROUP OF EVEN NUMBERS MORE THAN FOUR, THE THREE STEPS ARE THE SAME

❸ FOR GROUPS OF ODD NUMBERS MORE THAN FOUR, TWO STUDENTS SHOULD PAIR AND FUNCTION AS A SINGLE STUDENT

IDEAS FOR USING THREE-STEP INTERVIEW IN SOCIAL STUDIES

Teambuilding: Elizabeth Coelho (1994) suggests a number of interview questions about names that can help students become better acquainted in English as a Second Language classes. In any social studies class questions similar to the ones below could also be an anticipatory set leading into a discussion of the culture of families, male-female roles or family history.

- What is your given name? How do you pronounce it? How do you spell it?
- What is your family name? How do you pronounce it? How do you spell it? In your culture, is your given name your first name, or is your family name your first name?
- Does your family name have any religious significance?
- Does your family name tell something about where your ancestors come from or what their occupation was?
- Does any part of your name show what clan or kinship group your family comes from?
- In your culture, do women usually keep their own family name after they marry?
- In your culture, how do people give names to children?
- Is it usual to be named after someone else, living or dead?

Anticipatory Sets: Many topics can build on students' prior knowledge. The questions for interview might be broad such as "What experience have you had with..." or "What would you like to learn about..."

The questions also might be more focused, although still open-ended, such as "Try to think of all the influences of the introduction of the car (or television or computers?" "Think of a conflict that you have witnessed or been involved in. Discuss all the possible sources of conflict and possible ways it might be settled." Another set before a unit on migration could start with "Have you moved and what was it like?"

Role Plays: Assuming that students have enough knowledge of a topic to play roles, they could extend their knowledge if they discuss it while playing roles. For example, a unit on the forest industry could have one pair playing the role of a logger and an environmentalist and the other pair with the roles of government official and a native Indian activist.

Differing Perspectives: Similar to a role play, students might try to answer questions taking a different perspective. For example, one student might be interviewed on how history plays a role in a current event, another on geography, others on government or economics.

Exploring a Topic or Expressing Opinions: Possible questions might be similar to ones in Values Lines or Corners such as "What are the three most important things that you would want in a government?" "What period of time would you like to live in?" or "What do you or your family do about the environment—do you recycle, reuse, avoid any products or talk about the environment at all?"

Predictions: For example, "Interview your partner about what you think will happen in the next few weeks with the current event that we've been following."

Review of Homework: "What did you find most interesting about last night's reading? Most difficult?"

Review of a Lesson or Unit: "Interview your partner about what they have learned this week in social studies" or "Interview your partner about what they think would be a fair question to ask on the up-coming exam and how they might answer it."

Talk about writing: A teacher might ask students, "Take turns sharing with your partner what you are trying to do with your writing, where you think it is strong, and where you think you could improve it."

Structure 23   THREE-STEP INTERVIEW

NARRATIVE OF LESSONS USING THREE-STEP INTERVIEW

Personal and Political Change

Themes

- Individual development, and identity
- Individuals, groups, and institutions
- Power, authority, and governance
- Time, continuity, and change
- Civic ideals and practices

"The greatest compliment that was ever paid to me was when one asked me what I thought, and attended to my answer."

(Henry David Thoreau)

Tony Davidson was following the "structure of the month" approach to implementing cooperative learning. For his grade nine unit on political reform movements he wanted to use the Three-Step Interview. He started by giving a quick outline of the steps and explaining the following rationale. First, the Three-Step Interview is a good way for the students to find out what they know about a topic and to make personal connections. By building on what they already know, the topic can be more real and they can deepen their learning, he explained. Second, talking is good for reviewing what they have studied in class. Third, when students really listen to their team members, this helps build a good feeling of caring about others. He referred to the quotation from Thoreau that he wrote on the board and the number of ways listening is important in families, with friends and at work.

To begin the unit Mr. Davidson showed the steps of the structure on the overhead projector and introduced the topic for the interview: "You already know about changing things. It's not just something in a textbook. I want you to think about a time when you wanted something or wanted to change something or stop someone from doing something. What did you do to get what you wanted or to change things. You might also think about your feelings or the reaction of other people. If you can't think of anything you did, think about something you would like to change and how you might do it." He paused for a few seconds before saying, "Now let's follow the steps of Three-Step Interview to interview our partners about change in our own lives. Each of you take two or three minutes to interview. If your partner stops before then, really work on follow-up and open-ended questions."

As this was the first time he had used the structure, Mr. Davidson wanted to get some feedback on how it went. He wrote on the overhead the following questions and asked students to write and hand in their responses:

1. Did you have time to think about the questions?
2. Did you feel listened to?
3. Did you listen to your partner?
4. Did anyone interrupt?
5. Did you take turns in the proper order?
6. Did you have enough time, too much time to talk, or about the right length of time?
7. Did anybody praise or put down the ideas of someone else?
8. Was this activity worthwhile? What did you gain from it?

The material that the class studied was mainly about the suffrage movement, trade unions and the struggles for the improvement of working conditions in the early 20th century; however, Mr. Davidson also wanted to stress that the steps in democratic change begin with very simple and very personal steps, such as learning about the different sides to a problem, talking with others about what to do and building support for your ideas. So he returned to Three-Step Interview to consider case studies of situations at the school that they might want to change. His examples included a situation where the student hears racist name calling, a locker theft that they witness, a fight after school, and bullying.

Mr. Davidson also used the structure to review what the students studied from their text and lessons. He usually included some kind of review at the end of Friday's classes so it was easiest to use Three-Step Interview at that time. Over the course of the four week long unit the students Three-Step Interviewed five times.

Structure 24
VALUE LINES

Steps at a Glance

1. Start by posing, to students, a values question on which there is likely to be some diversity of opinion.
2. Students line up from one end of the classroom to another, based on their opinion.
3. The Folded Line: One end walks down to meet the other end with the others in line following so that each student has a partner.
4. Ask pairs to discuss their opinion using Paraphrase Passport.
5. The Split and Slide: Unfold the line, split it at the midpoint, and have one half of the line 'slide' down to find a new partner.

In Value Lines students are given a values question and order themselves in a line according to their opinions on that question. Next, they fold the line to talk to a partner about their reasons for their choice. A Value Line is a way for students to reflect on values questions and practice active listening.

Social Skills
- Paraphrasing

Variations
- Line-Ups
- Human Graph
- Pro-Con Dialogue

Value Lines can accomplish several goals: they can provide a theme question for the beginning of a unit, give an opportunity to practice paraphrasing, and build respect for different opinions. Above all, they can help students deal with values questions.

The Curriculum Standards for Social Studies (1994) of the National Council for Social Studies says that some values, like the right to life and liberty and freedom of worship and expression, are so key to our way of democratic life that we want to develop a strong student commitment to them. At other times, however, we want students to consider situations where they must weigh priorities where values conflict. As the NCSS says, democratic societies are characterized by hard choices and social studies should not dictate answers in these cases. Instead with structures like Value Lines it should teach students how to analyze and discuss these dilemmas with quality thinking and respect for differences of opinion.

Cooperative Learning and Social Studies: Towards Excellence and Equity by Tom Morton

Structure 24 VALUE LINES

STEPS FOR VALUE LINES

❶ START BY POSING TO STUDENTS A VALUES QUESTION ON WHICH THERE IS LIKELY TO BE SOME DIVERSITY OF OPINION

If possible, have students record their answer on a sheet of paper, for example, a number on a scale of 1–5, from strongly agree to strongly disagree.

❷ STUDENTS LINE UP FROM ONE END OF THE CLASSROOM TO ANOTHER, BASED ON THEIR VALUES

Designate one end of the classroom to be for those in favor and the other to be for those opposed. The student who agrees most strongly should be at one end while the student who disagrees the most should be at the other end. The remaining students stand in between towards one end or another depending on whether they agree or disagree or are divided in their opinion.

❸ THE FOLDED LINE

One end walks down to meet the other end with the others in line following so that each student has a partner. (With big senior secondary students, you will need to ask them to stretch out the line to give space.) The end partners will have strongly opposite viewpoints, while the students who were in the middle of the line may be paired with someone who has a similar viewpoint.

```
                FOLDED LINE
Agree ◄─Ⓐ─○─○─○─○─❓─❓─○─○─○─○─Ⓓ─► Disagree

                                 ❓─○─○─○─○─Ⓓ─► Disagree
                                 ❓─○─○─○─○─Ⓐ─► Agree
```

Teacher Tip: When students are crowded together, it is sometimes hard to see that they each have a partner so one option is to ask them to touch right toes with their partner and then check that everyone is paired up.

❹ ASK PAIRS TO DISCUSS THEIR OPINION USING PARAPHRASE PASSPORT

To play this game the teacher needs to explain briefly how to paraphrase. In the game students express their viewpoints on the values question, but after someone has spoken, the other person must correctly restate what was said before giving his or her own idea. This is to ensure that each person is listening and not just talking.

❺ THE SPLIT AND SLIDE

If we just fold the line, students in the middle miss the opportunity to interact with those different from themselves. However, the step of unfolding, splitting, and sliding may give a fence straddler a chance to talk with someone willing to take a strong stance, or the person who sees an issue from only one perspective may have the chance to interact with someone who sees it from a more complex point of view.

Fold back the line and then break it at the midpoint. (The Folded Line will have told you where the middle is.) Ask one half of the line to stand where they are. The other half should take two steps forward to create two separate lines. Ask the students to number themselves in order along the line. Then ask the new line to walk down to be opposite a partner who has the same number. Now everyone is facing someone with a different point of view.

Repeat the discussion with the new pairs using Paraphrase Passport.

Notes

Structure 24 VALUE LINES

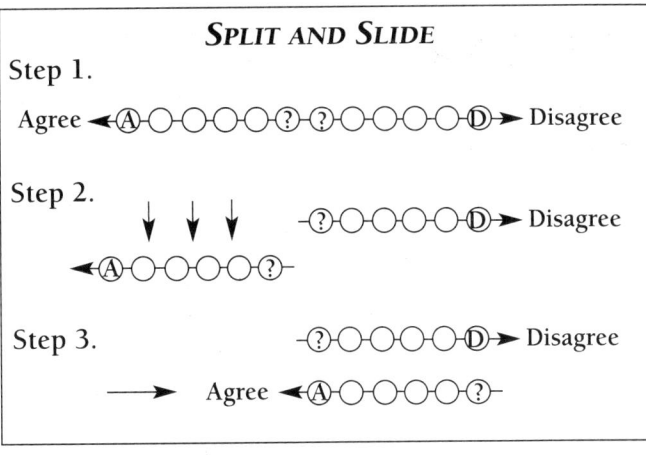

Variations

Line-Ups

In Line-Ups, the teacher states a characteristic (such as birthday, or distance of home from school). Students then line up based on the characteristic. If students were to line up on birthdays, January 1st would be at one end of the line, and December 31st at the other end. If they were to line up based on distance of home from school, a student who lives across the street from school would be on one side of the line, and a student who lives 10 miles from school would be on the other.

Team Formation Line-Ups: Whether you do a Line-Up or a Value Line, making teams or discussion groups based on these lines may provide some interesting conversation. You can create homogeneous teams by counting the first four students in the line and making that a group, and then the next four for the next group, and so on. You can also make heterogeneous groups by picking the students from each side to form a group, then the next two from each side, and so on.

Human Graph

This exercise is both a classbuilder and a discussion opener. For younger students it can be part of a unit on graphing.

Once asked a question like "Should we raise the minimum wage?" students express an opinion by standing next to a designated spot on a wall like the ones below:

Strongly Disagree	Disagree	Unsure	Agree	Strongly Agree

Students line out at right angles from these positions on the wall to form a bar graph.

The teacher then asks for students to discuss their reasons in pairs and then share them with the class. An exercise in paraphrasing like in Corners can follow or the teacher can lead a class discussion.

The same questions that are used for a Values Line can be used with a Human Graph with the same set of responses: the agree/disagree scale above. However, a Human Graph can also have the same kind of questions as Corners, like which is the best metaphor for the decade? In this case students stand next to responses quite unlike the agree/disagree scale.

Cooperative Learning and Social Studies: Towards Excellence and Equity by Tom Morton
Kagan Publishing • 1(800) 933-2667 • www.KaganOnline.com

Pro-Con Dialogue

This structure comes from Bert Bowers of the Teachers' Curriculum Institute in California. It combines features of the Line Up and Values Line with role play. Students order themselves in a row as they would in a Line Up and then fold the line to form pairs. The teacher then poses a Values Question and asks students on one side of the line to role play an advocate of one position and the other side to take the opposite position.

Students are given openers—introductory words to begin the argument and are instructed to practice paraphrase passport.

After a few minutes they switch roles and argue the other side.

IDEAS FOR USING LINE-UPS IN SOCIAL STUDIES

- **Birthdays**
  Ask the class to line up without speaking, using only non-verbal communication. Once they have done so, ask them to talk to each other to find out how accurate they were. (Use only the day and month and not the year of the birthdays as some people are sensitive about their age.)

  This could also be done with the years of birth of historical figures provided references were readily available.

- **Timeline**
  Give students historical events and ask them to line up according to the order of their occurrence.

- **Distance Born from the Room**
  Use a world wall map and ask students to estimate or they may spend more time than you want trying to calculate distances.

- **Distance of Home from School**
  Again ask students to estimate the distance. Note that around some schools there may be low status areas and students may not want to acknowledge where they live.

- **Alphabetical Order**
  Older students will find little fun in lining up in the alphabetical order of their last names so try this with the order of the historical figure they most admire or city or country in Asia that they would most like to visit.

- **Number of Times**
  For example, students line up by the number of times in the last week that they watched the television news or read the newspaper before starting a current events unit; by the number of times they have visited a certain country or state before studying that area; or the times they consumed a certain product in the last 24 hours—paper, food, or oil based product, for example—as part of an environmental or economics study. This can also give an indication of students' prior knowledge.

IDEAS FOR VALUE LINES

- **Important Issues for the Community, Country, or World**
  For example, in a unit on the American Civil War, Québec separatism, immigration or any other involving relations among different nationalities or ethnic groups, the teacher could begin with questions like these:

  Should an ethnic or linguistic group ever have the right to separate from a country? Should a provincial or state government ever have the right to do so?

  When, if ever, should English be the only language allowed?

Is it ever right to use violence in rebelling against an injustice?

Should someone break the law to help someone else escape from a terrible condition, like slavery or torture?

- **Issues for Personal Action**
The same issues could be phrased more personally with these questions:

Would you ever make a special effort to talk to a newcomer whose English is hard to understand? (Never to very often)

Would you ever insist that someone speak English and not their native language? (Never to always)

Would you ever take up arms against the government? (Definitely yes to definitely no)

If you knew a refugee was going to be deported and you were sure that his or her life would be in danger if this happened, would you break the law and hide that refugee? (Definitely yes to definitely no)

IDEAS FOR OPENERS IN A PRO-CON DIALOGUE

- **Should the minimum wage be raised?**
Openers for the side in favour of raising minimum wage:

"People who support themselves deserve a decent living. At minimum wage they have to live in poverty…" or

"If we put more money in the hands of the poor, they will spend it and help the economy for everyone…"

Openers for those opposed to raising it:

"Small business, who are the ones who pay the low wages, won't be able to afford to keep the workers at a higher wage. So a higher minimum wage will create unemployment…" or

"If those who work at minimum wage don't like it, they can look for other work or go back to school…"

Structure 24 VALUE LINES

Narrative of a Lesson Using a Line-Up

Case Studies on Violence and Rebellion

Themes
- Power, authority, and governance

Recurring Issues
- When, if ever, is violent rebellion justified?

Values
- Respect for different opinions
- Societies need laws that are respected by the majority of people

Skills
- Decision making

William Arthur and Frances Lorraine team teach a humanities course in a senior secondary school. They start a unit entitled War and Peace by writing on the blackboard, "Violence is always wrong." This provocative statement will form a thread that they will refer to several times over the next few weeks as they look at war and peace in history, sociological studies, contemporary events and literature.

One of their first academic goals is to have students understand and be able to identify values in public issues. An early cooperative goal is for students to practice active listening. Towards these ends they give students the handout of case studies on the use of violence that follows and ask each student to read and complete it individually.

Frances then asks the class to vote on where they stand on each of these cases. If they strongly agree, they wave their arms in the air; if they only agree, they just raise their arms; if they are unsure, they must fold their arms; if they disagree, they make the gesture of thumbs down with their hand; if they strongly disagree, they motion up or down with their hand.

This energizes the class and also gives Frances some feedback as to which case has the most disagreement and thus is most likely to generate discussion.

She sees that the third case study has the most potential and so she uses it for a Values Line. The class lines up according to their opinions for and against the violent rebellion and then goes through the steps of a Fold, Passport Paraphrase, and Split and Slide, interspersed with some whole class discussion.

Notes

William then takes over and divides the line into groups of two. Once they are settled, he identifies in the earlier student answers references to values and uses these to define values and explain their importance in clear thinking about what is right and wrong. Next, the students work in pairs to identify the values in conflict in the other case studies.

The class shares its answers using Stand Up and Share. Finally, students write in their journals about how well they listened and how much they felt listened to during their Values Line and their work in pairs.

Structure 24 VALUE LINES

Student Handout

Case Studies on Violent Rebellion

Instructions: When, if ever, is violent rebellion justified? Read the following situations. Even if you have a strong opinion for one side, try to set it aside at first to consider arguments both for and against the use of violence in these situations and write these underneath.

1. In 1831 in Virginia, a black slave named Nat Turner led six other slaves to murder their owner, his wife and children. They then marched from plantation to plantation gathering rebels to attack the nearby town of Jerusalem killing all whites on the way except one very poor white family. White militia defeated the rebels before they reached the town. Turner was captured, tried, and hanged.

Arguments for violent rebellion   *Arguments against violent rebellion*

2. To keep their slaves as property and to gain independence, American Southerners seceded from the federal union and attacked Fort Sumter, a federal fort in Southern territory, starting a civil war.

Arguments for violent rebellion   *Arguments against violent rebellion*

3. As white settlers began farming on Indian and Métis (mixed white and native) land driving away the buffalo, the native food source, the Indians and Métis started petitions and wrote letters to convince the government to help them. They were ignored. After a hard winter with many dying of starvation, they attacked the police, stole food, and set up their own government.

Arguments for violent rebellion   *Arguments against violent rebellion*

4. In an effort to gain independence for Québec and to preserve its culture, militant French-Canadian separatists started a campaign of bombings and eventually kidnapped a British trade representative and a Québec cabinet minister, Pierre Laporte. The federal government called out the army to help find them, but the kidnappers killed Laporte first.

Arguments for violent rebellion   *Arguments against violent rebellion*

Part 3
CONCLUSION

Teaching is an ephemeral profession. Teaching is a lickety-split, no time for reflection profession. Even when our work is rewarded with a smile or a stack of successful essays and we really feel we are building a community of learners, we soon have to plunge into the next class or the next pile of marking.

This book, however, has been a chance for me to do something different: to reflect on, struggle with, and refine my teaching practice and philosophy and arrive at a tangible end. Getting there was half the fun (and pain), but it is good to have arrived at this destination, the finished book.

That said, I still invite the reader to send me any corrections or ideas for improving the book, to help me return to the voyage for a further edition. Send all corrections and ideas to my e-mail address: **tmorton@cln.etc.bc.ca**, or my mailing address: **4019 Dunbar, Vancouver, B.C. V6S 2E5**.

Despite the wide acceptance of cooperative learning as a desirable practice, its use, especially at the secondary level, seems to be infrequent. Part of the reason may be a lack of teaching material that is specific to the subject and grade level. This book and others from **Kagan Cooperative Learning** may help. Additional ideas for improvement can only help.

Another reason for the low level of implementation of cooperative learning may be lack of support. I hope that the reader will find that support at his or her own school and through a local association of cooperative learning. The International Association of Cooperative Learning (IASCE, Box 1582, Santa Cruz, CA 95061-1582, USA), as well as producing an excellent magazine, can provide the names of local chapters of IASCE and venues for workshops and conferences.

References

All references to Spencer Kagan are to *Cooperative Learning* (1992). San Juan Capistrano, CA: Kagan Cooperative Learning, unless otherwise noted.

Part One

ACKNOWLEDGEMENTS

Goodlad, J. (1984). *A Place Called School*. NY: McGraw-Hill.

Orwell, G. (1984). Such, such were the joys. *The Penguin Essays of George Orwell*. Markham, Ontario: Penguin Canada, p. 449.

CHAPTER ONE

Gardner, H. (1993). Interviewed by Brant, R. On teaching for understanding: a conversation with Howard Gardner. *Educational Leadership*. vol. 30, no. 7, pp. 4–7.

Johnson, D. and Johnson, R. (1994). In Stahl, R., ed. *Cooperative Learning in Social Studies*. Menlo Park, CA: Addison-Wesley, p. 60.

Kagan, M. and Kagan, S. (1992). *Advanced Cooperative Learning: Playing with Elements*. San Juan Capistrano, CA: Kagan Cooperative Learning.

Kagan, S. (1992).

National Council for the Social Studies (1994). *Expectations for Excellence: Curriculum Standards for Social Studies*. Washington: National Council for the Social Studies.

Newmann, F. and Wehlage, G. (1993). Five standards of authentic instruction. *Educational leadership*, vol. 30, no. 7, pp. 8–12.

CHAPTER THREE

Burns, M. (1981). Groups of four: solving the management problem. *Learning*. September, pp. 46–51.

Cohen, E. (1994). *Designing Groupwork*. 2nd ed. NY: Teachers College Press, p. 123.

Johnson, D. and Johnson, R. (1994). In Stahl, R., ed. *Cooperative Learning in Social Studies*. Menlo Park, CA: Addison-Wesley, p. 60.

Morris, R. (1977). *A Normative Intervention to Equalize Participation in Task-Oriented Groups*. Unpublished doctoral dissertation, Stanford University, cited in Cohen, E. (1994). *Designing groupwork*. 2nd ed. NY: Teachers College Press, p. 53.

CHAPTER FOUR

Bennett, B., Rolheiser-Bennett, C., and Stevahn, L. (1991). *Cooperative Learning: Where Heart Meets Mind*. Toronto: Educational Connections, p. 154.

Bower, B, Lobdell, J., and Swenson, L. (1994). *History Alive!* Menlo Park, CA: Addison-Wesley, p. 168.

Clarke, J., Wideman, R., and Eadie, S. (1990). *Together We Learn*. Scarborough, Ontario, p. 107.

Johnson, D., Johnson, R., and Johnson Holubec, E. (1990). *Cooperation in the Classroom*. 4th ed. Edina, MN: Interaction, 1994.

Kagan, S. (1995). "Group Grades Miss the Mark." *Educational Leadership*. vol. 52, no. 9, pp. 68–71.

Sophocles, cited in Rolheiser-Bennett, C. and Stevahn, L. "Expanding Visions of Evaluation in Cooperative Learning." *Cooperative Learning*, vol. 13, no. 1, p. 3.

References

Part Two

STRUCTURE 1. COLOR-CODED CO-OP CARDS

MacGlobe. (1991). Tempe, AZ: PC. Globe, Inc.

SuperPaint. (1993). San Diego, CA: Aldus Corporation.

STRUCTURE 2. CO-OP CO-OP

Dippong, J. (1992). Lesson plan: evaluation forms. *Cooperative Learning.* vol. 13, no. 1, p. 50.

Nuñez, L. (1993). *Why Do People Move? Migration from Latin America.* Stanford, CA: Latin America Project/SPICE.

STRUCTURE 4. CREATIVE CONTROVERSY

Johnson, D. and Johnson, R. (1992). *Creative Controversy: Intellectual Challenge in the Classroom.* Edina, MN: Interaction.

Parker, W., McDaniel, J., and Valencia, S. (1991). Helping students think about public issues: instruction versus prompting. *Social Education.* Jan., 1991, pp. 41–67.

Wright, R. (1992). *Stolen Continents.* Toronto: Penguin Canada.

STRUCTURE 5. FIND MY RULE

Bruner, J. (1961). *The Process of Education.* Cambridge, MA: Harvard University Press.

Bruner, J., Goodnow, J.J., and Austin, G.A. (1967). *A Study of Thinking.* New York: Science Editions. In Joyce, B. and Weil, M. (1986). *Models of Teaching.* Englewood Cliffs, New Jersey: Prentice-Hall, pp. 25–39.

STRUCTURE 6. FIND-SOMEONE-WHO...

Armstrong, T. (1994). *Multiple Intelligences in the Classroom.* Alexandria, VA: ASCD, p. 44.

Pike, G. and Selby, D. (1988). *Global Teacher, Global Learner.* Seven Oaks, Kent, England: Hodder and Stoughton, p. 114.

Robertson, L. cited in Kagan (1992), p. 9.5.

STRUCTURE 7. FORMATIONS

Chu, R. (1993). *Along the Silk Road.* Stanford, CA: China Project/SPICE.

STRUCTURE 9. JIGSAW

Beer, B. (1983). *Patterns of Civilization.* Englewood Cliffs, NJ: Prentice-Hall.

Bowers, V. and Garrod, S. (1987). *Our Land: Building the West.* Toronto: Gage.

Coelho, E. (1991). *Jigsaw.* Markham, Ontario: Pippin.

Coelho, E., Olsen, J., and Winer, L. (1989). *All Sides of the Issue.* Hayward, CA: Alemany Press.

Coelho, E., Winer, L. (1991). *Jigsaw Plus.* Markham, Ontario: Pippin.

Commonwealth. July 17, 1863, and *Freeman's Record*, March, 1865, pp. 34–38. In Blockson, C. (1987). *The Underground Railroad.* NY: Prentice-Hall.

Kagan, S. (1992). *Cooperative Learning.* San Juan Capistrano, CA: Kagan Cooperative Learning.

Ross, A. (1875). *Recollections.* Toronto: Rowell and Hutchinson, pp. 32–55. In Blockson, C., (1987). *The Underground Railroad.* NY: Prentice-Hall.

VanSickle, R. (1994). Jigsaw II: Cooperative Learning with "expert group" specialization. In *Cooperative Learning in Social Studies.* Stahl, R., ed. Menlo Park, CA: Addison-Welsley, pp. 98–132.

Structure 10. Mix-N-Match

Graceland. (1987). Director: Michael Lindsay-Hogg. 90 minutes. Warner Reprise, 3300 Warner Blvd, Burbank, CA 91510.

Rhythm of Resistance. (1979). Part of the *Beats of the Heart* series. Director: Jeremy Marre. 53 minutes. Shanachie, P.O. Box 208, Newton, NJ 07860.

Thanks to **Valerie Dare** of the World Music Project, Britannia Secondary School, Vancouver, for these references in Structure 10 and numerous ideas on teaching socials with music.

Structure 11. Mystery Game

Pardoe, D. (1982). *Tommorow's World.* Canadian Red Cross, p. 142.

Stafford, G. (1990). *Developing Effective Classroom Groups: A Practical Guide for Teachers.* Bristol: Acora.

Structure 12. Numbered Heads Together

Shaw, V. (1993). *Communitybuilding in the Classroom.* San Juan Capistrano, CA: Kagan Cooperative Learning.

Structure 13. Pairs Check

Dunlop, S. (1987). *Towards Tomorrow: Canada in a Changing World, Geography.* Toronto: Harcourt Brace Jovanovitch.

Structure 14. Pairs Compare

Coelho, E., and Winer, L. (1991). *Jigsaw Plus.* Markham, Ontario: Pippin.

Structure 15. Pairs Read and Pairs View

Zemon Davis, N. (1983). *The Return of Martin Guerre.* Cambridge: Harvard University Press.

Structure 18. Simultaneous Sharing

Stone, J. (1992). *Cooperative Learning and Language Arts: A Multi-Structural Approach.* San Juan Capistrano, CA: Kagan Cooperative Learning. p. 39.

Structure 19. Sort

Joyce, B. and Weil, M. (1986). *Models of Teaching.* Englewood Cliffs, New Jersey: Prentice-Hall, pp. 40–54.

Structure 20. Team Discussion

McClung, N. (1972, originally 1915). *In Times Like These.* Toronto: University of Toronto Press. In Bennett, P. and Cornelius, J. (1986). *Emerging Identities.* Scarborough, Ontario: Prentice-Hall, pp. 379–380.

O'Reilly, K. and Splain, J. (1987). *Critical Viewing.* Pacific Grove: CA: Midwest Publications, p. 11.

Rhoades, J. and McCabe, P. (1992). *Outcome Based Learning: A Teacher's Guide to Restructuring the Classroom.* Sacramento, CA: ITA Publications.

Sedgewick, R. (1856). *The Proper Sphere and Influence of Women in Christian Society.* A lecture to the YMCA, Halifax, Nova Scotia. In Bennett, P. and Cornelius, J. (1986). *Emerging Identities.* Scarborough, Ontario: Prentice-Hall, pp. 386–387.

Structure 21. Team Web

Pike, G. and Selby, D. (1988). *Global Teacher, Global Learner.* Seven Oaks, Kent, England: Hodder and Stoughton, p. 141.

Structure 22. Think-Pair-Share

Bellanca, J. and Fogarty, R. (1990). *Blueprints for Thinking in the Cooperative Classroom.* Palatine, IL: Skylight, pp. 40–41.

References

Clark, P. (1991). Helping students to analyze, evaluate, and judge information. *Horizon.* vol. 29:1, pp. 26–34.

Elbow, Peter. (1983). Critical thinking is not enough. In Berman, S. (1991). Thinking in context: teaching for openmindedness and critical understanding. In Costa, A., ed. (1991). *Developing Minds: A Resource Book for Teachers.* vol. 1. Alexandria, VA: ASCD, p. 13.

Hou, C. and Hou, C. (1995).*Great Canadian Political Cartoons.* Unpublished manuscript.

STRUCTURE 23. THREE-STEP INTERVIEW

Coelho, E. (1994). *Learning Together in the Multicultural Classroom.* Markham, Ontario: Pippin, pp. 54–55.

STRUCTURE 24. VALUE LINES

Bowers, Bert. Teachers' Curriculum Institute, Mountain View, CA.

Recommended Sources

Books

For social studies teachers who wish to learn more cooperative structures than those described in this book, Spencer Kagan's *Cooperative Learning* (San Juan Capistrano, CA: Kagan Cooperative Learning, 1992.) is the most complete resource. The author also includes chapters on team and class building, thinking skills, communication skills and cooperative projects that are readily adaptable to the social studies class.

Kagan Publishing
P.O. Box 72008
San Clemente, CA 92673-2008
Phone: 1 (800) 933-2667

Robert Stahl and Ron Van Sickle have edited a collection of essays for the National Council for the Social Studies (NCSS), *Cooperative Learning in the Social Studies Classroom: An Introduction to Social Study*. This is not a "how-to book," but rather a look at research and issues in the use of cooperative learning in social studies.

NCSS Publications, c/o Maxway Data
Corp, 225 W. 34th St, Suite 1105
New York, NY 1001
Phone: 1 (800) 683-0812

Cooperative Learning in Social Studies: A Handbook for Teachers, edited by Robert Stahl (Menlo Park, CA: Addison-Wesley, 1994) is the practical companion to the NCSS book above. Most of the major schools of cooperative learning have a chapter. Structures are explained by Jeanne Stone and Spencer Kagan in "Social Studies and the Structural Approach" and Robert Stahl, John Meyer, and Nancy Stahl in a chapter on Co-op Co-op. Other chapters look at forms of Jigsaw, Robert Slavin's Teams-Games-Tournament and Student Teams-Achievement Divisions, and the Johnsons' Creative Controversy.

Addison-Wesley
Jacob Way
Reading, MA 01867
Phone: 1 (800) 447-2226

Bert Bower, Jim Lobdell and Lee Swenson in *History Alive* (Addison-Wesley, 1994) have applied the work of Elizabeth Cohen's Program for Complex Instruction (PCI) to history teaching. PCI combines cooperative learning with activities that use multiple intelligences. The structural approach can enhance what is already a cooperative focus in *History Alive*. The authors also run an institute that provides curriculum materials and training.

Teachers Curriculum Institute
201 San Antonio Circle, Suite 105
Mountain View, CA 94040, USA
Phone: 1 (800) 497-6138

The Stanford Program on International and Cross-Cultural Education (SPICE) produces some of the most rich and rigorous curriculum material available, much of which is built on cooperative learning. Especially worthwhile are the materials built on the Program for Complex Instruction such as *Nationalism and Identity in a European Context* (Steinbeck, R. 1993), *Why Do People Move?: Migration from Latin America* (Nuñez, L. 1993), and *Along the Silk Road* (Chu, R. 1993).

SPICE, Institute for International Studies
Room 14 C, Stanford University
Stanford, CA 94305-5013
Phone: (415) 723-1114

A popular teacher's guide with an international focus is Graham Selby and David Pike's *Global Teacher, Global Learner* (1988, London: Hodder and Stoughton). Along with explanations of concepts in global education like human rights and

Recommended Sources

interdependence, the authors draw together a collection of extremely creative activities for team building, role playing, discussion and the like.

Hodder and Stoughton
Mill Road, Dunton Green
Sevenoaks, Kent, England, TN13 2YA

Cooperative Learning, Cooperative Lives (Schniedewind, N. and Davidson, E. 1987. Dubuque, Iowa: W. C. Brown Co.) includes a number of lessons and worksheets suitable for upper elementary and middle school that teach content related to themes of cooperation, competition and respect for diversity while using the cooperative process. The lessons start with issues from the classroom and school like the use of put-downs and peer pressure and then expand to national and international topics like food and workers' cooperatives, trade, and war and peace.
Order from:

Circle Books
30 Walnut Street
Somerville, MA 02143
Phone: (617) 623-7863

Elizabeth Coelho is the author or coauthor of several powerful books for developing a community of learners in a multicultural classroom at the middle and high school level: *Learning Together in the Multicultural Classroom* (1994. Markham, Ontario: Pippin), a teachers guide; *Jigsaw* (1991. Markham, Ontario: Pippin), student materials and lesson plans that focus on reading skills and constructive controversy with a reading level of grades 3–7; *All Sides of the Issue* (with Winn-Bell Olsen, J. and Winer, L. 1989. Hayward, California: Alemany Press), the American version of *Jigsaw*; and *Jigsaw Plus* (1991. Markham, Ontario: Pippin), similar to *Jigsaw*, but at a higher reading level, grades 6-10.

Pippin Publishing
150 Telson Road
Markham, Ontario, L3R 1E5
Phone: (416) 513-6966

All Sides of the Issue can be ordered from
Prentice-Hall
PO Box 11071
Des Moines, IA 50336-1071
Phone: 1 (800) 223-1360

Another source of strategies and teaching materials is *Creative Controversy* (Johnson, D. and Johnson, R. 1992. Edina, MN: Interaction). The book includes a number of short, involving exercises designed to encourage perspective-taking, processing forms, a self-evaluation questionnaire, and student materials on diverse controversies like the debate over the contents of the Constitution of the United States, the hunting of the timber wolf, and James Wolfe, the British general at the Battle of Quebec.

Interaction Book Company
7208 Cornelia Drive
Edina, MN 44535
Phone: (612) 831-9500

Lesson Plans for Cooperative Learning (secondary social studies) (Alberts, M., Caldwell, J., and Schmidt, C. 1989. Monticello, Minnesota: Learning Incentives.) gives five detailed lessons based on the Johnsons' Learning Together model for topics like three world religions and propaganda.

Learning Incentives
Rt. 1, Box 104
Monticelloe, MN 55362
Phone: (612) 878-2336

Other useful resources for teachers who use team learning to develop quality thinking about public issues are the booklets from the Public Issues Series of the Social Science Education Consortium (SSEC). There are booklets on religious freedom, immigration, and the New Deal. There is some treatment of discussion skills but the focus is on critical thinking such as using analogies or identifying and weighing values. Cooperative structures would enhance this focus. SSEC also produces the CREST series, role playing exercises on science-related social issues like nuclear fuel storage and AIDS and drug research.

SSEC Publications
3300 Mitchell Lane, Suite 240
Boulder, CO 80301-2272

Collections of Articles, Theme Issues

Several national journals and magazines in Canada and the United States have featured the structural approach to cooperative learning along with other models in theme issues. Those relating to Social Studies include the following:

The International Association for Cooperation in Education (IASCE), a group of teachers and researchers from around the world, produces a magazine, *Cooperative Learning*. Number 3, volume 12, 1992, is a theme issue on social studies. It includes lesson plans and classroom examples such as "Teaching for the Bleachers" (Morton, T.) that includes a creative controversy on the Pig War, a bizarre conflict between Canada and the United States from days past, and "Who Killed JFK?" (Foyle, H.), using group investigation (similar to Co-op Co-op).

Number 3, volume 2, 1990, of *Social Studies and the Young Learner*, published for K-8 teachers by the National Council for the Social Studies (NCSS) features cooperative learning and illustrates the use of Co-op Co-op and Jigsaw in several articles.

The History and Social Science Teacher, now called *Canadian Social Studies*, produced a theme issue on cooperative learning in the 1991, winter issue. Among the articles is a piece by Myers, Cox and Evans called "Getting Started Strategies" using Kagan's Structural Approach and an account by Rosemary Evans on the use of group investigation.

Single Articles

Social Education, the major publication of NCSS, has contained a number of articles on cooperative learning applied to social studies classrooms. Most of these have focused on the use of Jigsaw. For example, there is a lesson on the Electoral College (Palmer, J. in number 4, volume 52, 1988) and one on modernization in Meiji, Japan (Ferguson in number 5, volume 52, 1988).

The Social Studies features Jigsaw in "Where in Western Europe Would You Like to Live? A cooperative lesson for world geography" (Richburg and Nelson in number 3, volume 82, 1991).

The History and Social Science Teacher has also provided individual articles on classroom practice of cooperative learning. For example, Morton applies creative controversy to a key episode in World War Two in "Decision at Dieppe" (number 4, volume 21, 1986) and the Mystery Game structure to buffalo hunting by native North Americans (number 4, volume 25, 1990). Myers and Lemon also look at native North Americans using Jigsaw (number 1, volume 24, 1988).

Professional Development!

Kagan Proudly Offers Top-Notch Professional & Staff Development Opportunities...

★ Consulting Services

★ Graduate Courses

★ Summer Academies

★ Workshops in Your Area

Bring Kagan to Your School or District!

Kagan makes it easy to set up the best in-service your school or district has ever experienced! Bring in a certified member of the dynamic Kagan consulting team for one of the following fantastic workshops:

- **Cooperative Learning**
- Block Scheduling & Secondary Restructuring
- **Brain-Based Learning**
- **Character Development**
- Creating the Cooperative School
- **Emotional Intelligence**
- Hands-On Science
- Higher-Level Thinking
- Math with Manipulatives
- Multicultural Classroom
- **Multiple Intelligences**
- Peer Coaching for Teachers
- Second Language Learning (ESL)
- **Silly Sports & Goofy Games**
- Social Studies
- Strategies for Inclusion
- Surpassing the Standards
- Teambuilding & Classbuilding
- **Win-Win Discipline**
- Writing Process

Come learn how to boost achievement, prevent discipline problems, and make learning more fun and meaningful for you and your students!

Call for More Info!

1 (800) 266-7576

Or Visit Us Online!

www.KaganOnline.com